VOLUME 429                                            JANUARY 1977

# THE ANNALS

*of* The American Academy *of* Political
*and* Social Science

RICHARD D. LAMBERT, *Editor*

ALAN W. HESTON, *Assistant Editor*

## THE NEW RURAL AMERICA

*Special Editor of This Volume*

**FRANK CLEMENTE**
*Senior Research Associate*
*Center for the Study of Environmental Policy*
*Pennsylvania State University*
*University Park, Pennsylvania*

PHILADELPHIA

Library of Congress Catalog Card Number 76-27028

77- 493

The articles appearing in THE ANNALS are indexed in the *Reader's Guide to Periodical Literature*, the *Book Review Index*, the *Public Affairs Information Service Bulletin*, *Social Sciences Index*, and *Current Contents: Behavioral, Social, Management Sciences* and *Combined Retrospective Index Sets*. They are also abstracted and indexed in *ABC Pol Sci*, *Historical Abstracts*, *United States Political Science Documents*, *International Political Science Abstracts* and/or *America: History and Life*.

International Standard Book Numbers (ISBN)

ISBN 0-87761-209-9, vol. 429, 1977; paper—$4.00
ISBN 0-87761-208-0, vol. 429, 1977; cloth—$5.00

*Issued bimonthly by The American Academy of Political and Social Science at 3937 Chestnut St., Philadelphia, Pennsylvania 19104. Cost per year: $15.00 paperbound; $20.00 clothbound. Add $1.50 to above rates for membership outside U.S.A. Second-class postage paid at Philadelphia and at additional mailing offices.*

*Claims for undelivered copies must be made within the month following the regular month of publication. The publisher will supply missing copies when losses have been sustained in transit and when the reserve stock will permit.*

*Editorial and Business Offices, 3937 Chestnut Street, Philadelphia, Pennsylvania 19104.*

# CONTENTS

iii

BOOK DEPARTMENT

## INTERNATIONAL RELATIONS AND POLITICS

## AFRICA AND ASIA

## EUROPE

## UNITED STATES HISTORY AND POLITICS

## SOCIOLOGY

## ECONOMICS

# PREFACE

The almost awesome growth of metropolitan areas in this century has often diverted attention from small towns and rural areas. In the 1960s, for example, the problems associated with rapid urban growth drew significant research attention and discussion in both the professional and the popular media. To the extent that rural areas were examined, they were often done so as the residual of urban studies. Even the title, *The People Left Behind*, of the President's Commission on Rural Poverty conveyed the impression that rural America was an anachronism in a rapidly industrializing and modernizing society. Such a perspective did much to lend credence to one sociologist's comment that rural America "is like a fished out pond, full of bullheads and suckers."

In recent years, however, there has been an increasing recognition among researchers and popular commentators that rural America is alive and generally doing well. Exactly how well, and what we can expect for the future, is the subject of this series of papers.

FRANK CLEMENTE

ANNALS, AAPSS, **429**, Jan. 1977

# The Place of U.S. Food in Eliminating World Hunger

By G. E. BRANDOW

ABSTRACT: Hunger in the sense of severe malnutrition is a fact for hundreds of millions of people in the less developed countries. Though the countries collectively have made impressive gains in agriculture, potential benefits in the form of more food production per person have been wiped out by rapid population growth. The United States has become by far the world's leading food exporter while providing large quantities of prized foods for its own population. Experts disagree on whether the food situation of the less developed world will worsen, but few expect elimination of hunger in this century. Among the means by which the United States might give assistance are help to poor countries in developing their agriculture and direct food aid. Costs of food aid include higher food prices in the United States, reduced foreign exchange earnings, and higher taxes and, together with dismay about population growth in recipient countries, are likely to limit food aid to much less than is technically possible. Suggestions for policy to provide more food aid than the modest amount now supplied include: enlist cooperation of other advanced nations; direct food aid where it is most needed; avoid piling up unpayable debts for food; encourage expanded production, especially of food grains, in the United States; and maintain reserves of strategic foods.

*G. E. Brandow is Professor of Agricultural Economics at the Pennsylvania State University specializing in food and agricultural policy. He is a Fellow and former President of the American Agricultural Economics Association and served as Executive Director of the National Commission on Food Marketing in the mid-1960s.*

HUNGER is a symbolic word for chronic, severe malnutrition and, in the extreme case, starvation. Chronic malnutrition means not only physical distress from lack of food but also high susceptibility to diseases, shortened life span, and general misery. It is estimated that in 1970 one-fourth of the people living in the less developed countries of the world—or nearly half a billion people—had insufficient food to maintain health.[1] In most less developed areas, agricultural production methods are still predominantly primitive, and productivity is low. Productivity in most nonagricultural activities is also low, with the result that comparatively few goods are available for exchange for food in international trade.

In the developed countries, hunger is much less frequent though not absent. Nations produce sufficient food for themselves or are productive enough in other pursuits to be able to buy food abroad. High average incomes, traceable to high productivity, enable people to gratify to some extent their preferences for livestock products (meat, poultry, eggs, and dairy products) and for other relatively expensive foods.

An outstanding fact about the capacity of cropland and related resources to feed people is that a given quantity of grain can feed the maximum number of people when consumed directly as human food. When grain is used as the primary

1. Food and Agriculture Organization, United Nations. The developed countries are usually taken to be the United States, Canada, Europe including Russia, Australia, New Zealand, South Africa, and Japan. China is not included in the estimate here cited for the less developed world but is included in some other statistics given later.

source of feed for livestock, perhaps 70 percent or more of the energy and protein in the grain is not recovered in the form of edible livestock product. Much land, of course, is unsuited to crops—it is too hilly or too dry, for example. Cattle and sheep grazing such land convert forage plants into edible products and add to the food supply. Livestock can also utilize some other materials not suitable for human food. Furthermore, some animal protein in the human diet improves its quality. In general, however, feeding substantial amounts of grain to livestock yields products highly desired by most people but incapable of sustaining nearly as large a population as would the original grain.

The worldwide tendency for populations to upgrade their diets in energy intake (at least up to a point), in nutritional quality (again, up to some point), and in pleasurability as income per person rises is demonstrated by the following estimates of food consumption patterns (see fig. 1).

Income per person is much higher, of course, in the developed than in the less developed countries and higher in the United States than in the developed countries as a whole. The substitution of livestock products for cereal grains and such starchy foods as cassava and sweet potatoes as level of living rises is obvious. The data are United Nations' estimates for the early 1960s and include the Communist countries. Probably the most significant change since then has been an increase in consumption of livestock products in the developed world other than the United States.

Trends over the past decade or two point to major problems that the less developed world (as a whole, not every country) will face in the

| ECONOMIC GROUP OF COUNTRIES | DAILY CALORIES PER PERSON | PERCENTAGE OF CALORIES FROM | | |
| --- | --- | --- | --- | --- |
| | | CEREALS AND STARCHY FOODS | FRUITS AND VEGETABLES | MEAT, FISH, EGGS, MILK |
| Less developed | 2,100 | 71 | 3 | 8 |
| Developed, including U.S. | 3,040 | 43 | 4 | 24 |
| United States | 3,160 | 24 | 6 | 35 |

FIGURE 1

future. The less developed countries have done much better in increasing their food production than is commonly believed: between 1961–65 and 1973–75, agricultural production rose by 34 percent in the less developed world (excluding China) compared with 28 percent in the developed countries. But the much faster rate of population growth in the less developed than in the developed countries caused production per person to be virtually stagnant in the less developed world while increasing 15 percent in the already better-off developed countries. Population growth averages 2.3 percent per year in the less developed countries (including China) and poses an enormous difficulty for them as they struggle to improve the diets of their people.

It will be impossible to maintain the pace of production increase in the less developed countries without more advanced agricultural technology and more nonfarm inputs such as fertilizer. The developed countries generally have achieved higher food production over the past two decades by applying new technology and more nonfarm inputs to an approximately stable area of cropland. The less developed countries, collectively, have used both these methods (starting from a low base) and expansion of crop acreage. The option of more cropland is rapidly disappearing in important less developed countries, forcing them to turn more completely to ways of increasing yields per hectare.

Looking to the future, the less developed countries can attempt to deal with hunger in several ways. One of the most important is to increase their own food production, including, conceivably, some unconventional sources of food. Another is to increase their productivity in nonagricultural lines so that higher exports can pay for food imports. The possibility of monopolizing a vital raw material, as the Organization of Petroleum Exporting Countries (OPEC) does petroleum, is tantalizing but not widely available. At least some food aid will be available from the developed nations. Population control is imperative but cannot be quickly achieved.

A complicating factor will be shifts in food consumption patterns if and as levels of living rise. Higher real incomes in the less developed countries will increase demand for food internally; a "food problem" will persist even if hunger diminishes. Still-rising population and further advances in levels of living in the advanced nations will increase their demand for food, especially livestock products. As a result, additional food production in developed countries and even in poor countries will not automatically become available for alleviating hunger where hunger is most prevalent.

The experts disagree on the probable food situation of the less developed countries during the remainder of this century. Some fear that population will so outpace food production that hunger will much increase and that famine will be frequent in years of general crop failure. Such fears are heightened by the possibility that weather will become less favorable to crop production. Some other experts believe that trends of the past decade or two will continue: food production in the less developed world will, on the whole, keep up with population growth, and food from the developed nations will fill the largest gaps in the food supply of developing countries. Virtually no one expects hunger to be eliminated in this century.

### THE PLACE OF THE U.S. IN WORLD FOOD SUPPLY

The United States has 5.4 percent of the world's population. In the years 1973–75, the nation's share of world production and consumption of two leading groups of food and feed products was as follows:

|  | PRODUC-TION (%) | CONSUMP-TION (%) |
|---|---|---|
| All grains | 19.7 | 13.6 |
| Oilseed and fish meal | 45.7 | 22.4 |

(includes meal equivalent of oilseeds not processed)

Grain is a basic food material because of its importance in direct consumption by humans and its place as a livestock feed. The meal component of such oilseeds as soybeans is high in protein, most of it is usable as human food, and though some is so used (for example, whole soybeans), most is used for livestock feed. The United States produces far more than its population share of both basic materials, consumes large but smaller shares, and supplies substantial amounts to other countries. Net exports of grain from the United States amounted to 7.4 percent of the grain consumed elsewhere in the world during 1973–75. For oilseed and fish meal, the figure was 30.7 percent.[2]

Individual grains are classified in the advanced nations as food grains (principally wheat and rice) and feed grains (principally corn, sorghum, barley, and oats). But feed grains are used mainly as human food in areas of the less developed world suited to their production. In tonnage, feed grains are more important than food grains in the United States: feed grains were 75 percent of the nation's grain production and 55 percent of its grain exports in the years 1973–75. Crop acreage could be shifted from feed grains to wheat if high wheat prices in relation to feed grain prices warranted the change. Average grain yield per acre, however, would be reduced by substitution of wheat for feed grains.

The dominant position of the United States as a supplier of food is a comparatively recent development. As table 1 shows, Canada exported as much grain as the United States in the early 1950s. Australia, South Africa, and Southeast Asia (mainly Thailand) together exported about half as much as the United States. Latin America had a small export surplus principally because of large grain exports by Argentina. Russia's modest export surplus about matched the net imports of Eastern Europe, and China had small net exports. Western Europe was the principal importer of grain; Japan imported about one-fifth as much.

2. Calculations of production, consumption, and export percentages were based on data compiled by the U.S. Department of Agriculture, including preliminary or partially forecast data for 1975.

TABLE 1

NET EXPORTS OR IMPORTS (−) OF GRAIN, ANNUAL CROP-YEAR AVERAGES
1952–54, 1960–62, AND 1973–75

| REGION OR COUNTRY | 1952–54 AVERAGE (THOUSAND METRIC TONS) | 1960–62 AVERAGE (THOUSAND METRIC TONS) | 1973–75 AVERAGE (THOUSAND METRIC TONS) |
|---|---|---|---|
| Developed countries | | | |
| United States | 10,661 | 32,756 | 74,075 |
| Canada | 11,868 | 9,700 | 13,879 |
| Australia, New Zealand, South Africa | 2,595 | 8,839 | 14,305 |
| Japan | −3,892 | −5,357 | −18,856 |
| Western Europe | −20,375 | −26,032 | −20,148 |
| Russia | 1,748 | 7,299 | −10,544 |
| Eastern Europe | −1,072 | −6,721 | −7,719 |
| Less developed | | | |
| China (People's Republic) | 364 | −3,639 | −3,963 |
| Latin America | 538 | 788 | −617 |
| Africa, ex. S. Africa | −82 | −6,251 | −17,639 |
| South Asia | −3,497 | −6,117 | −8,981 |
| Southeast Asia | 3,034 | 3,938 | 3,100 |
| Far East and other Asian countries | −1,890 | −5,336 | −11,869 |
| Statistical discrepancy | — | −3,867 | −5,023 |

SOURCE: Compiled from data published by the U.S. Department of Agriculture. Averages for 1973–75 include partial forecasts for 1975.

Among the less developed areas, only South Asia, including India, was a fairly large net importer of grain.

By 1973–75, no other country was even close to the United States as an exporter of grain (or of oilseed protein). Canada's exports were about the same as in the early 1950s. Though Australia and South Africa had achieved large proportionate increases in grain exports, their combined tonnage was about the same as Canada's. Southeast Asia's exports remained near the level of the early 1950s. Russia, Eastern Europe, and China were net importers and together absorbed more than 20 million tons of other countries' grain production.[3] Western Europe imported about as much

3. Both Russia and the United States suffered one unusually poor grain production year during 1973–75.

grain as in the early 1950s, and Japan's imports nearly matched Western Europe's. Africa, the Far East, and the rest of Asia had become large importers, and South Asia's grain imports were more than double those of the early 1950s. Of the less developed regions listed in table 1, only Southeast Asia still had an export surplus (though Argentina remained an important exporter).

Emphasis on grain and oilseeds obscures the fact that the United States is also a food importer. Coffee and bananas are examples of imported foods not produced in the United States; sugar and beef are examples of imported foods that add to domestic production. For all foods collectively, imports amount to slightly more than half as much as exports; net food exports (exports less imports) are just short of one-tenth of production.

As experts consider where larger supplies of food might come from in the future if demands of import countries should continue to grow, their attention again turns to the United States. The nation's demonstrated capacity to increase yields per acre on its vast harvested acreage has not come to an end. More land could be put under the plow, though the productivity of most of it would be well below the current average. Some areas outside the United States—for example, Brazil—seem to have high potential for agricultural expansion. Usually they also have high rates of population growth. The United States, already by far the leading exporter, is a leading potential source of additional exports.

### U.S. ALTERNATIVES IN ALLEVIATING HUNGER

Transferring food from the rich and agriculturally productive United States to poor countries short of food is an obvious approach to alleviating hunger. But as has already been suggested, there are other alternatives, and they should at least be recognized in appraising the direct use of U.S. food.

The foremost alternative is assistance by the United States in helping poor countries to develop their own food production. This means, principally, increasing production in agriculture and fisheries, but it can also include development of non-conventional food sources, new foods to make better use of existing materials, and improved methods of handling and storing food to reduce post-harvest losses. The assistance can take two principal forms. First is help in developing and applying new knowledge about superior crops, livestock, cultivation methods, soil management, nutrition, food handling, and the like. Second is assistance in providing physical inputs, such as fertilizer and certain farm equipment, or for developing soil and water resources.

Aid in checking population growth is another approach. The task is enormously difficult even for governments of the poor countries themselves; it is even more difficult for outsiders. Still another alternative is making U.S. markets more accessible to products from poor countries so that the countries can increase their ability to buy food from the United States.

Alternative means exist for transferring food from the United States to the less developed countries. By far the most important method in the first half of the 1970s was the same method used in exporting food to developed countries: commercial sale. The existence of an exportable food surplus in the United States, Australia, Thailand, or other nation is helpful to food-short poor countries even if they have to pay full price for what they get. The problem, of course, is that their opportunity to participate in the commercial market is greatly limited by their lack of purchasing power. Thus another alternative is to supply food to them on concessional terms. These range all the way from outright grants or gifts to long-term loans at less than commercial interest rates.

Though this is not the place to develop the point, it should be noted that all the alternatives to food aid have limitations as means of eliminating hunger, as does food aid itself. The U.S. government has had a substantial program of agricultural development assistance for poor countries since about 1950, and foundations, the United Nations, and some countries other than the United States have also supplied assistance. Success has been mixed, at best;

though some less developed countries have done well, others—including India and Bangladesh—remain in a precarious food situation. Exports of nonfood products from the less developed to the developed countries often are limited by low productivity at the source and may be further limited by resistance in developed countries to admission of competitive imports. Even if birth rates should fall promptly to replacement levels in the less developed world, the high proportion of young people would assure further population growth for years to come.

## U.S. Food Aid, Past and Present

Food aid—exports under concessional terms—played a small role in the huge shipments of food from the United States in the early 1970s. Sixty-two percent of all agricultural exports (mostly food) went to developed countries in fiscal year 1975 (approximately the crop year 1974). Of the agricultural exports to less developed countries (excluding China, which received no aid), 14 percent was on concessional terms. There were exceptions to the modest role of food aid: for example, about three-fourths of agricultural exports to Bangladesh and substantially all of agricultural exports to some African countries were concessional. Aid exports were 28 percent of all agricultural exports to India.

A continuing program of food aid began in 1954 under Public Law 480, later called Food for Peace. Originally, the principal or at least crucial incentive for the program was agricultural surpluses accumulating in the hands of the government under farm price supports. Some aid took the form of food grants, but until the late 1960s the principal concessional device was to accept currencies of recipient countries, not convertible to dollars, as payment for agricultural products. The high-water mark for P.L. 480 was reached in fiscal 1965, a year of crop failure in India, when concessional sales accounted for 26 percent of all agricultural exports.

Among the criticisms of the program was the contention that food aid, which usually became additions to market supplies in recipient countries, tended to hold down prices there and thus to discourage local food production. Probably a more important result of food aid was the tendency for a number of recipient countries to rely upon it and to slight their own agriculture in allocating resources for economic development. P.L. 480 terms were made more stringent: sales to be paid for in dollars over 20 to 40 years gradually replaced nonconvertible currency sales, and recipient countries were expected to make progress in developing their own food production. Provision for grants continued. Tighter terms and Green Revolution successes in several developing countries reduced the dollar value of food aid by 30 percent between 1965 and 1972. Further shrinkage occurred in fiscal 1973 and 1974 as commercial markets abroad expanded sharply. Aid exports increased modestly in fiscal 1975 and 1976.

Included in U.S. aid are foods distributed through voluntary relief agencies, such as CARE (15 percent of the total in fiscal 1975), and through the international World Food Program (8 percent).

The principal achievement of food aid has been to increase the food supply in situations where more food was badly needed. To the extent that aid can be targeted on nutritionally vulnerable groups such as children or on particularly impoverished segments of the population, the food is effective in alleviating the worst aspects of hunger. When food aid is essentially a general addition to the food supply of the recipient countries, as most of it has been in the past, the benefits are widely diffused. Confining large-scale food aid to those who need it most probably is not possible. There are modest opportunities to use distribution of food aid to stimulate nutrition or community improvement programs, and some funds (in local currency) realized from general sale of food may be useful in supporting economic development. Political stability resulting from more food probably is favorable to sustained economic progress. A common contention is that food aid buys time for a less developed country to slow its population growth and to invigorate its agriculture.

## SOME EFFECTS OF LARGE-SCALE FOOD AID

What would a large-scale food aid program involve for the United States, one capable of making a substantial impact on hunger in the less developed world in the future? To avoid excessive generality, let us assume 50 million metric tons of grain as the average annual amount to be transferred to poor countries for little or no payment.[4] This amount of grain is approximately double the grain-equivalent of all aid provided under P.L. 480 at the peak of the program in the mid-1960s. On paper, 50 million tons could correct the food deficiency estimated for non-Communist less developed countries in 1970, but in practice the grain could not be distributed precisely to those who needed it most.

4. Grain is used illustratively because it would make up most of actual food aid, but other foods would displace some grain in a realistic program.

Given time, three sources of food for aid purposes would appear. One would be reduced food consumption in the United States. As the government attempted to purchase grain for aid, grain prices would rise sharply, livestock production would be curtailed, and retail prices of livestock products would increase. Higher prices to consumers would cause voluntary reduction of meat, poultry, egg, and dairy consumption commensurate with reduced production. Problems of providing adequate nutrition for the poor in the United States would intensify, but total food supplies for the nation would still be more than adequate for good nutrition.

A second source of grain for food aid would be reduced commercial exports of grain in response to high prices in the United States. The response might be slight at first but large after foreign countries had time to adjust their own production of livestock and grain.

The third source would be expanded grain production in the United States. Producers could intensify production (for example, use more fertilizer) and shift a little cropland from other crops to grain in a year or two. Given, say, five or more years and assurance of continued high prices, farmers might increase total crop acreage by 5 to 10 percent. This is considerably less than appears possible from an inventory of soil resources made in 1967, but expansion of total harvested acreage faces several economic— and environmental—obstacles.

There is little doubt that 50 million tons of grain could be obtained for aid purposes. The question is how high food prices would have to go to free up 50 million tons and how much grain would come from each of the three sources. As a rough estimate intended only to be illustrative, the difference in overall retail food prices would perhaps amount to 10 percent—that percentage would be added to the level of retail food prices that would otherwise exist.

Such outcomes suggest the impact of large-scale food aid upon the American people, whose support for the policy would be necessary if the policy endured. Higher food prices for consumers is one obvious impact. A second effect would appear in foreign exchange earnings. In the short run, commercial exports probably would not decline enough to offset higher prices, with the result that foreign exchange earnings would increase; over several years, the loss of commercial exports probably would be great enough to reduce foreign exchange earnings. Foreign exchange, of course, is needed to pay for imports of such products as petroleum and for other international uses. A third effect would be the cost of purchasing grain for aid purposes: possibly the domestic cost of grain and payment for at least part of the ocean transportation would amount to 10 billion dollars (another rough estimate). If the U.S. government paid all the bill, that amount would be added to taxes (or would increase the budget deficit, probably stimulating general inflation). A fourth effect would be sharply higher farm prices for grain (much more in percentage terms than the 10 percent estimated for retail food prices) and higher incomes for grain producers; but producers of hogs, feedlot beef, poultry, eggs, and milk would be in a price-cost squeeze and forced to reduce output.

American citizens would have differing evaluations of these results. Many who strongly favor food aid would be willing to accept the resulting strains upon the economy. Others would be unwilling to accept the costs imposed upon them. It is important to note that satisfactions of giving food aid are not distributed among the people as are the personal costs and (in the case of grain producers) gains of providing it. Also, the satisfactions of giving food aid tend to be abstract, while the costs show up in daily concerns about the cost of living, taxes, and (in the case of many livestock producers) earning a living. An issue like food aid, accordingly, strains the capacity of the American political system to make and execute public policy.

The issue would be further complicated by circumstances abroad. Inevitably, substantial amounts of food aid would go to individuals who want more or better food but do not physiologically require it. Corruption and obvious waste are sure to be associated with distribution of food in some recipient countries. Political turmoil will at times cause setbacks in local food production. Experience shows that receipt of aid is not necessarily accompanied by gratitude toward donor countries. In the past, international policies of the United States have much influenced the choice of countries to which aid was given. There is disagreement, of course, about these policies and the extent to which they should affect the distribution of aid. Obviously, large-scale food aid requires firm resolution on the part of those who provide it to bear many disappointments.

Probably the most inhibiting obstacle to all-out support for food aid is the ultimate inadequacy of this solution to hunger if population growth is not checked and if food production is not much increased in the less developed world. The United States, or the developed countries collectively, cannot alone supply all the food to care for the added population to appear in the less developed countries in this century if there are no restraints on population. Fifty million tons of grain is not enough to feed for one year the added population to appear in the less developed regions three years from now. To the argument that food aid gives time for recipient countries to curb population increase and to accelerate agricultural development, some opponents of aid reply that food aid in the next decade will only increase the number of people to know famine in following decades.

Thus, the United States finds itself in a situation where (1) humanitarian motives and international policy considerations prompt it to respond to the needs of less developed countries by giving food aid, (2) the United States cannot be sure of the long-term effectiveness of its aid, and (3) the effects of large-scale food aid on U.S. citizens will almost surely mean that food aid will be substantially less than the nation is technically capable of supplying.

## POLICY IMPLICATIONS

Hunger will exist in the world for a long time. Policy to combat hunger should therefore be framed for the long run and made responsive to changing situations as they appear. Food shipments to poor countries will play a part in a balanced policy, but so also will assistance in expanding their food production, help in curbing their population growth, and greater willingness to accept their products in international trade.

U.S. food will and should continue to be exported to the less developed countries both as commercial sales and on concessional or aid terms. Some of the countries can buy enough to meet essential requirements, and others can buy some of the food they need. Reserving food aid to food-short countries that cannot pay for it without seriously impairing their own economic de-

velopment will help assure that the limited aid likely to be available will go where it will do the most good.

Though the United States is in a unique position with regard to food, the responsibility for alleviating hunger extends to all developed countries. Western Europe, Russia, Japan, and the richest OPEC nations should expect to assume reasonable shares of the financial burden of food aid even if they are net importers of food. Given the political divisions in the world, food aid probably will continue to be provided on an individual country basis as well as through international organizations.

Conditions attached to food aid are a touchy matter for both donor and recipient countries. In light of all the possibilities of misuse of food aid, tough terms by the United States to ensure (so far as that is possible) that aid is properly used seem warranted. But financial terms probably should be relaxed for countries not capable of buying commercially. Food to alleviate hunger is not an investment creating increased production out of which payment can be made. It seems unlikely that long-term dollar loans for food aid can be paid; their extensive use only piles up difficulties for the future. Also, in 1973 Congress provided that the choice of nations to receive aid should be based more on need and less on U.S. political objectives than at times in the past; further shift of policy in this direction may be desirable.

Agricultural production must continue to expand in the United States, especially if food aid is to play a substantial role in alleviating hunger abroad. Experience demonstrates that willingness to supply aid is much influenced by the availability of food that can be exported without increasing domestic prices or forcing consumers to turn to less preferred, if still nutritional, diets. Agricultural production cannot be greatly accelerated in the short run, for farmers are wary that short-term price increases may not persist, output-increasing investments take time, and research on production methods ordinarily requires years to produce results. In a highly uncertain world where future needs cannot be clearly known, it will probably be better to err on the side of having a little too much food production rather than a little too little. Too much food would mean using more food for aid than targeted and/or programs to support farm incomes; too little would mean less aid than desired and higher food prices, together with the stimulus of higher food prices to general inflation.

Two moderate means of encouraging agricultural production for food aid are favorable income-support assurances to food grain producers and more agricultural research. Research would be aimed at more efficient food production generally and would include work on environmentally acceptable ways of increasing output. More drastic measures might include higher income assurances for food grain producers, low-cost loans for new land development, guarantees of as much natural gas as needed for manufacture of nitrogen fertilizer, and similar methods. The more drastic measures probably should be used only if the United States has a strong determination to give much food aid or if future events show that total demand for food, including some aid, outruns production. Closely related to efforts to expand production of conventional foods is research to develop new foods from conventional and new sources.

Food aid increases the need for reserve stocks, especially of grains; only if reserves exist will food be available as needed. International cooperation is highly desirable in maintaining food reserves, and some combination of international and domestic programs seems likely.

Many Americans are moved by humanitarian and moral reasons to want much more food aid than public policy will provide. They therefore look for private means of alleviating hunger abroad. Even if participated in by fairly large numbers, such actions as eating less meat are not very effective by themselves, for the market response is lower prices, higher consumption by other consumers, more grain exports to developed countries, and, perhaps, less production of grain. Little of the "saved" grain may in fact go to hungry people. An alternative (or supplement) is to use private funds for purchase and shipment of food. It seems possible to revise and expand current provisions of P.L. 480 for food aid through voluntary relief agencies so as to attract more private funds and to give greater assurance that food aid is thereby increased.

The time is at hand, if not overdue, for a reappraisal of food aid policy. Several of the circumstances leading to retrenchment after the mid-1960s no longer apply. Prospective needs for food aid are large and have become an international concern to which the United States must respond. Though the World Food Conference of 1974 was suggested by the United States, no positive food aid policy going beyond ad hoc application of old programs has yet emerged in the United States. In light of the unique position of the nation as a food producer, no international policy on the question of hunger will be formulated until the United States knows what it wants to do and takes leadership in developing effective international arrangements.

# The Changing American Farm

## HAROLD F. BREIMYER

ABSTRACT: The American farm has never been as homogeneous or as stable as it appears in nostalgic recollection. Its
historic emphasis on fee ·simple ownership by operating
proprietors was nevertheless a marked departure from its
feudal antecedent and remains relevant today. Farmers'
desires for status and for managerial independence have not
mitigated. They are subject to (1) changes, such as increase
in size, that have no deep significance; and (2) other changes,
such as increased dependence on nonfarm inputs, that bring
more specialization of enterprise, including growing detachment of livestock (and poultry) farming from crop farming,
and that make farming more sensitive to the terms of relationship with input-supplying as well as market industries. Encroachment of those industries via vertical integration
(ownership or contract) along with internal growth of some
farms to larger than family size gradually shrink the dominance of the traditional family farm. Even so, the most viable
unit may be the part-time or retirement farm, which does not
depend heavily on farm income. The ultimate question relates to what national policy is to be. Past policy has been
ambivalent, and no clear direction for the future is to be seen.

*Harold F. Breimyer is Perry Foundation Professor of Agricultural Economics at
the University of Missouri-Columbia. His duties include teaching, research, and
extension. For 30 years he was staff economist for the United States Department of
Agriculture and the Council of Economic Advisers. His books are* Individual
Freedom and the Economic Organization of Agriculture *and* Economics of the
Product Markets of Agriculture. *He was President of the American Agricultural
Economics Association, which has also named him a Fellow.*

POPULAR ideas about the American farm are wreathed in emotion and haloed by nostalgia. Most institutions of our day are viewed and judged more or less rationally. Not so the farm. It carries various affective associations, many of them lodged in memory. Some of them mislead.

It is common, for example, to think of the farm of the past as comparatively uniform and stable. That recollection then contrasts with the variability and insecurity of today. Some difference exists, and the stresses of our time will be noted below. But, significantly, the American farm of the past was less distinguished for stability or homogeneity than for its revolutionary departure from its antecedent, the European feudal system. And although the farm of today is indeed being tugged from various directions and its future is uncertain, the more serious threat does not arise from publicized trends such as larger size, greater technology, or even increased financial capitalization. Of greater import are pressures to fractionate the organizational structure of farming, creating sharp divisions between who owns, manages, and works on American farms.

The place and fate of the farm enter the consciousness of most Americans. Many families had rural forbears. All recognize their dependence on the food and fiber products of the farm. In addition, our citizens hold an almost mystical regard for the life-sustaining biological processes contained in farming. Human beings marvel at the regenerative features of crop and animal husbandry, which, unlike all mechanical processes, yield an increase in substance and not a mere change in form.

## DEFINITION OF A FARM

Definition of a farm suffers from both familiarity and obscurity. Everyone knows what a farm is until he tries to define it. Scholarly sources are of little help. The *Encyclopedia of the Social Sciences* discourses informatively about the plantation but omits the farm. Webster's dictionary tells us only that the verb, to farm, comes from the Old French *fermer*, to fix or make a contract, which in turn derives from the Latin *firmare*, to make firm.[1] James Horsfall translates this into the role of the farmer as a renter: "a farmer in the old French was a share cropper, a peasant, a serf."[2]

Our own focus shifts back and forth from the impersonal word, farm, to the personal, farmer. Our concerns properly involve how the identity of the farm affects the place and welfare of the farmer.

Our dual interest is illustrated in the popular notion of a farm as a unit for producing crops and/or livestock (including poultry). Is the unit basically managerial or operational? In other words, is an individual farm defined as a unit coming under a single management, or one that is operated from a single headquarters?

Similar but more important is the consideration of sovereignty. The idea of a farm implies managerial control, that is to say, autonomy in deploying resources and accepting associated risk and return. Sometimes this aspect of definition is put in terms of linkage of a farm with its two adjoining sectors, the sup-

1. *Webster's Seventh New Collegiate Dictionary* (Springfield, Mass.: G. and C. Merriam Company, 1970), p. 302.
2. James G. Horsfall, "Agricultural Strategy in the Tragedy of the Commons," *Agricultural Science Review*, vol. 10, no. 1 (First Quarter 1972), p. 19.

pliers of inputs and marketers of products. If the linkage is via buying and selling, the farm is said to be autonomous, to enjoy sovereignty. If, instead, contractual integration prevails, sovereignty is compromised or even lost.

A sharply different orientation is how the concept of a farm involves the unique resource of farming, the land. How is land to be held, how farmed, and under what terms? In this sense, a farm is viewed in terms of the relation of man to land, or of land to man.

But that does not close the issue. What kinds of enterprises belong on a farm or in farming? To the extent institutions of the land define farming, are livestock and poultry included? The word "agriculture" literally means land culture. We can equivocate on whether it includes grazing of animals on native pasture, but it almost surely excludes feeding harvested crops to animals in confinement. Yet the traditional American farm has included the raising and feeding of livestock and poultry.

Now, though, livestock and poultry operations are increasingly being detached from the source of feed. Some, such as tiering hens in cages, are located on plots of land no larger than a site for manufacturing—which, in fact, the system resembles. Perhaps such operations no longer qualify as a part of farming.

It is not necessary to arrive at definitional purity. It may be sufficient to recognize the uncertainties of definition.

## ALTERNATE KINDS OF FARMING

We next consider the alternate organizational forms of farming. These are useful for inventorying the present but even more so for projecting the future. This approach

was followed by Extension economists of north central states who addressed the subject.[3] Their selected categories of farms may be expanded to the following:

1. Less than family size
2. Family size, open market
   a. Primarily owner operated
   b. Primarily tenant operated
3. Larger than family size, open market
4. Cooperative
5. Contractually integrated
6. Large corporate

The smallest farms are usually part-time or retirement farms. These are the first category. They are numerous.

Family-size farms that are predominantly operated by their owner, and that buy and sell in the market, are the epitome of the traditional U.S. family farm. These form category 2a. A number of farms are similar but are owned by a retired farmer or his widow or a nearby nonfarm investor. These are category 2b.

A third category is of farms larger than family size but owned and operated within farming, not by nonfarm people or firms. The dividing line between family- and larger-than-family-size is indistinct. One rule of thumb is that a farm of more than one and a half family workers and an equal number of hired workers no longer classifies as "family." Sometimes two family and two non-family workers are the breaking point.

Although family farmers implicitly assume that the principal threat

3. *Who Will Control U.S. Agriculture?* A *Series of Six Leaflets*, North Central Regional Extension Publications 32-1 to 6, University of Illinois at Urbana-Champaign, Cooperative Extension Service Special Publication 28, March 1973.

to them arises externally, Thomas Stout has long pointed out that farming already has a large contingent of super-size units within it. In 1967 he observed that "we have more severe concentration ratios in agriculture" than in many manufacturing industries.[4]

Cooperative farming (category 4) requires that individual farms, though still modest proprietorships, be bound together by full-contract commitments for cooperative procurement of inputs and marketing of products. Farmers would have a voice in policy-making by their cooperatives, and they would be autonomous over their individual farming operations. Few farms of this kind now exist, but they are a reasonable possibility for the future.

Contractual integration (category 5) is identified by production contracts between the farm and the supplier of inputs, marketer of products, or both. The farmer has relatively little managerial discretion. Integrated production of broilers may be the clearest example.

Corporate farming (category 6) refers to total control by industrial type corporations. The corporation owns and operates the farm. Workers are wage employees.

The six kinds of farming allow further variations. Distinctions among them are not clear-cut. For example, a trend of the 1960s and 1970s has been toward part-owner farming, in which the operator owns a base or "home" farm and rents one or several tracts that he farms. This kind of farm blurs subcategories 2a and 2b.

## FORCES OF CHANGE, 1776

Forces bearing on the American farm today have old antecedents. They begin with the early history of our nation. Then as now, a powerful driving force was farmers' striving for recognition, status, opportunity. That plea was recognized in the colonial period. It has never been silenced since.

Colonizers of America sought to break loose from the restrictive land-holding and land tenure rules of medieval Europe. Those clearly pertained to both man and land. According to George Geiger, a distinction can be drawn between the earlier feudalism and the later manorial system. In the former, land was held in a succession of service relationships to higher authorities (nobles and, at the summit, the sovereign). In the latter, the manor was more nearly independent. It was also nearly self-sufficient, and master-servant relationships within it were proprietary rather than fealty.[5]

Don Paarlberg points out that it was our national wish to build a "free and open system of tenure" into our agriculture. Steps were taken to "prevent the development of a hereditary land-owning class." This was done, for example, by laws prohibiting primogeniture—the "bequeathing of the farm, intact, to the eldest male heir"; and entailment—"specifying . . . that a piece of property must stay in the family through subsequent generations."[6]

It would be heroic to say that in the yeasty setting of the time the aspirations of our forefathers them-

4. Thomas T. Stout, "Effect of Changes in Market Structure on Ownership Patterns of Wealth and on the Distribution of Incomes, Rights and Privileges," *Implications of Changes on Farm Management and Marketing Research* (Iowa State University: CAED Report 29, 1967), p. 362.

5. George Raymond Geiger, *The Theory of the Land Question* (New York: Macmillan and Company, 1936), pp. 156–59.
6. Don Paarlberg, "Providing Capital for Tomorrow's Farms," remarks at Presidents' Council Conference (Springfield, Mass.: U.S., Department of Agriculture 3661–74, December 1974), p. 2.

selves were the controlling force. More accurate is that accessibility to new, virgin, limitless, undefended land made it easy to act. In the words of Louis Hartz, "Where land was abundant and the voyage to the New World itself a claim to independence, the spirit which repudiated peasantry and tenantry flourished with remarkable ease."[7]

Our land laws have provided for ownership in fee simple. Through a combination of law and circumstance, the majority of farms in the United States came to be of the kind usually called the family farm. Only the plantations of the south and the Spanish haciendas of the southwest were notable departures from that basic type.

## FORCES OF CHANGE, 1976

Two centuries after the signing of the Declaration of Independence, U.S. farming is still subject to forces that impel change. Those forces, also invite if not impel public decision as to which directions of change are to be accommodated and which restrained.

Early aspirations for status and for managerial independence have not been mitigated. Those hopes and strivings are now expressed in the language of "Who Will Control . . . ?" U.S. farming. They convert to a choice among the six kinds of farming listed above. What is different today is not the goals for farming held by farmers or even by nonfarm people; it is rather the broad and diverse mix of forces that are being brought to bear on the structure of farming.

Some of those forces arise internally. They are usually classed within the broad term "technology."

7. Louis Hartz, *The Liberal Tradition in America* (New York: Harcourt, Brace and World, 1955), pp. 17–18.

A more exact explanation is that the techniques of farming, the skills required of the farmer, and the kind and source of resources employed have all gone through transformation.

This is not to say that farming is more difficult now, nor that such changes as the increase in size of a typical farm are particularly significant. Farming now requires that the farmer possess more scientific knowledge than his predecessors did. It is a substitution of how to lubricate a tractor for how to fit a collar on a horse; or of application rates and rules for chemical pesticides versus knowing what wood ashes repel potato bugs.

The increase in size of a midwest farm from a pre-tractor 80 acres to a highly mechanized 320 acres means only that big machines till a larger area.[8]

Other inferences are more important. Obviously, the kind of knowledge needed today is more formally acquired. Hence there is a greater role for formal education, both in-school and continuing. The complexity of modern techniques has led to a significant change to more specialization of enterprise on farms and among farmers. This increases a farmer's risk as contrasted with the evening-out of diversification. It in turn can lead to interest in cooperative or governmental measures to reduce risk.

8. A corroboration comes from Philip M. Raup: "It has been a truism that until this generation the revolution in agriculture had not made any basic change in the functional characteristics of farms; only the size was different. With exceptions in the cotton South, the ranching West, and California, the big farm of the 1930s or even the 1950s was in most cases a large-scale version of the universal peasant farm. . . ." "Urban Threats to Rural Lands: Background and Beginnings," *Journal of American Institute of Planners,* vol. 41, no. 6 (November 1975), p. 372.

Specialization helps to account for the gradual detachment of livestock and poultry enterprises from crop farming. A major consequence of specialization is political. Even though farming has never been politically unified—it has always had its internecine wars—the trend toward specialization of enterprise exacerbates conflicts. It has enhanced the political role of commodity organizations, which threaten to overshadow general farm organizations politically. And insofar as general organizations are incapable of reconciling diverse interests, the conflicting demands of individual commodity groups go forward to the Congress and Executive branch for resolution. Thus does internal structure affect political process.

Still another consequence of technical change comes from the shift to more resources of nonfarm origin. Farmers now obtain many of their resources from off the farm. According to some estimates, the fuel, machinery, chemicals, fertilizers, veterinary services, and other inputs obtained from outside farming amount to almost two-thirds of all resources used. Land and the farmer's labor are now scarcely more than one-third.

As a result, farming is now highly subject to the terms of relationship with the source of nonfarm inputs. The connection with input suppliers is one of the criteria governing the kind of farming that is to prevail.

To be sure, this trend toward more use of nonfarm inputs and sensitivity to the terms of getting them is only the opposite face of the commercialization coin. Several generations have passed since farming became commercial on the selling side. It is now commercial on the procurement side also.

A final development may be ambiguously classed as internal. Due in part to new means of transportation and communication, the farm and farmer have lost not only their isolation but most of their cultural identity. Farmers and their families are now virtually indistinguishable from city and town residents. They have melded with them in cultural, recreational, educational, and religious activities. They even coalesce somewhat politically.

## EXTERNAL INFLUENCES ON FARMING

Although it is tempting to say that farming is affected mainly by what happens within it, the opposite is more nearly the truth. Perhaps more than ever before in our history, farming is affected by events arising from outside its borders—outside the borders of farming, but even, it may be added, outside the borders of the nation.

Now that agriculture draws on the nonfarm economy for so many of its resource inputs, as well as for its markets, it is subject to developments in that economy. Most visible there is the ever greater concentration of size and power among firms. The farming sector is notable for its uniquely small-scale organization that contrasts so sharply with the large firms in most farm-related industries.

Those industries have not been static but have been moving toward conglomeration, which centralizes economic power even more, and toward vertical integration. Insofar as firms integrate vertically into farm production, they convert farming to the fifth or sixth types named above (contractual or ownership integration).

But that is not the end of it. Primarily in order to resist the market

TABLE 1

NUMBER OF FARMS BY CENSUS CLASSIFICATION, 1969

| | NUMBER OF FARMS | |
|---|---|---|
| ECONOMIC CLASS | NUMBER (THOUSANDS) | PERCENT OF TOTAL |
| 1—$40,000+ sales | 211 | 7.1 |
| 2—$20,000–39,999 sales | 357 | 12.0 |
| 3—$10,000–19,999 sales | 505 | 16.2 |
| 4—$5,000–9,999 sales | 389 | 13.1 |
| 5—$2,500–4,999 sales | 286 | 9.6 |
| Less than $2,500 sales Part-time Part-retirement Abnormal | 1,223 | 41.2 |
| Total | 2,971 | 100.0 |

SOURCE: 1969 Census of Agriculture, U.S., Department of Commerce.

power or vertical encroachment of industrial firms, farmers have instigated collective defensive action. These may take the form of governmental programs to influence production, price, and income; or group action by farmers through marketing orders, large cooperatives, or collective bargaining.

Modern farming has become vulnerable to increasing scarcity and the rising price of its industrial input materials, particularly petroleum and chemical fertilizer. For many years they were highly available and their price trends lagged behind most industrial prices. Not so in the 1970s. At times some materials have been physically scarce. They have continuously been more expensive than before.

Higher priced inputs act to restrain gross productivity of farming. They also have a feedback effect. It is to accentuate the scarcity, and therefore the price, of land. Cheap fertilizer substituted for land and made it more plentiful. Its higher cost now makes land relatively scarcer.

Land has become more dear for another reason, namely, increased competition arising from actual or potential nonfarm use. A growing population draws more land into a myriad of uses ranging from home and industrial sites to highways to recreational areas. Although the three-fourths million acres lost each year probably include no more than one-third million acres of good farmland, the attrition over time helps sustain an uptrend in land prices.

Land price inflation yields a bonanza return to present owners, moves it out of the reach of younger farmers or any would-be farmers of modest means, and attracts speculative buyers and particularly those aided by a tax shelter. And insofar as land is assessed for taxes at higher than its farming value, it is driven out of ownership by operating farmers and perhaps entirely out of farming.

Farming has always been sensitive to fluctuations in demand for its products. When most of the market was domestic, attention focused on it. In the 1970s, domestic demand has been stabilized by unemployment benefits, social security pay-

FIGURE 1

CONCENTRATION OF AGRICULTURAL PRODUCTION IN 1969 (PERCENTAGE OF TOTAL
MARKET VALUE OF PRODUCTION FROM FARMS WITH $100,000
OR MORE IN GROSS SALES)

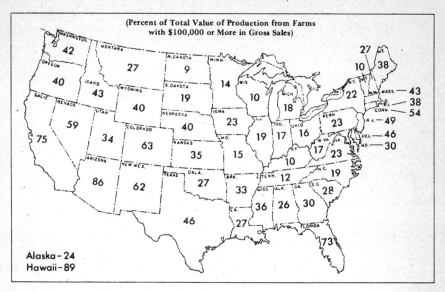

SOURCE: U.S. Census of Agriculture, 1969.

ments, and supplemental food programs. In 1976 the food stamp program alone added about $6 billion a year to retail demand for food. Export demand was, instead, the big variable. It became subject to economic and political events worldwide.

Of all the influences felt upon farming in the 1970s, the most newly prominent one was that of environmental concerns. These had the impact of restraining some yield-increasing techniques in farming (for example, application of some chemicals) and of imposing unwelcome regulations on farming practices. The regulations were not merely annoying; their form and application could affect the relative viability of various kinds of farming.

Last of external influences to be named here is financial. Terms of access to capital now exert a power-ful influence over the performance of farming and especially the kind of farming that is to prevail. Those terms are no longer expressed solely as loan versus equity capital. New is the role of income tax laws in affecting both the total supply of capital to farming and the competitive advantage of one kind of farming over another. In general, tax regulations have worked to the competitive disadvantage of the traditional family farm. A self-financed family farmer cannot compete with a "tax-loss" nonfarm investor who can absorb an operating loss in farming as a write-off from tax obligations in his other undertakings.

## EMERGING STRUCTURE OF FARMING

The Bureau of the Census has classified farms according to value

TABLE 2

NUMBER OF FARMS AND INCOME, BY VALUE OF SALES PER FARM, 1974

| VALUE OF SALES | NUMBER OF FARMS (THOUS.) | INCOME PER FARM* | | | PERCENT OF U.S. TOTAL NUMBER OF FARMS | PERCENT OF U.S. TOTAL INCOME* | | |
| | | FROM FARMING | | | | FROM FARMING | | |
| | | CASH RECEIPTS | NET | TOTAL | | CASH RECEIPTS | NET | TOTAL |
|---|---|---|---|---|---|---|---|---|
| $100,000 and over | 115 | $391,600 | $83,234 | $93,904 | 4.1 | 47.4 | 34.5 | 20.1 |
| $40,000–99,999 | 355 | 63,493 | 20,192 | 25,806 | 12.5 | 23.7 | 25.9 | 17.0 |
| $20,000–39,999 | 588 | 30,133 | 11,234 | 16,078 | 20.8 | 18.7 | 23.8 | 17.6 |
| $10,000–19,999 | 325 | 15,625 | 6,015 | 12,157 | 11.5 | 5.3 | 7.1 | 7.3 |
| $5,000–9,999 | 246 | 7,874 | 3,341 | 11,491 | 8.7 | 2.0 | 3.0 | 5.2 |
| $2,500–4,999 | 494 | 3,783 | 1,745 | 11,085 | 17.4 | 2.0 | 3.1 | 10.2 |
| Less than $2,500 | 707 | 1,071 | 1,022 | 17,209 | 25.0 | 0.9 | 2.6 | 22.6 |
| Total or average | 2,830 | 33,545 | 9,789 | 19,021 | 100.0 | 100.0 | 100.0 | 100.0 |

SOURCE: *Farm Income Statistics*, U.S., Department of Agriculture, Economic Research Service, Statistical Bulletin No. 547, July 1975.
* Includes government payments.

of sales, with separate categories for part-time and part-retirement farms. Data for 1969 show a high number of small farms including part-time and part-retirement farms (see table 1).

Class 1 farms in 1969 were only 7 percent of all farms, but they had 51 percent of all sales.

Concentration in the largest farms varies by type of farm and by area. The percent of all sales in 1969 originating in Class 1 farms varied as follows by type of farm. (Data exclude sales from part-time and part-retirement farms, which are usually almost negligible.)[9]

| | | | |
|----------------|------|-----------|------|
| Vegetable | 85.0 | Cotton | 54.4 |
| Poultry | 84.6 | General | 45.7 |
| Misc. field crop | 74.6 | Dairy | 41.1 |
| Livestock ranch | 72.8 | Cash grain | 35.4 |
| Fruit and nut | 68.8 | Tobacco | 18.6 |
| Livestock | 61.2 | | |

Concentration differs widely by states. The map in figure 1 is confined to value of production on farms selling more than $100,000 of product per year. In five states—Nevada, California, Arizona, New Mexico, and Florida—more than half of all production is on farms of that large size.

The Economic Research Service publishes annual estimates of farm sales and income according to volume of sales per farm. Data in table 2 apply to 1974. These data also show the high concentration in a relatively small number of large farms that Thomas Stout reported a decade ago. The 115,000 largest farms (sales volume of $100,000 or more) in 1974 were only 4 percent of all farms but made 47 percent of all sales and earned 34 percent of

9. U.S., Department of Commerce, *Census of Agriculture, 1969* (Washington, D.C.: U.S. Government Printing Office).

TABLE 3

PERCENT OF FARM OUTPUT PRODUCED
UNDER PRODUCTION CONTRACTS, 1970

| | |
|-----------------------------|------|
| Feed grains | 0.1 |
| Food grains | 2.0 |
| Vegetables for fresh market | 21.0 |
| Vegetables for processing | 85.0 |
| Potatoes | 45.0 |
| Citrus fruits | 55.0 |
| Other fruits and nuts | 20.0 |
| Sugarbeets | 98.0 |
| Sugarcane | 40.0 |
| Cotton | 11.0 |
| Tobacco | 2.0 |
| Oil bearing crops | 1.0 |
| Seed crops | 80.0 |
| Fed cattle | 18.0 |
| Sheep and lambs | 7.0 |
| Hogs | 1.0 |
| Eggs | 20.0 |
| Broilers | 90.0 |
| Turkeys | 42.0 |

SOURCE: Ronald L. Mighell and William S. Hoofnagle, *Contract Production and Vertical Integration in Farming, 1960 and 1970*, U.S., Department of Agriculture, Economic Research Service, ERS-479, 1972.

all net income from farming. Those selling $40,000 or more accounted for 71 percent of all sales and 60 percent of net income.

The 1.2 million smallest farms contributed only 2.9 percent of sales and 5.7 percent of net income earned in farming. Many of the smallest farms are part time and part retirement. A high proportion have sizable income from other sources. In 1974 the 707,000 farms with least net income from farming had off-farm income averaging more than $16,000.

Off-farm income received by the smallest farms increased rapidly in the 1960s and early 1970s. In 1960, farms receiving less than $2,500 net income from farming had an average off-farm income of only $2,732. By 1970 the off-farm income was up to $7,433. It more than doubled in the next four years.[10] It should be recognized, however, that individual farms moved into and out of the lowest income category according to changes in farm product prices.

Scattered data relate to how much farm production takes place in contractual integration and by large industrial-type corporations. Estimates for 1970 regarding contractual integration are shown in table 3. The proportions are highest for broilers, sugar beets, vegetables for processing, and seed crops.

The extent of direct farming by large corporations is more difficult to measure. The Economic Research Service estimated that in 1970 about 4.8 percent of all crops and likewise 4.8 percent of all livestock were produced under vertical integration, a term referring to direct operations by input-supplying or marketing firms.[11]

A selected and impressive statistic, reported by Donn Reimund, is that "large multiestablishment firms with farming operations" accounted for "7 percent of the total value of U.S. farm production as reported in the 1969 Census of Agriculture."[12] But as these "large multiestablishments" by no means comprise all the large corporate entities engaged in farming, we must conclude that big-scale corporate farming has reached substantial proportion. Certainly more than 10 percent of all farm output must be credited to big corporations.

10. *Farm Income Statistics*, U.S., Department of Agriculture, Economic Research Service, Statistical Bulletin No. 547, July 1975.

11. Ronald L. Mighell and William S. Hoofnagle, *Contract Production and Vertical Integration in Farming, 1960 and 1970*, U.S., Department of Agriculture, Economic Research Service, ERS-479, 1972.

12. Donn A. Reimund, *Farming and Agribusiness Activities of Large Multiunit Firms*, U.S., Department of Agriculture, Economic Research Service, ERS 591, 1975, p. v.

A summary judgment is that the American farm is devolving into a number of kinds of units. The traditional family farm (type 2a in the listing above) has not dominated as much in the past as generally believed, and it is being compromised and displaced persistently. Paradoxically, the farming likely to show the most staying power may be the part-time or retirement farm that does not depend solely on farm income for its viability.

Also encroaching on the owner-operated family farm are nonfarm landlord ownership (category 2b), the larger than family farm (category 3), the contractually integrated farm (category 5), and the industrial type corporate farm (category 6). The relative growth rate for each is difficult to predict.

This review must conclude with a note in the realm of policy. What happens to the American farm will depend in large measure on what is done to influence it. Policies in the past have been ambivalent. Many policies ranging from cooperative credit to publicly supported research and education definitely have favored the traditional owner-operated family farm. Some others have worked in the opposite direction. It is generally believed that price and income programs have, on balance, favored larger units. This was most clearly true prior to the imposition of a dollar limit on size of payment going to a single farmer. Working most in favor of larger, nonfamily, farms have been the various income tax rules.

To date, only the most marginal kinds of public action have been taken to redirect trends in the American farm. It remains to be seen whether the U.S. public, farmers and nonfarmers alike, will choose to exercise direction-giving control in the future.

ANNALS, AAPSS, **429**, Jan. 1977

# The Price of Farm Products in the Future

By WILLARD W. COCHRANE

ABSTRACT: The central focus of this article is on the behavior of U.S. grain prices in the context of prospective world developments over the next several decades. We first look at the process of farm price determination. We next look at the dramatic movements in farm prices, particularly grain prices, in the period 1970–75. Given this background, we explore in some depth what is likely to be the trend in world grain prices over the next 25 years and the bases of that trend development. The conclusion is reached that world grain prices are likely to trend upward over the period 1975–2000. It is argued, however, that grain prices are not likely to move along a smooth trend; to the contrary, grain prices are likely to fluctuate widely, sharply, and unpredictably around trend. Finally, the policy implications of future grain price behavior are explored and some tentative policy suggestions presented.

---

*Willard W. Cochrane is Professor of Agricultural Economics and Professor of Public Affairs at the University of Minnesota. He received a B.S. degree from the University of California at Berkeley in 1937, an M.S. degree from Montana State College in 1938, and a Ph.D. degree from Harvard University in 1945. He is the author of numerous books and articles, the most recent being* American Farm Policy, 1948–1973 *(with Mary E. Ryan), University of Minnesota Press, August 1976. He is past President of the American Agricultural Economic Association and a Fellow of that association. He served as Director of Agricultural Economics, U.S. Department of Agriculture, 1961–64, and as Dean of International Programs, University of Minnesota, 1965–70.*

THIS paper focuses on farm product prices in the United States. But because the agricultural sector of the United States is inextricably linked to the world market, the discussion of future U.S. prices will be in the context of expected world developments (about 50 percent of the grain moving in world trade comes from the United States, and about 35 percent of the grain produced in the United States is exported). Further, to an important degree this discussion will be concerned with grain prices. Grains are the basic food and feeding stuff at home and abroad and the leading farm commodity moving in international trade. Through the ubiquitous process of substitution, all farm prices are tied to and move with (after a period of adjustment) grain prices. Thus, the central focus of this article is on U.S. grain prices in the context of world developments over the next several decades.

## HOW FARM PRICES ARE DETERMINED

Farm prices in the United States are typically determined in markets with many buyers and many sellers; this is particularly the case in the grains. Prices are determined by the interaction of those impersonal forces: supply and demand. The determination of farm prices, particularly in the mid-1970s, probably comes closer to satisfying the conditions of the elementary textbook case of market price determination than is the case in any other sector of the economy. But having made this generalization, we must immediately make some qualifications and additions to the above statement.[1]

For many years, the federal government has exerted an important influence on farm prices. It has exerted this influence in several ways. First, it supported the prices of major commodities (such as wheat, corn, and cotton) at prices above or approaching short-run equilibrium levels. This it did by standing ready to take over the commodities of farmers participating in related programs whenever the market price of the commodity involved fell below the price support level. Second, the government affected the supply of major commodities coming into the market by numerous and varied production control programs. Third, the government affected the demand for a large number of commodities by acquiring those commodities in the market and disposing of them outside commercial channels (for example, through the operation of Public Law 480). By these various devices, the federal government caused the prices of farm commodities to be higher, at least in the short run, than they otherwise would have been. Government played an active role in the determination of farm prices from the end of World War II to 1972.

The markets for all farm commodities do not satisfy the condition of many buyers and many sellers. In the case of certain fruit and vegetable crops for processing and certain livestock products—dairy and poultry products—the markets have become increasingly monopolistic in the twentieth century. In the processing markets, strong monopsonists have emerged. In the dairy markets, a form of bilateral monopoly

1. For a good discussion of farm price behavior in differently structured markets, see William G. Tomek and Kenneth L. Robinson, *Agricultural Product Prices* (Ithaca, N.Y.: Cornell University Press, 1972), chs. 5, 8, 9, and 10.

has emerged. And in the case of poultry meat, open markets at the farm level have all but disappeared through integration. Thus, various types of monopolistic structures have come to dominate price formation in the markets for fruits, vegetables, dairy products, and poultry.

In the case of the grains, the U.S. market is one segment, albeit a large segment, of an international market. The price of corn or wheat in Chicago reflects growing conditions and demand changes in the Soviet Union almost as readily as it does such conditions in the United States. The supply of and demand for corn, which interact in the Chicago market to determine the price of corn, reflect worldwide supply and demand conditions. Thus, the spatial boundaries of the market for U.S. grain are worldwide.

Because of the growth period of a crop season or longer required in agricultural production, the supply response to price for agricultural commodities is delayed by a period of a crop season or longer. This delayed response gives rise to a price-supply-price sequence which has become known as the "Cobweb Theorem."[2] Price in one period induces a production response in a second period, which gives rise to a new price in the second period; the price determined in the second period once again induces a production response in the third period. this cobweb interaction goes on and on through time. Price movements through time will be sharp, extreme, and explosive where the elasticity of demand is low absolutely and low

relative to the elasticity of supply. And price movements through time will be moderate and tend to dampen down where the elasticity of demand is large absolutely and large relative to the elasticity of supply.

Further, because the principal product of agriculture, food, is required by consumers for physiological reasons in reasonably fixed amounts day after day, the demand for food in the aggregate is highly inelastic, and the demand for staple food products is strongly inelastic. This means that for any small change in the supply of food in the aggregate, or any of the staple food products, the prices of those products must move in the opposite direction by a large amount. This tends to give a "feast or famine" aspect to the food-agricultural sector. A little food surplus causes farm product prices to fall drastically; a little shortage causes farm prices to shoot skyward.

Although the basic forces of supply and demand, in markets with many buyers and many sellers, dominate the process of price formation in most agricultural commodities, each of these markets has characteristics which are peculiar to it. Some markets have been or are greatly influenced by government programs, some are becoming increasingly monopolistic in structure, and all, because of the natural growth process in agricultural production and the regular demands of the human stomach, tend to react haltingly through time and often in an extreme fashion. We must understand the unique aspects of farm commodity markets to understand the varied and often extreme behavior of farm product prices.

2. See, Mordecai Ezekiel, "The Cobweb Theorem," *Quarterly Journal of Economics*, February 1938, pp. 255–80; and Willard W. Cochrane, *Farm Prices: Myth and Reality* (Minneapolis: University of Minnesota Press, 1958), ch. 3.

## THE HECTIC 1970s

The international grain market began to tighten and grain prices began to rise during the period 1970–72. Any number of specific reasons may be given for this market tightening: major production control programs in Canada and the U.S.A.; a leveling off of the "Green Revolution" in South and Southeast Asia; important increases in grain exports from North America to other parts of the developed world. But the basic cause was to be found in the divergent trends in world grain production and consumption.[3] The growth in world grain consumption exceeded the growth in world grain production by about 1 million tons each year from 1961 to 1976, with the result that annual world grain consumption in the period 1970–72 exceeded world grain production, on a trend basis, by about 10 million tons per year. This excess in the world consumption of grains over world production, on a trend basis, was large enough to have a significant impact on world grain stocks. Total world stocks of wheat and coarse grains declined from 187 million tons in 1969–70 to 148 million tons at the beginning of the 1972–3 crop year, and, as a share of the total consumption of wheat and coarse grains, those stocks had declined from 22 percent in 1969–70 to 16 percent at the beginning of 1972–73. In sum, the period 1970–72 set the stage for the dramatic developments in 1972–73.

The world production of grain declined about 2 percent from trend during the crop year 1972–73 and declined between 2 and 3 percent from the level of production realized in 1971–72. The crop in the Soviet Union was particularly poor in 1972–73, declining from 181 million

3. This phenomenon is fully described and discussed in the *World Agricultural Situation*, Economic Research Service, USDA, December 1975, WAS-9, pp. 33–43.

tons in 1971–72 to 168 million tons in 1972–73. As a result of this poor crop, the Soviet Union entered the world market and purchased huge quantities of wheat, corn, and other grains. Its total imports of grain reached 24 million tons in calendar year 1973, as compared with some 2 million tons in 1970. The generally poor crop around the world and Soviet purchases, in the context of the generally tightening international market described above, set off a wave of buying and speculation around the world which drove grain prices to record highs.

The average price of corn received by farmers in the United States increased from $1.19 per bushel in October 1972 to $2.68 per bushel in August 1973. Since August 1973, corn prices received by farmers have fluctuated widely, reaching a high of $3.37 per bushel in August 1974 and falling back to $2.37 per bushel in December 1975. The movement in wheat prices was sharper and even more dramatic. The average price of wheat received by farmers in the United States increased from $1.32 per bushel in July 1972 to $4.62 in September 1973. Since September 1973, wheat prices too have fluctuated widely, reaching a high of $5.52 per bushel in February 1974 and falling back to $3.41 per bushel in December 1975.

World grain crops were well below trend in 1974–75 and 1975–76, causing the world grain situation to remain extremely tight during those years. As a result, the high level of grain prices realized in 1973 was maintained through the crop year 1975–76. Information regarding crop growing conditions around the world, the imposition of informal export controls by the U.S. government, changes in livestock feeding rates, and other supply-demand factors caused grain prices in the United States to fluctuate rather widely over the period 1972–76, as we have observed. But in a trend sense, grain prices in the United States and for the world moved sideward between July 1973 and July 1976.

The very high grain prices realized during the period 1973–76 were pleasantly received by grain producers, but they worked great hardship on certain groups. Livestock producers in the United States caught between skyrocketing feed grain prices and consumer resistance to high meat prices experienced great financial difficulties, and many livestock producers were forced out of business. Less developed countries on a grain import basis also experienced serious difficulties during this period. At times they could not obtain grains at any price; all free supplies were tied up by contracts. And when they could obtain supplies, the high prices which they were forced to pay for those supplies caused them serious balance-of-payment difficulties. For purchasers of grain, the period 1973–76 was a trying time, indeed.

The question posed by supply-demand developments in the grains for the early 1970s is the following. Do the three poor crop years out of four in the period 1972–76 represent some sort of weather aberration? And with the return to a favorable cycle of weather, will adequate supplies of grains become available to world consumers at reasonable prices? Or does the somewhat longer period 1970–76, with its ups and downs in production, and with world grain consumption clearly outdistancing world grain production, represent the true long-run demand and supply balance for grains? If the latter is the correct picture,

we may expect the long-run trend in the real price of grains to rise in world markets.

## LONG-RUN FUTURE TREND IN PRICES

If food and agricultural policies and investment policies in agriculture in countries around the world in the period 1975–2000 are not greatly different from those of the early 1970s, then, in the judgment of this writer, the trend in the real price of grains will be upward over the long period, 1975–2000.[4] How sharply prices will trend upward it is difficult to say. The slope of the upward trend will depend upon several unknowns and imponderables. An increase in the real price of grain is defined to mean that the share of the average consumer's income spent on grain or grain products will increase.

The argument that the real price of grain will rise over the long period 1975–2000 rests on several strands of thought or sets of factors. Three sets of factors are considered here: supply factors, demand factors, and conjectural factors.

*Supply factors.* Total cultivated land in the world is a small percentage of the total land mass—some 11 percent. But this does not mean that the arable land in the world can easily or readily be expanded. It is estimated that the total potentially arable land in the world amounts to about 24 percent of the total land mass.[5] But much, if

4. International Food Policy Research Institute, *Meeting Food Needs in the Developing World: The Location and Magnitude of the Task in the Next Decade*, Research Report No. 1, International Food Policy Research Institute, Washington, D.C., February 1976.
5. *The World Food Problem*, a Report of the President's Science Advisory Committee, vol. 2, White House, May 1967, pp. 429–36.

not most, of this land can be made arable only at considerable cost—costs required for draining, clearing, leveling, or terracing to transform nonarable land into arable land. Further, the land so transformed is very likely to be less productive than land already in cultivation. If this were not the case, investments would already have been made in the land to convert it to an arable status. This means that the supply function for arable land has slope, and for most of the developed world and the less developed regions of Asia, it is highly inelastic. It may be that the supply of arable land in Africa and South America is elastic, but even in those areas the supply function must be positively inclined. What the precise elasticity of supply of arable land in the world is may be debated, but not the fact that the supply function is positively inclined. This means, in turn, that at the present state of technology additional land will be brought into cultivation only at higher product prices or, as we have hypothesized here, as the real price of grain in the world market trends upward.

The line of reasoning presented above with respect to land holds with even greater force with respect to water available for irrigation. Water has become an exceedingly scarce resource around the world. This is not to say that water available for irrigation cannot be increased in supply. It can. But only at considerable cost—costs required to pump water from greater depths, to transport water greater distances, to impound water in less efficient ponds and reservoirs, and to move water through or around natural barriers. This means that the supply curve for water for irrigation is positively inclined. It is further argued here that the supply of water for irrigation

is inelastic in almost every region of the world where irrigation water is required.

The public recognition of the limited oil reserves in the world relative to demand in the early 1970s, the skyrocketing prices of petroleum products, and the general and significant increase in energy prices had a direct and adverse effect on agricultural production. The prices of all nonfarm-produced inputs that are dependent on energy in their production (for example, machinery, nitrogenous fertilizer) rose significantly, as did the prices of direct energy inputs (electricity, gasoline). This, of course, increased the cost of producing agricultural products in the 1970s. In the long run, the prices of agricultural products must increase sufficiently to cover the higher costs of energy, direct and indirect, to agricultural producers. Further, most signs point to a long-run increase in the cost of energy to users, not a decrease. Thus, the growing scarcity of that easy-to-use source of energy, petroleum, in particular, and the rising cost of energy, generally, must be viewed as additional deterrents to the rate of growth in agricultural production around the world.

But it is the interaction of the growing scarcities of land, water, and energy that operates as an important drag to increased production. Energy is required in ever larger amounts to increase total agricultural production where dwindling supplies of water must be pumped and moved to new lands that have been leveled and diked to produce crops that make heavy use of fertilizer. The whole process is technically feasible, but it can only take place at higher and higher costs. This is the meaning of the increased scarcity of conventional resources which confronts producers of agricultural products whether in the United States, India, or Brazil.

*Demand factors.* Short of some demographic miracle or the general onset of Malthusian controls, the population of the world is expected to double by the year 2010. This means that total food production in the world must approximately double by the year 2010. It is sometimes observed that most of this increase in population will occur in the less developed world, with the direct or indirect implication that the surplus-food-producing developed world will not help feed the food-deficit less developed world. This could be the way the tightening food situation in the world is resolved; the developed world holds down the real cost of food to its consumers by restricting food aid shipments while the Malthusian controls of starvation and increased death rates among the very young and very poor take over in the less developed world. But at least in its crudest form, this, in the view of this writer, will not be the course of world developments. Strong, but not always effective, efforts will be made in the less developed world to keep the rate of growth in food production from lagging behind population growth in those areas. And sincere, but not always wise, efforts will be made in the developed world to assist the less developed regions in meeting their increased food requirements. These efforts will include economic assistance, technical assistance, and food aid.

Whether all of these efforts will prove successful in meeting the food requirements of a world population that has doubled in size remains to be seen. But the important point to be made here is that those efforts will exert a strong pull, or a strong demand, on the scarce productive resources described in the previous section. This strong pull will operate to increase the prices of those inputs. It must to induce them to move into the agricultural productive system. And to cover the increased costs of production resulting from the higher input prices, the real price of the product must in the long-run rise. This is the way that a doubling of the world population will operate to create an upward movement in the real price of food.

But this is not the end of the demand story. Developments in the developed world seem likely to create a further upward pressure on food prices. Rising real incomes in Japan, Western Europe, Eastern Europe, the Soviet Union, and in certain newly rich areas have resulted in important increases in the per capita consumption of animal products—particularly meat. But, typically, those areas cannot produce all of the raw products out of which the animal products they require can be produced, namely, feed grains and oil meals. Thus, these regions have turned increasingly to North America for the needed raw materials of animal production.

If the real incomes of peoples in the developed world continue to increase with economic development, we must expect: (1) the per capita consumption of animal products in the developed countries involved to increase and (2) the imports of grain and oil meals into numerous developed countries from North America to continue to increase. This means that developed nations will, in the future, be competing strongly with the nations of the less developed world for surplus grains of North America. This action will further serve to tighten the international grain market and drive up the price of grain to all those dependent on grain imports.

In sum, the income effect on consumption behavior will cause the per capita consumption of animal products to increase in the developed nations with the further economic growth of those nations.[6] The countries involved must typically go into the international market and purchase much of the raw materials (such as feed grains, oil meal) out of which to produce the increased supplies of animal products. These countries also possess the foreign exchange to purchase those commodities at prevailing market prices and under conventional commercial terms. Thus, they are in a strong position to bid free supplies available for export away from the needy less developed countries that suffer from chronic shortages of foreign exchange. And this element of foreign demand, when added to world population growth, must result in an extraordinarily strong total world demand for grains in the period 1975–2000. This strong total demand interacting with a lagging supply could create a persistent upward pressure on the world price of grains over the long-run future.

*Conjectural factors.* The confirmed optimists will argue that the economic force of the physical resource scarcities discussed above will be overcome by research, technological development, and farm technological advance. This may turn out to be the case. At this writing it is impossible either to prove or disprove this argument. But there are bits and pieces of evidence that should give proponents of this argument some pause. First, farm technological advance and the resulting rate of increase in agricultural productivity have been uneven and inconsistent in the United States in the 1970s. The "Green Revolution" and the resultant increase in yields per acre in South and Southeast Asia have slowed down and leveled off in the 1970s. Thus, in the developed world and the less developed world, that great force, farm technological advance, of the 1950s and 1960s, is sputtering in the 1970s.

Second, although much research in agricultural production is taking place around the world and continuous improvements in agricultural production practices and technologies are being made, there does not appear to be any production development in the offing comparable to the revolution in corn production in the United States from 1935 to 1965, or to the revolution in wheat production in Asia in the 1960s. With respect to agricultural production developments, we appear to be in a period of refinements, not major breakthroughs.

Third, world grain production lagged behind world grain consumption in the 1960s—a decade of great technological development and rapid farm technological advance.[7]

---

6. It should be recognized that the growing scarcity of natural resources in a finite world could operate to slow rates of overall economic growth in all countries around the world. Such developments would tend to vitiate the specific argument being made at this point, but they do not weaken the general argument that growth in food production for the world as a whole is likely to lag behind growth in food requirements over the long period 1975–2000. See, Mihajlo Mesarovic and Eduard Pestel, *Mankind at the Turning Point, Second Report of the Club of Rome* (New York: Reader's Digest Press, 1974).

7. The counter argument may be made that production controls in the United States and Canada contributed to a lag in world grain production in the 1960s, and without those controls in operation it will be easier to overcome the lag in the 1970s. This is a reasonable argument, but the fact remains that the lag in grain production in the 1970s is not being overcome.

To cope with this lag in world grain production and growing resource scarcities, research, technological development, and farm technological advance must be more pervasive and more effective in the 1970s, '80s, and '90s than they were in the 1960s. And this is one possible outcome. But in the judgment of this writer, the odds are strongly against such an outcome. We will have farm technological advance in the 1970s, '80s, and '90s and the resulting increases in agricultural productivity, but such technological advances and such increases in productivity are not likely to be great enough to increase world grain production sufficiently to meet the increased demands at a constant level of real grain prices.

Finally, there is that great conjectural factor, the weather. There is an argument being developed and advanced by the climatologists that the climate is changing, and adversely for crop production in the Northern Hemisphere. The argument states that the Northern Hemisphere has been cooling slowly since the 1940s. This cooling trend affects the flow and direction of wind currents in such ways as to make the monsoon areas of the world drier and growing conditions in steppe areas, such as the American plains, more variable and uncertain.

Whether this argument proves correct remains to be seen. But it does suggest that crop growing conditions around the world are not likely to be any better over the next 25 years than they were during the past 25 years, and there is some possibility that they will be worse— perhaps much worse, perhaps only a little worse. In any event, the argument being advanced by prominent climatologists does not give comfort to agricultural experts who argue that the rapidly growing world food requirements will be easily and readily met by increased food production. To the contrary, it suggests one more important cause for concern with regard to the future food supply-demand balance for the world.

In summary, it is argued here that it is most probable (although not certain) that the long-run trend in the real price of grains in the world, hence in the United States, will be upward. All the important forces that will be at work over the next 25 years would seem (as of 1976) to point in this direction. Higher real prices of grain will be required to pull the additional and very scarce productive resources into the agricultural production system, and these higher real prices will serve to restrict consumer demands for food around the world. In the United States, this will mean higher livestock product prices and cereal product prices with the consequent consumer frustration and anger. In the rapidly developing developed areas of the world (for example, Japan, Soviet Union), this will mean a reduced rate of increase in animal product consumption and consumer unrest. In the less developed areas of the world, this will mean reduced food grain consumption among the very poor and increased death rates among the very young.

This view of the long-run future is similar to the views advanced by the English classical economists of the nineteenth century.[8] The opening up of the great grain basket in North America in the nineteenth century and the technological revolution in agriculture in the twentieth century threw the timing of their

8. Benjamin Higgins, *Economic Development: Problems, Principles and Policies*, rev. ed. (New York: W. W. Norton & Co., 1968), ch. 3.

argument off by 100 years or more. But the finite world, it is argued here, once more is closing in upon the expanding number of consumers and the expanding wants of those consumers.

## PRICE FLUCTUATIONS AROUND TREND

We should not expect world grain prices, hence U.S. food product prices, to trend upward in a nice, smooth configuration. Rather, we should expect world grain prices and U.S. food product prices to fluctuate sharply, widely, and unpredictably around trend unless governments intervene with effective stabilization programs and policies.

This is the logical expectation for the following reasons:

1. The world demand for total grains is highly inelastic—possibly approaching −.1.
2. The world production of grains varies from trend by 1 to 4 percent per year as the result of variations in the weather, hence in crop growing conditions. These annual variations in the weather are completely unpredictable.
3. The world is linked together by international trade in the grains so that a shortfall in production in one area (say, the Soviet Union) is reflected very quickly in the price of grain around the world (say, the United States).

What we have in the grains is thus an international market, albeit not a perfect one, in which total grain production varies modestly from year to year, around trend, as the result of variations in the weather. These modest variations in production, given the severe inelasticity of demand for grain, result, in turn, in wide swings in grain prices; and,

since the variations in the weather are unpredictable, the fluctuations in grain prices are unpredictable.

This phenomenon of wide and unpredictable price fluctuations in world grain prices may be expected whether the real price of grains is trending upward or downward or is constant, so long as governments do not intervene with some form of effective price stabilization. In a free international grain market, sharp, wide, unpredictable price fluctuations are the norm.

Sharp, wide, and unpredictable grain price fluctuations may be welcomed by a few (grain traders and speculators with superior information), but for most people such fluctuations create problems. Consumers rightly observe that retail food prices rarely decline in one period by as much as they advanced in a previous period; increased margins tend to get built into the retail price in periods of high prices. Grain producers must be cautious in their investment decisions when their product prices fluctuate widely and unpredictably. And livestock producers can be ruined financially where grain prices advance sharply and dramatically but increases in their meat product prices lag behind the upturn in grain prices by a production period or two.

Sharp, wide, and unpredictable price fluctuations in agriculture create risk for the producer, and the greater this risk the more cautious the producer will be with respect to making new and costly investments in his business. Thus, the effect of unpredictable price variability in agriculture is to slow down the rate of growth in agricultural production. And if the long-run trend argument presented in the previous section is correct, then the consequences of sharp, wide, and unpredictable fluctuations in the price of grains in the world market will be to slow down the rate of growth in world grain production, particularly in the highly commercial, surplus-producing areas, and exacerbate the long-run supply-demand balance for grains. The long-run supply-demand balance problem and the short-run price fluctuation problem are thus related.

## POLICY IMPLICATIONS

The policy implications of the foregoing analyses are many and varied. The policy ideas and prescriptions for dealing with the problems identified and discussed will depend upon through whose eyes the problems are being viewed— U.S. consumers, U.S. farmers (and which farmers—grain producers, or livestock producers), consumers in the rapidly developing developed countries (for example, Japanese consumers), or consumers in the less developed countries (for example, consumers living in poverty in India), and on and on. Since it is not possible to consider the policy perspectives of every group in the world in this short paper, or perhaps in any single paper, we will focus on the policy needs of United States consumers and producers with an eye on the international consequences.

If the world price of grains in real terms is to trend upward over the next 25 years, but with sharp, wide, and unpredictable annual fluctuations, then the United States needs to find ways and means of moderating that upward trend in world grain prices and to dampen down annual fluctuations around trend. It must find ways and means to moderate the upward trend in world prices unless it tries to isolate itself from the world

market. But the latter action is impractical, since the United States is the leading grain exporter in the world. It, thus, turns out that the United States, if it is to deal effectively with its domestic food price level problem, must find ways to deal effectively with a world price level problem (namely, the world grain price level).

One approach to moderating the upward trend in the real price of grains in the world market for the United States would involve finding ways and means of increasing the total supply of grains in the world relative to the total demand for grains. It might seek to do this in any number of ways. We suggest three possibilities:

1. Increase the support for research and development on agricultural production and energy production within the United States.
2. Increase the support for research and development in agricultural production and energy production under various kinds of international arrangements.
3. Offer economic assistance to less developed nations as an inducement to them to effectuate population control measures; such a policy might be undertaken unilaterally or in cooperation with other developed nations.

Another approach to moderating the upward trend in the real price of grains on the part of the United States could involve certain redistribution policies which have the effect of contracting effective demand or increasing supplies. We suggest three possibilities:

1. Limit food aid and other forms of economic aid to less developed nations that are pursuing effective

agricultural development policies and population control policies. In effect, this is the John Smith doctrine that says, those who won't work must starve.

2. Limit the exports of grain to developed nations in accordance with some internationally agreed-upon formula.

3. Develop an international agreement involving the oil exporting and importing nations with the objective of subsidizing the use of energy in agricultural production.

The pursuit of some combination of the above policies would have the effect of expanding supplies or contracting demand in the world market, hence operate to moderate the upward trend in world grain prices. This would benefit consumers of grain products and animal products around the world, including consumers in the United States. But the pursuit of such policies would not benefit producers of grain in the United States, and the pursuit of such policies with too great vigor could force grain prices downward and create income problems for domestic grain producers.

To protect the economic interests of grain producers in the United States and thereby induce them to continue to expand output, it would appear both desirable and necessary to guarantee grain farmers a fair price for their product. This might be achieved through a price support program or an income support program involving target prices and deficiency payments. Such programs could well be nonoperational in many, if not most, years if the price and income support features of such programs were established just below, and moved along with, the world trend in grain prices. But the programs would be available on a standby basis to protect farmers against a downturn in world grain prices. In other words, it is argued here that farm producers must be provided with price and income protection if the national society expects them to produce at full capacity year after year.

To this point we have been concerned only with the trend problem, and the policy discussion has been limited to ways and means of moderating the long-run upward trend in the real price of grains in the world market. But what about the short-run fluctuations in the price of grains? To cope with this problem, the United States acting alone or in cooperation with other important importing and exporting nations must implement a reserve stock program for the grains with the capacity to even out supplies between crop seasons and thereby stabilize prices over time. There is really no alternative to such a policy, where crop production varies unpredictably as the result of unpredictable variations in the weather.

Any number of reserve stock programs might be conceptualized, each with a specific price stabilization objective and each with specific decision rules for acquiring and releasing stocks. We cannot in this brief paper explore the many policy ramifications of a reserve stock program for the grains.[9] We can and do argue, however, that a reserve stock program to stabilize world grain prices is both economically desirable and operationally feasible. But whether agreement can be reached with regard to price stabilization objectives within a country, such as the United States, or among

9. See, Willard W. Cochrane and Yigal Danin, *Reserve Stock Grain Models, the World and the United States* (Minneapolis: University of Minnesota Agricultural Experiment Station Technical Bulletin 305, March 1976).

such countries as the U.S.A., the U.S.S.R., the E.E.C., and Japan, remains to be seen. To date, little has been achieved in the way of reaching an agreement with regard to price stabilization objectives. Producer interests seek a high price ceiling; consumer interests want a low floor price. And there matters stand.

## CONCLUSION

A compromise on U.S. farm policy that was reasonably acceptable to all concerned was reached in 1965 after 20 years of struggle. But in the period 1970–75, the world of food and agriculture turned upside down; the general surplus condition gave way to a general deficit situation. It is the principal point of this paper that this general deficit situation will be with us for a long time to come. And this is a world problem from which the United States cannot divorce itself. It cannot and remain the leading supplier of grains to a deficit world.

So now the United States and the world are in need of a viable food and agricultural policy. But such a policy has not been forthcoming. Some of the elements of such a policy have been outlined above. But the arduous task of working out the compromise between consumer and producer interests within the United States is just beginning to be talked about. And the even more difficult task of effecting a compromise on food and agricultural policy among the importing and exporting nations, too, is in the very early discussion stage. Thus, we can think and talk about the elements of an international food and agricultural policy, as we have done above, but the shape and substance of the policy that must emerge is not at all clear. Perhaps its shape and substance will become clear in response to the unfolding future. But if the arguments presented in this paper are valid, we need policy guidance *now* to make the future more tolerable. As of 1976, that policy guidance is lacking.

ANNALS, AAPSS, 429, Jan. 1977

# Rural-Urban Differences in Attitudes and Behavior in the United States

By NORVAL D. GLENN AND LESTER HILL, JR.

ABSTRACT: Recent American data reveal moderate to substantial farm-nonfarm differences on a few kinds of attitudes and behavior, but since farm people now are only about 4 percent of the population, the farm-nonfarm distinction cannot account for much of the total variation of any kind of attitudes or behavior. The kinds of attitudes and behavior which differ substantially between farm and nonfarm people usually differ monotonically by community size; hence, "ruralism" seems to some extent to characterize residents of the smaller dense settlements and, to a lesser extent, those of intermediate-sized cities. Furthermore, city residents with rural backgrounds tend to retain rural attitudes and behavior characteristics, size of community of origin being a stronger predictor of some attitudes than size of community of current residence. Although the association of community size with a more or less representative list of attitudinal variables is weak, such correlates of community size as age and socioeconomic status do not largely account for the larger associations, which probably reflect a tendency for social and cultural change to occur earlier in the larger communities. The explanatory utility of size of community of origin and of residence seems less than that of age and education but at least as great as that of several other explanatory variables favored by social scientists, such as family income and occupational prestige.

Norval D. Glenn is Professor of Sociology at the University of Texas at Austin. Formerly on the faculties of Miami University and the University of Illinois at Urbana, his publications include four books and more than 80 journal articles and book chapters, primarily on social stratification, political sociology, the family, aging and the life cycle, and urban sociology. He is author of a forthcoming monograph on the methodology of cohort analysis.

Lester Hill, Jr., a doctoral candidate in the Department of Sociology at the University of Texas at Austin, is writing a dissertation on the relationship between attitudes and behavior.

THERE is considerable disagreement among social scientists concerning the importance of the rural-urban distinction in modern societies. At least three rather distinctive viewpoints have some prominence. The first, exemplified in Louis Wirth's classic essay on "Urbanism as a Way of Life," posits direct, universal effects of population size, density, and heterogeneity on important aspects of social structure, culture, and personality.[1] According to this view, the concentration of people of diverse characteristics and backgrounds into large, dense settlements necessarily produces social isolation, individualism, social disorganization, and a number of other phenomena.

A second major viewpoint, exemplified in the writings of Richard Dewey[2] and Herbert Gans,[3] among others, is that few if any social, cultural, and personality characteristics are necessarily and invariably associated with the size, density, and heterogeneity of settlements. Critics of the Wirth thesis also often point out that population size, density, and heterogeneity are imperfectly correlated with one another and that the effects of each may not be the same as the effects of the other two. According to this view, the correlates of urbanization vary from society to society and from time to time in any one society and are often little more than the results of historical accident. For instance, it is pointed out that many present rural-urban differences in the United States result from inclusion among the later immigrants—who arrived after the closing of the frontier and thus generally settled in the industrial cities—of a relatively large percentage of Catholics, Jews, and persons from southern and eastern Europe. Hence, rural-urban differences tend to reflect religious and ethnic differences.

Related to this second view is the thesis that rural-urban differences, whatever their source, tend to disappear during the advanced stages of urbanization and industrialization.[4] This view, which the senior author has called the "massification thesis,"[5] is that due to such influences as standardized education, improved means of transportation which break down rural isolation, and saturation of small towns and the countryside with stimuli from the mass media, urban culture and lifestyles are diffused to the hinterland—that rural people become almost indistinguishable from their city cousins. So far as we know, no social scientist has denied that considerable urban-to-rural cultural diffusion has occurred in modern societies, but the extent to which this diffusion has obliterated rural-urban differences remains an issue of debate.

An intermediate viewpoint—articulated most completely and clearly in a recent essay by Claude Fischer[6]

1. Louis Wirth, "Urbanism as a Way of Life," *American Journal of Sociology*, vol. 44 (July 1938), pp. 3–24.

2. Richard Dewey, "The Rural-Urban Continuum: Real but Relatively Unimportant," *American Journal of Sociology*, vol. 66 (July 1960), pp. 60–6.

3. Herbert J. Gans, "Urbanism and Suburbanism as Ways of Life: A Re-Evaluation of Definitions," in Arnold M. Rose, ed., *Human Behavior and Social Processes* (Boston: Houghton-Mifflin, 1962), pp. 625–28.

4. For instance, see Kenneth Boulding, "The Death of the City: A Frightened Look at Post-Civilization," in Oscar Handlin and John Burchard, eds., *The Historian and the City* (Cambridge, Mass.: MIT and Harvard University Press, 1963), p. 143.

5. Norval D. Glenn, "Massification versus Differentiation: Some Trend Data from National Surveys," *Social Forces*, vol. 46 (December 1967), pp. 172–80.

6. Claude Fischer, "Toward a Subcultural Theory of Urbanism," *American Journal of Sociology*, vol. 80 (May 1975), pp. 1319–41.

but presented in at least embryonic form in several earlier publications —is that whereas population size, density, and heterogeneity do not have all of the effects attributed to them by Wirth, they are conducive to innovation and unconventional behavior. According to Fischer, population concentration "produces a diversity of subcultures, strengthens them, and fosters diffusion among them. . . ." Presumably, the concentration of diverse people into dense settlements is conducive to a cross-fertilization of ideas, to an awareness of and tolerance of diverse values and lifestyles, and thus to innovation and unconventionality.

If in each society the cities tend to be the sources of innovation and to be in the vanguard of social and cultural change, appreciable rural-urban differences are likely to exist even if much urban-to-rural diffusion of culture has occurred and is occurring. During the initial phases of any particular process of change, the urban population will tend to change more rapidly, leading to rural-urban divergence. Later, "ceiling effects" will tend to limit the rate of change in the urban population, and urban-to-rural diffusion will lead to more rapid change in the rural population and to rural-urban convergence. Thus, as older rural-urban differences diminish or disappear, new ones will appear. Whereas no particular culture traits, aside from those closely associated with receptivity to change, will invariably be associated with rural or urban communities, important rural-urban differences of some kind will tend to persist even in the most highly urbanized and industrialized societies.

The social scientific literature does not provide the evidence (at least not in a systematic fashion) which would allow a definitive choice among the differing viewpoints. Although the preponderance of evidence seems to suggest that the Wirth thesis is not correct without important qualifications, survey data from virtually all modern societies reveal remaining rural-urban differences in regard to a variety of kinds of attitudes and behavior. There is evidence that in the United States some rural-urban differences have recently increased rather than diminished,[7] but the evidence does not allow any conclusion about the magnitude or direction of the overall change. The evidence that social and cultural change typically originates in cities and proceeds more rapidly among urban than rural people is convincing but not definitive. It is easy to demonstrate that change often has occurred in this fashion, but we do not know that it has always done so, even in modern societies, or that it usually has done so in most societies.

Even though the Fischer thesis is not undeniably correct, presently available evidence, as we assess it, makes it more credible than any competing theoretical perspective. We suspect that it (or some slight variant) will soon become the most widely accepted view among students of rural-urban differences (if it is not already), and we provisionally accept it. However, even a developing consensus on the basic sources of rural-urban cultural and behavioral differences will not still debate concerning the practical and theoretical importance of these differences in modern societies. For instance, the importance of differences created by any differing receptivity

7. Glenn, "Massification versus Differentiation," and Norval D. Glenn, "Recent Trends in Intercategory Differences in Attitudes," *Social Forces*, vol. 52 (March 1974), pp. 395–401.

to change depends in large measure on whether the receptivity varies in a more or less linear fashion with community size or whether the main difference is a disjunctive one between the most truly rural people (those who both live and work in the open countryside) and the remainder of the population. If the latter should be correct, the resulting rural-urban differences would be of rapidly diminishing practical importance in most modern societies as the rural-farm population becomes a very small proportion of the total. Furthermore, as Fischer is careful to point out, if his theory is correct, it does not necessarily follow that rural-urban differences are usually large enough to be of much practical importance or that the rural-urban distinction accounts for a large proportion of the variation in attitudes, behavior, and lifestyles in any society. To those who would understand, or who would utilize knowledge of, variations in attitudes and behavior in the United States, an important question remains unanswered: does the rural-urban distinction make enough difference to warrant serious attention? Our purpose here is to provide a provisional answer to that question.

## THE MAGNITUDE AND NATURE OF CONTEMPORARY RURAL-URBAN DIFFERENCES

The magnitude of rural-urban differences in attitudes and behavior shown by American national surveys varies according to kind of attitudes and behavior and according to the way the rural-urban distinction is made. Usually, although not always, the largest differences appear when farmers (and their families), or rural-farm people, are compared with the rest of the population. Although students of rural and urban society and culture do not agree on just how the rural-urban distinction should be made (or whether it should be conceived of as a continuum rather than a dichotomous distinction), there are compelling reasons for considering rural-farm people the most truly rural segment of the population and for considering the farm-nonfarm distinction the most theoretically meaningful of any dichotomous rural-urban distinction. As an aggregate, the farm population differs to an important degree in many demographic characteristics from even the residents of the smaller dense settlements, and farmers are the only major segment of the population for which both place of work and place of residence are usually in the open countryside. Residents of the open countryside who are in nonfarm occupations often (perhaps usually) both work and maintain most of their social relations in dense settlements of some size. Therefore, it is useful to begin a treatment of rural-urban differences with a farm-nonfarm comparison.

Recent national survey data show that farmers (and their families) do not differ substantially from other occupational categories in a large proportion of the kinds of attitudes and behavior covered by the surveys. However, differences not likely to have resulted from sampling error appear in responses to at least a large minority of the questions. For instance, Norval Glenn and Jon Alston drew on data from 92 questions asked on American opinion polls from 1953 to 1965 and found farmers, as a whole, to be relatively prejudiced, ethnocentric, isolationist, intolerant of deviance, opposed to civil liberties, distrustful of people, traditionally religious, ascetic, work-oriented, Puritanical, uninformed, and favorable to early

TABLE 1

Responses (in Percent) to Selected Attitudinal Questions Asked on American Gallup Polls, by Occupation of Head of Household

| | Professional and Business | White Collar | Farm | Manual |
|---|---|---|---|---|
| **Religious beliefs** | | | | |
| believe in the Devil (1968) | 57 | 56 | 75 | 61 |
| believe in life after death (1968) | 76 | 66 | 86 | 71 |
| believe in hell (1968) | 60 | 56 | 86 | 68 |
| believe in heaven (1968) | 77 | 81 | 93 | 89 |
| **Issues concerning personal morals and vices** | | | | |
| think that birth control information should be available to anyone who wants it (1968) | 86 | 81 | 64 | 76 |
| think use of marijuana should be made legal (1969) | 18 | 22 | 5 | 10 |
| would like to see stricter state laws concerning sale of obscene literature on newsstands (1969) | 71 | 69 | 81 | 79 |
| would find pictures of nudes in magazines objectionable (1969) | 64 | 64 | 89 | 76 |
| have smoked cigarettes in past week (1972) | 48 | 54 | 29 | 48 |
| **Minority-majority issues** | | | | |
| would vote for a well-qualified Jew for president (1969) | 95 | 92 | 73 | 87 |
| would vote for a well-qualified Catholic for president (1969) | 95 | 93 | 80 | 91 |
| would vote for a well-qualified Negro for president (1969) | 76 | 74 | 56 | 70 |
| would vote for a well-qualified woman for president (1969) | 55 | 58 | 47 | 54 |
| think the U.S. would be governed better if women had more say in politics (1969) | 21 | 21 | 13 | 25 |
| would vote for a well-qualified woman for Congress (1970) | 90 | 90 | 71 | 82 |
| approve of marriage between Catholics and Protestants (1969) | 73 | 67 | 46 | 62 |
| approve of marriage between Jews and non-Jews (1968) | 71 | 69 | 34 | 59 |
| approve of marriage between whites and nonwhites (1968) | 28 | 24 | 9 | 20 |
| **Political issues** | | | | |
| consider themselves conservative (1972) | 37 | 34 | 41 | 41 |
| favor lowering voting age to 18 (1969) | 60 | 62 | 72 | 67 |
| think law enforcement agencies should be tougher in dealing with crime and lawlessness (1972) | 80 | 81 | 93 | 84 |
| would favor a law requiring a police permit to buy a gun (1971) | 76 | 69 | 47 | 71 |
| think college students should have a greater say in the running of colleges (1969) | 29 | 33 | 16 | 27 |
| have favorable view of Red China (1972) | 30 | 20 | 17 | 22 |
| have favorable view of Russia (1972) | 54 | 40 | 35 | 38 |

Source: Various issues of the *Gallup Opinion Index*.

marriage and high fertility.[8] These differences existed not only in the adult population as a whole but also among young nonsouthern Protestants. Although these differences tend to confirm popular stereotypes of rural-farm people, most of them were fairly small, and in many cases only a small minority of farmers exhibited the characteristics which were more prevalent among farmers than among persons in other occupations.

Rural-farm people have become such a small proportion of the total population that the most recent national surveys do not give reliable estimates of the characteristics of the remaining farmers. For instance, the American Institute of Public Opinion (the American Gallup Poll) stopped reporting separate data for the farm respondents late in 1973. However, data from the late 1960s and early 1970s show that farmers were still the most distinctive (and usually the most conservative) segment of the population in regard to many kinds of attitudes (see table 1). For instance, farmers tended to be more fundamentalist in religious beliefs, Puritanical, prejudiced, and conservative on political issues than persons in any other occupational category. In general, they resembled manual workers more than they resembled persons in higher-status occupations (although Glenn and Alston found farmers' attitudes on labor-management issues to resemble those of business and professional people).

8. Norval D. Glenn and Jon P. Alston, "Rural-Urban Differences in Reported Attitudes and Behavior," *Southwestern Social Science Quarterly*, vol. 47 (March 1967), pp. 381–400. See, also, Norval D. Glenn and Jon P. Alston, "Cultural Distances among Occupational Categories," *American Sociological Review*, vol. 33 (June 1968), pp. 365–82.

Although a few of the farm-nonfarm differences in table 1 are fairly large, it should be kept in mind that we generally selected for reporting the largest differences we could find; therefore, the reported differences should not be considered representative of farm-nonfarm differences in general. Furthermore, the farm-nonfarm distinction accounted for only a small proportion of the total variation in responses even in the case of the items for which the differences were the largest. Since the rural-nonfarm population was no more than about 5 percent of any of the samples, even categorical differences between farmers and nonfarmers would not have produced substantial variation in the total samples.[9] Thus, in many respects the practical importance of even the largest farm-nonfarm differences is not very great. For instance, farmers do not constitute a "market" distinctive and large enough to be of much concern to most manufacturers and retailers, except those whose goods are specifically for the agricultural industry. On the other hand, farm-nonfarm differences do have some practical importance, the best example perhaps being in regard to politics. Farmers retain political influence disproportionate to their numbers (for instance, because "agricultural states," such as the Dakotas, with small populations but relatively large numbers of farmers, have two U.S. senators, the same as the populous industrial states), and any small portion of the electorate can be crucial to the outcome of a close election.

The theoretical importance of the farm-nonfarm attitudinal differences

9. Rural-farm people were about 5 percent of the total U.S. population in 1970 and are now only about 4 percent.

TABLE 2

RESPONSES (IN PERCENT) TO SELECTED ATTITUDINAL QUESTIONS ASKED ON
AMERICAN GALLUP POLLS, BY SIZE OF COMMUNITY*

| | UNDER 2,500, RURAL | 2,500– 49,999 | 50,000– 499,999 | 500,000– 999,999 | 1,000,000 AND OVER |
|---|---|---|---|---|---|
| **Religious beliefs** | | | | | |
| believe that religion is old-fashioned and out-of-date (1975) | 12 | 18 | 20 | 19 | 35 |
| have a great deal of confidence in the church or in organized religion (1975) | 51 | 48 | 41 | 44 | 32 |
| are very religious (1975) | 30 | 29 | 24 | 27 | 20 |
| **Issues concerning personal morals and vices** | | | | | |
| think abortion under any circumstances should be legal (1975) | 9 | 19 | 23 | 29 | 31 |
| would favor anti-abortion constitutional amendment (1975) | 53 | 43 | 45 | 38 | 38 |
| think use of marijuana should be made legal (1974) | 21 | 21 | 27 | 33 | 35 |
| believe it is wrong for people to have sex relations before marriage (1973) | 61 | 50 | 44 | 41 | 34 |
| would find topless nightclub waitresses objectionable (1973) | 68 | 69 | 58 | 51 | 46 |
| **Minority-majority issues** | | | | | |
| favor Equal Rights Amendment (1975) | 53 | 59 | 55 | 65 | 67 |
| would vote for woman for president (1976) | 68 | 73 | 73 | 76 | 80 |
| consider being married, with children, and no full-time job to be ideal lifestyle (women only, 1976) | 53 | 39 | 45 | 38 | 38 |
| **Political issues** | | | | | |
| favor registration of all firearms (1975) | 50 | 64 | 71 | 77 | 81 |
| would favor conservative over liberal political party (1975) | 42 | 43 | 39 | 44 | 36 |
| feel that war is outmoded as a way of settling differences between nations (1975) | 37 | 45 | 48 | 51 | 48 |
| are politically liberal (1974) | 16 | 26 | 28 | 27 | 35 |
| favor unconditional amnesty for draft evaders (1974) | 29 | 26 | 38 | 39 | 40 |
| favor reestablishing diplomatic relations with Cuba (1974) | 58 | 62 | 60 | 70 | 71 |
| have a great deal of confidence in labor unions (1973) | 11 | 14 | 16 | 15 | 18 |

SOURCE: Various issues of the *Gallup Opinion Index.*
* Suburban residents are classified according to the size of their central cities.

TABLE 3

SIZE OF COMMUNITY LIVED IN AT AGE 16, U.S. ADULT POPULATION, BY AGE, COMBINED DATA FROM SURVEYS CONDUCTED IN 1972, 1973, 1974, AND 1975

| | AGE | | | | | | | |
|---|---|---|---|---|---|---|---|---|
| | 18–29 | 30–39 | 40–49 | 50–59 | 60–69 | 70–79 | 80 & UP | TOTAL |
| Open countryside | 22.3 | 28.5 | 30.2 | 38.9 | 44.6 | 46.9 | 55.6 | 32.9 |
| Dense settlements with less than 50,000 residents | 30.4 | 30.2 | 34.1 | 27.3 | 29.8 | 31.4 | 22.2 | 30.3 |
| Cities with 50,000 or more population and their suburbs | 47.3 | 41.3 | 35.7 | 33.7 | 25.6 | 21.6 | 22.2 | 36.8 |
| Total | 100.0 | 100.0 | 100.0 | 100.0 | 100.0 | 100.0 | 100.0 | 100.0 |
| N | 1,565 | 1,119 | 1,027 | 989 | 781 | 462 | 117 | 6,060 |

SOURCE: The General Social Surveys conducted by the National Opinion Research Center (James A. Davis, principal investigator).

depends largely on whether they reflect largely socioeconomic, demographic, and religious-ethnic differences or whether they are in some way causally related to population concentration. Glenn and Alston conclude that most of the differences they found did not reflect differences in age, religious preference, region, income, or education; the differences existed among young nonsouthern Protestants as well as in the total population, and farmers often differed from manual workers, whom they resembled in income and education. Although we have not subjected the data in table 1 to the controls used by Glenn and Alston, we are confident that the controls would not eliminate most of the differences, since the topics are similar to those studied by Glenn and Alston. Furthermore, socioeconomic differences can hardly account for most of the attitudinal differences, in view of the often substantial attitudinal differences between the farm and manual classes.

It is apparent from community-size breakdowns of responses to the items used for table 1 (not shown) and from responses to a number of questions asked on more recent national surveys (table 2) that the farm-nonfarm distinction is not the only rural-urban distinction useful for explaining attitudes and behavior. Again, it must be pointed out that we tended to select for reporting the items showing the greatest variation in responses by our independent variable, and thus the data do not indicate the typical degree of variation in expressed attitudes among communities of different sizes. However, the reported data are very nearly representative of all of the data we examined in one important respect:[10] when there is any appreciable variation in responses by community size, the variation is usually monotonic rather than being a disjunctive difference between the smallest communities and all others. That is, the largest communities usually differ from the medium-sized

10. We examined all of the data in recent (since the late 1960s) issues of the *Gallup Opinion Index*.

communities about as much (and in the same direction) as the medium-sized communities differ from the smallest communities. This pattern of variation suggests that it is useful to conceive of a rural-urban continuum rather than a dichotomous rural-urban distinction. It also indicates that attitudinal and behavioral variation associated with degree of population concentration will not become unimportant simply because the most truly rural people become a very small proportion of the population. A rather substantial proportion of the population lives, and probably will long continue to live, in inter-mediate-sized communities;[11] and the differences between these people and the residents of the largest cities (and their suburbs) constitute rural-urban differences in one sense. Furthermore, there is no immediate prospect that rural-nonfarm people (residents of dense settlements of less than 2,500 population and non-farm residents of the open country-side) will soon become an insignifi-cant segment of the population.[12]

## THE IMPORTANCE OF RURAL BACKGROUND

Even if the only important differ-ences associated with population concentration were between the "truly rural" people and others in the society, "ruralism" would not soon virtually disappear from Ameri-can society, assuming that early socialization has enduring effects on individuals. Although few Ameri-cans are now "truly rural," a sub-

stantial proportion of the adults have rural backgrounds (see table 3), vary-ing from around half of the elderly to about a fourth of the young adults.

Rural-urban differences in back-grounds undoubtedly contribute to the attitudinal and behavioral dif-ferentiation of the urban population, although apparently not in quite the way that some social scientists have speculated. For instance, Leo Schnore speculates that class differences in attitudes reflect to a large extent the fact that a larger percentage of the people in the lower than in the higher classes have rural back-grounds.[13] To test this hypothesis, we did a regression analysis of 19 attitudinal and behavioral variables from the 1974 General Social Survey (see table 4).[14] We first regressed each variable on prestige of occupa-tion (males) or prestige of spouse's occupation (married females), and then we added size of place of resi-dence at age 16 (rural-urban di-chotomy) as a control variable. For most of the dependent variables, adding the control variable did reduce the strength of the associa-tion, but in no case was the reduction more than slight (see table 4). For males, the mean correlation coef-ficient (which is equivalent to the zero-order beta) is .115 and the mean partial beta (standardized regression coefficient) is .107. For females, the values are .104 and .094, respec-tively. Therefore, at least in regard to the variables included in this

11. Thirty-one percent of the respondents to two national surveys conducted in 1974 and 1975 (the General Social Surveys conducted by the National Opinion Research Center) lived in cities with populations of from 2,500 to 249,999.

12. In 1970, rural-nonfarm people were 21.3 percent of the total U.S. population.

13. Leo F. Schnore, "The Rural-Urban Variable: An Urbanite's Perspective," *Rural Sociology*, vol. 31 (June 1966), pp. 131–43.

14. Since we were concerned with repre-sentativeness rather than with illustrating extreme cases, we selected the variables before we examined the data in order to avoid biasing the results via the selection process. For discussion of the "no peeking" rule, see Herbert H. Hyman, *Secondary Analysis of Sample Surveys* (New York: John Wiley, 1972).

TABLE 4

Relationship of Occupational Prestige (Males) or Spouse's Occupational
Prestige (Married Females) to Selected Dependent Variables,
with and without Rural-Urban Background Controlled,
Whites, United States, 1974

| Dependent Variable | Males | | Females | |
|---|---|---|---|---|
| | Zero-Order Correlation | Partial Beta | Zero-Order Correlation | Partial Beta |
| Frequency of church attendance | .116 | .134 | .021 | .023 |
| Republican party identification | .088 | .112 | .113 | .118 |
| Political conservatism | −.026 | −.019 | −.043 | −.034 |
| Belief that luck is more important than hard work in getting ahead | .017 | .018 | .038 | .032 |
| Frequency of socializing with relatives | −.167 | −.155 | −.112 | −.121 |
| Frequency of socializing with neighbors | −.005 | .023 | .046 | .045 |
| Frequency of socializing with friends who are not neighbors | .023 | .006 | .211 | .191 |
| Frequency of going to bar or tavern | .011 | −.014 | .067 | .056 |
| Expressed ideal family size | .023 | .044 | −.021 | −.005 |
| Permissiveness concerning premarital sex | .135 | .095 | .111 | .089 |
| Permissiveness concerning extramarital sex | .200 | .178 | .133 | .125 |
| Permissiveness concerning homosexual sex | .191 | .171 | .162 | .151 |
| Tolerance of communism | .148 | .134 | .142 | .126 |
| Belief in greater expenditures for education | .015 | −.003 | .084 | .072 |
| Belief in greater expenditures for welfare | −.058 | −.042 | .017 | .007 |
| Belief in greater expenditures for the military | −.249 | −.230 | −.155 | −.142 |
| Willingness to invite a black to dinner | .068 | .055 | .037 | .021 |
| Vocabulary test score | .473 | .444 | .317 | .292 |
| Number of children (persons age 45 and older) | −.181 | −.169 | −.138 | −.127 |

Source: The 1974 General Social Survey conducted by the National Opinion Research
Center (James A. Davis, principal investigator).
Note: Data in this and subsequent tables are limited to whites in order to control race.
Truncation is used for control since race interacts with some of the predictor variables. All
dependent variables are scored to form ordinal or interval scales with at least three categories.

TABLE 5

RELATIONSHIP (PARTIAL) OF SIZE OF COMMUNITY LIVED IN AT AGE 16 AND OF SIZE OF
COMMUNITY OF CURRENT RESIDENCE TO SELECTED DEPENDENT
VARIABLES, WHITES, UNITED STATES, 1974

| | STANDARDIZED PARTIAL REGRESSION COEFFICIENT (BETA) | | | |
| | MALES | | FEMALES | |
| DEPENDENT VARIABLE | COMMUNITY OF ORIGIN | COMMUNITY OF RESIDENCE | COMMUNITY OF ORIGIN | COMMUNITY OF RESIDENCE |
|---|---|---|---|---|
| Frequency of church attendance | −.007 | −.051 | .051 | −.103 |
| Republican party identification | −.067 | −.038 | −.020 | −.017 |
| Political conservatism | −.088 | −.051 | −.115 | −.035 |
| Belief that luck is more important than hard work in getting ahead | .062 | −.004 | .034 | −.033 |
| Frequency of socializing with relatives | .009 | −.041 | .065 | −.033 |
| Frequency of socializing with neighbors | −.066 | −.022 | .093 | −.055 |
| Frequency of socializing with friends who are not neighbors | .059 | .082 | .087 | .019 |
| Frequency of going to bar or tavern | .072 | .083 | .008 | −.110 |
| Expressed ideal family size | −.081 | .034 | −.081 | −.001 |
| Permissiveness concerning premarital sex | .073 | .039 | .050 | .128 |
| Permissiveness concerning extramarital sex | .095 | .137 | .077 | −.011 |
| Permissiveness concerning homosexual sex | .075 | .146 | .050 | .027 |
| Tolerance of communism | .084 | .015 | .055 | .019 |
| Belief in greater expenditures for education | −.032 | .126 | .091 | .023 |
| Belief in greater expenditures for welfare | −.028 | .010 | −.011 | .073 |
| Belief in greater expenditures for the military | −.074 | −.074 | −.074 | .014 |
| Willingness to invite a black to dinner | −.014 | .096 | .033 | −.055 |
| Vocabulary test score | .052 | .051 | .189 | −.027 |
| Number of children (persons age 45 and older) | −.096 | −.016 | −.119 | −.043 |

SOURCE: The 1974 General Social Survey conducted by the National Opinion Research Center (James A. Davis, principal investigator).

NOTE: Only the two community-size variables are predictor variables in the regression equations.

analysis (which, of course, are not necessarily representative of all attitudinal and behavioral variables), the higher proportion of low-status than of high-status people who have rural origins does not seem to be an important source of so-called class differences.

However, it is important that, in the case of several of the variables, size of community of residence at age 16 was a better predictor of the responses than size of present (at the time of the survey) community of residence (see table 5).[15] In the case of eight of the 19 variables for males and 14 of the 19 for females, the partial unstandardized regression coefficient is larger for size of community of residence at age 16 than for size of present community of residence. For males, the mean beta is .060 for size of community of residence at age 16 and .059 for size of present community of residence.[16] The corresponding means for females are .075 and .043.

Obviously, neither of the community size variables was an important predictor of most of the dependent variables we selected from the 1974 General Social Survey; most of the associations are neither statistically significant nor large enough to be important, even if they did not result from sampling error. This is true even for several variables which, according to the literature, should bear a rather strong relationship to community size. For instance, expressions of the ideal number of children for a family were virtually unrelated to size of present community of residence and only weakly related to size of community of origin. Some researchers require that a beta be at least .15 before it is considered worthy of interpretation; by that criterion, only the association among females of size of

community of origin with the vocabulary test scores was large enough to be important. However, several other betas do not fall far short of .15 and, thus, probably reflect associations of some importance in the population. For males, these include the associations of size of present community of residence with permissive attitudes toward premarital and homosexual sex and with favorable attitudes toward formal education. For females, these include the associations of size of present community of residence with permissive attitudes toward premarital sex and of size of community of residence at age 16 with number of children and with liberal political orientations.

## A MULTIVARIATE ANALYSIS

Of course, even the larger associations may not reflect direct effects of community size but rather may be spurious or reflect indirect effects through variables which intervene between community size and the dependent variables. If so, both the Wirth and the Fischer views of the effects of population concentration would tend to lose their credibility. To test for this possibility, we added nine background and current characteristics, all of which seemed likely to have some effect on some of the dependent variables, to the regression equation as predictors along with the two community-size variables.[17] We then selected each dependent variable with a zero-order correlation of at least .10 with one of the community-size variables and compared the correlation coef-

15. For this analysis, we used the same three-category community-size breakdown for community of origin and of current residence, namely, (1) open countryside, (2) dense settlements of less than 50,000 residents, and (3) cities of 50,000 or more population and their suburbs.

16. We disregarded the signs of the betas in computing these means.

17. We also recoded the community-size variables into the maximum number of categories consistent with retaining ordinal scales, which made the two variables incomparable with one another but allowed each to explain the maximum amount of variance in the dependent variables.

TABLE 6

ZERO-ORDER AND PARTIAL RELATIONSHIPS OF COMMUNITY-SIZE VARIABLES TO SELECTED DEPENDENT VARIABLES, WHITES, UNITED STATES, 1974

| | MALES | | | | FEMALES | | | |
| | COMMUNITY OF ORIGIN | | COMMUNITY OF RESIDENCE | | COMMUNITY OF ORIGIN | | COMMUNITY OF RESIDENCE | |
| DEPENDENT VARIABLE | ZERO-ORDER CORRELATION | PARTIAL BETA | ZERO-ORDER CORRELATION | PARTIAL BETA | ZERO-ORDER CORRELATION | PARTIAL BETA | ZERO-ORDER CORRELATION | PARTIAL BETA |
|---|---|---|---|---|---|---|---|---|
| Political conservatism | −.112 | −.091 | * | * | −.118 | −.058 | * | * |
| Frequency of socialization with friends who are not neighbors | .172 | .079 | .147 | .084 | .189 | .090 | * | * |
| Frequency of going to bar or tavern | .167 | .108 | .118 | .065 | .103 | .023 | * | * |
| Permissiveness concerning premarital sex | .171 | .093 | .118 | .036 | .212 | .042 | .211 | .137 |
| Permissiveness concerning extramarital sex | .162 | .073 | .204 | .152 | .101 | .045 | * | * |
| Permissiveness concerning homosexual sex | .173 | .064 | .204 | .148 | .132 | .016 | .109 | .060 |
| Belief in greater expenditures for education | .086 | .028 | .114 | .090 | .137 | .085 | * | * |
| Belief in greater expenditures for the military | −.158 | −.087 | −.110 | .048 | −.148 | −.059 | * | * |
| Vocabulary test score | .225 | .077 | .184 | .053 | .333 | .215 | .127 | .005 |
| Number of children (persons age 45 and older) | −.123 | −.101 | * | * | −.142 | −.100 | * | * |

SOURCE: The 1974 General Social Survey conducted by the National Opinion Research Center (James A. Davis, principal investigator).

NOTE: For the multiple regression analysis, the independent variables include all of the independent variables listed in table 7.

* Data not reported because zero-order correlation is less than .1.

ficient (zero-order beta) with the partial beta (see table 6).

Generally, the controls diminished the associations to an important degree, but only in a few cases were the associations reduced to virtually zero. We cannot be sure, of course, that we controlled all antecedent

TABLE 7

Mean Partial Relationship (Beta) of Two Community-Size Variables and Nine
Other Independent Variables to 19 Selected Dependent Variables,
Whites, United States, 1974

| Independent Variable | Males | Married Females |
|---|---|---|
| Size of community of origin | .067 | .069 |
| Size of community of residence | .059 | .040 |
| Region | .084 | .076 |
| Region of origin | .047 | .071 |
| Age | .159 | .131 |
| Family income | .049 | .044 |
| Subjective economic standing of family | .068 | .071 |
| Subjective economic standing of family at age 16 | .041 | .058 |
| Occupational prestige (of spouse in case of females) | .055 | .040 |
| Father's occupational prestige | .041 | .040 |
| Years of school completed | .103 | .102 |

Source: The 1974 General Social Survey conducted by the National Opinion Research Center (James A. Davis, principal investigator).

Note: Means are computed without regard to signs of the betas. All 11 of the independent variables are in the regression equations. The 19 dependent variables are those listed in tables 4 and 5.

and intervening variables which could account for the remaining associations, as indicated by the betas, but it appears likely that population concentration, or some very close correlates, had rather direct effects on some of the dependent variables, such as vocabulary (females), fertility, attitudes toward family size, attitudes toward communism, and attitudes toward premarital sex. If so, we speculate that, with the probable exception of the effect on vocabulary, the effects were mainly a matter of the people in the smaller communities lagging behind those in the larger communities as attitudes and behavior have changed.

The multivariate analysis also allows tentative conclusions about the relative explanatory power of the community-size variables and the other predictor variables, most of which are often used in social scientific research. The means in table 7 indicate that the explanatory power of age and education exceeded those of both size of community of origin and size of community of current residence by a considerable margin. Even region of residence had slightly better predictive power, on the average, than either of the community-size variables. On the other hand, the community size variables did not fare badly in competition with some other variables often used as explanatory variables in social scientific research, such as occupational prestige and family income. Of course, the 19 dependent variables used for these comparisons are not necessarily representative, and the relative predictive power of the different independent variables varies a great deal among the 19 dependent variables.[18]

## CONCLUSIONS

What, then, is the importance of the rural-urban distinction and of the community-size variable to those who would understand and deal with attitudinal and behavioral variation in the United States? The answer, clearly, is that the importance is more than negligible and

18. For a somewhat similar comparison, see George W. Lowe and Charles W. Peek, "Location and Lifestyle: The Comparative Explanatory Utility of Urbanism and Rurality," *Rural Sociology*, vol. 39 (Fall 1974), pp. 392–419. More recent research by Lowe and Peek, as yet unpublished, reveals that, for a large number of attitudinal variables from the General Social Surveys, a cluster of "status" variables has considerably greater predictive power than a cluster of rural-urban-community-size variables.

that there is little reason to believe that the importance is diminishing or will soon diminish very much. It would certainly be premature to suggest that students of rural-urban differences should find more fruitful topics to study.

On the other hand, the importance of rural-urban differences should not be exaggerated. The rural-urban variable, along with many other explanatory variables long favored by social scientists, is losing much of its apparent importance as researchers increasingly use "proportional-reduction-in-error" measures of association and interpret their findings in terms of proportion of variance explained. For most attitudinal and behavioral variables, the predictive utility of the rural-urban variable is modest at best; "overinterpretation" of rather small differences between percentages has often obscured the fact that on most issues the rural and urban populations each has almost as much internal differentiation in attitudes as does the total population.

Annals, AAPSS, **429**, Jan. 1977

# Political Structure of Rural America

By David Knoke and Constance Henry

Abstract: Historical rural American political behavior has revolved around the three themes of radicalism, conservatism, and apathy. Post-World War II research on urban-rural differences reveals little support either for contemporary rural radicalism or greater political apathy in rural areas. However, rural citizens, particularly farmers, exhibit more conservative political orientations than metropolitan populations. The reapportionment revolution of the 1960s, which proponents thought would reduce rural advantage in state and national government, has not noticeably altered social policy outputs of state legislatures or the Congress in a more liberal, urban-oriented direction. The Electoral College currently under-represents rural influence in electing the president, although various alternatives tend to discriminate in reverse. Future trends suggest a diminishing political difference between rural and urban populations. Exposure of rural residents to mass media and the interchange of populations between geographic areas imply a gradual homogenization of social, cultural, and political values which will ultimately render country and city indistinguishable in terms of political behavior. Other social dimensions play a more central role in political conflict than the rural-urban dimension. Leaving aside the possibility of an unforeseen crisis, rural interests are unlikely to capture national political attention.

---

*David Knoke is Associate Professor of Sociology at Indiana University in Bloomington. Educated at the University of Michigan, he is author of* Change and Continuity in American Politics *and many journal articles on political behavior. He was an Associate Editor of the* American Sociological Review.

*Constance Henry is a graduate student in sociology at Indiana University, where she also did her undergraduate work. She previously worked as a Research Associate in the planning department for the state of Indiana.*

THE political history of rural America interweaves three themes which appear contradictory on the surface but, on closer inspection, exhibit an underlying unity. Over the centuries, rural political behavior has alternated among agrarian radicalism, rural conservatism, and mass apathy. The wellsprings of these political styles arise in the social and economic conditions confronted by farmers and rural and small-town dwellers residing within a steadily urbanizing industrial nation.

Agrarian radicalism swept the Midwest and parts of the South for nearly half a century following the Civil War, as farmers responded to perceived depredations of an emerging hegemonic corporate capitalism. Indifference by the major political parties to farmers' crises in unreliable weather, uncertain markets, and unscrupulous financiers enabled third-party movements such as Populism to make sizable electoral inroads with proposals to limit the power of vested interests and expand control of the state over economic conditions. The cycle of agrarian protest triggered by economic downturns was finally broken only by the extended period of agricultural prosperity following World War II.[1]

Rural conservatism has been a more durable, pervasive orientation in the hinterland, suffusing not only politics but religion, morality, and lifestyle. Grounded in the values of moral integrity and individualistic self-help, rural Americans tradiionally have long been suspicious and disdainful of urban centers. The political manifestations—opposition to big government, big business, big labor; isolationism in foreign policy; hostility to non-Anglo-Saxon minorities; intense patriotism—may be seen as part of a general defense of status and a way of life threatened by the encroachment of the urban industrial sector. This traditional rural conservatism has provided the mainstay of the Republican party but has also periodically fueled extremist movements, from prohibition to McCarthy and Wallace, which aimed to restore the rural sector to its real or imagined pristine state.

Mass apathy, the third face of rural politics, was extensively documented in *The American Voter*, perhaps the most influential account of contemporary agrarian politics.[2] Rural inhabitants, particularly farmers, displayed great irregularity in political participation and party loyalty, a volatility presumed to arise from inadequate socialization to the role of political actor. Agrarian politics, unlike the more stable, integrated political behavior of urban workers, was depicted as short-term, transient, and prone to evaporation upon solution of immediate grievances.

The three themes of agrarian radicalism, conservatism, and apathy may be seen as different manifestations of an underlying social and cultural isolation of rural America from the dominant mainstream. Remote from and largely untouched by national political currents, rural

1. On agrarian radicalism, see John D. Hicks, *The Populist Revolt: A History of the Farmers' Alliance and the People's Party* (Lincoln: University of Nebraska Press, 1961). For a detailed examination and refutation of the thesis that McCarthyism has roots in the agrarian radicalism of the nineteenth century, see Michael Rogin, *The Intellectuals and McCarthy: The Radical Specter* (Cambridge, Mass.: Harvard University Press, 1967).

2. Angus Campbell et al., *The American Voter* (New York: John Wiley & Sons, Inc., 1960), ch. 13.

dwellers were prone to view political problems in simple, moralistic terms which called for direct, spontaneous action. The low salience of political action for most rural residents lay behind their predominant apathy and traditional conservatism. The weak tie to the larger political community made the rural mass a prime target for mobilization by radical appeals in economic and social crises. But the very ease with which rural folk could be shaken from lethargy presented tremendous obstacles to consolidating and sustaining any movement beyond the immediate resolution of crisis. Consistently, the mass bases of extremist movements sank back into apathy and traditional conservatism once the initial mobilization ran its course.

The rest of this paper focuses on rural political behavior since World War II. We are interested in evidence on the prevalence of radical, conservative, and apathetic modes in contemporary rural America. We present findings on the behavior and attitudes of the mass populace and the institutional structures of government, explicitly comparing rural and urban sectors for signs of convergence.

## POLITICAL PARTICIPATION

If rural Americans are more politically apathetic than urban residents, they should show substantially lower levels of voting turnout, irregular patterns of voting for party candidates, as well as less participation in all forms of political action. Based on surveys with nonsouthern respondents during the Eisenhower elections, authors of *The American Voter* concluded that rural persons, especially farmers, were more inconsistent than urban workers in always voting and in voting for the

same party's presidential candidates in all elections. Yet in replicating these analyses on later elections, we found the earlier findings to be atypical: more recent rural-urban differences in voting participation are not large and are sometimes reversed.

More damaging evidence against the rural apathy theme was presented in a major study of political participation by Sidney Verba and Norman Nie.[3] Their index of overall political participation showed that isolated villages and rural areas and isolated towns of fewer than 10,000 inhabitants had lower rates than any other type of community except small suburbs adjacent to large metropolises. However, such small places are populated with people whose lower education, occupation, and income levels make them less prone to political involvement. When the data were statistically adjusted to remove the effects of low social and economic status, the rural and isolated small communities were shown to participate politically more than the residents of large urban places.

The authors concluded that political activity was most prevalent in communities with well-defined political boundaries in which local participation could occur. As communities increased and began to lose their distinct boundaries from other communities, the general participation rates declined, particularly those actions aimed at influencing social issues in the community. Rather than being places devoid of political involvement, the rural areas, villages, and small towns offer their residents a greater chance for

3. Sidney Verba and Norman H. Nie, *Participation in America: Political Democracy and Social Equality* (New York: Harper & Row, Publishers, 1972), pp. 229–47.

civic involvement and meaningful political influence than do the larger, more "central" urban settings. But, with increasing urbanization, the small and relatively independent communities which foster citizen participation in politics are becoming rarer.

## PARTISAN POLITICS

For more than half a century, rural and small town America has been Republican in party support and voting behavior, while urban and especially metropolitan communities have generally been Democratic. Evidence from recent surveys does not show these partisan differences to be eroding.[4] As the South has edged closer toward two-party politics in state and national elections, signs of a similar rural-urban partisan cleavage have emerged there. Farmers in both the South and non-South are less likely than rural non-farmers to call themselves Independents. Thus, contrary to the assumption that farmers are apathetic, they are more likely than any rural or urban group to identify with one of the major political parties.

In both regions, farming families are more likely to be Republican than any other residential category, with rural nonfarmers the next most Republican. In fact, due to the low level of Independents, southern farmers are not only the most Republican group but also the only group in which a majority identified with the Democratic party.

Historically, rural areas have voted "Democratic when farm prices are low and Republican when they are high."[5] The American Voter's analysis of the 1956 presidential election indicated that farmers who had experienced downward trends in their crop prices voted against the incumbent Republican administration. However, a replication of this analysis in the next three elections failed to find evidence that downward price trends translate into votes against the incumbent party.[6] And in the 1972 contest, despite high farm prices and record wheat sales to Russia, Richard Nixon actually received fewer votes among farmers in both regions than he did from small urban communities. Perhaps the general prosperity of the post-World War II period has dampened the alleged political sensitivity of American farmers to short-term shifts in their economic fortunes.

## SOCIAL ISSUES

As well as continued preference for the Republican party, contemporary rural residents maintain traditionally conservative stances on a variety of political and social issues. In fact, a size-of-place gradient has frequently been observed, with rural residents the most conservative and liberal attitudes increasingly evident among town, small city, suburb, and large city residents in that order.[7]

4. The data used in this section and the next come from the 1973 and 1974 General Social Surveys conducted by the National Opinion Research Center and made available through the Roper Public Opinion Research Center. Neither organization is responsible for the interpretations made herein.

5. Hugh A. Bone and Austin Ranney, *Politics and Voters* (New York: McGraw-Hill, 1963), p. 47.

6. David Knoke and David E. Long, "The Economic Sensitivity of the American Farm Vote," *Rural Sociology*, vol. 40 (Spring 1975), pp. 7–17.

7. This gradient was found with regard to civil rights attitudes by Hart M. Nelsen and Raytha L. Yokley, "Civil Rights Attitudes of Rural and Urban Presbyterians," *Rural Sociology*, vol. 35 (June 1970), pp. 141–52. However, see the absence of a consistent

## TABLE 1

PERCENTAGE OF PERSONS TOLERANT OF CIVIL LIBERTIES FOR COMMUNISTS, BY REGION
AND SIZE OF PLACE, 1973–1974 GSS SURVEYS COMBINED

| REGION AND SIZE OF PLACE | WILLINGNESS TO ALLOW A COMMUNIST TO: | | |
|---|---|---|---|
| | TEACH IN COLLEGE | GIVE A SPEECH | HAVE A BOOK IN PUBLIC LIBRARY |
| South | | | |
| farm | 17 | 23 | 28 |
| rural non-farm | 30 | 44 | 39 |
| small city | 35 | 48 | 46 |
| large city | 42 | 58 | 61 |
| Non-South | | | |
| farm | 25 | 55 | 51 |
| rural non-farm | 43 | 63 | 65 |
| small city | 40 | 59 | 60 |
| large city | 46 | 69 | 68 |

SOURCE: General Social Surveys for 1973 and 1974, conducted by National Opinion Research Center, made available through the Roper Public Opinion Research Center.

NOTE: Size of place categories: Farm—head of household farmer; Rural non-farm—population less than 2,500; Small city—2,500 to 49,999; Large city—50,000 or more.

Perhaps the most revealing evidence on traditional rural conservatism can be found in data from Samuel Stouffer's classic *Communism, Conformity, and Civil Liberties*. Using a 15-item "intolerance" scale of willingness to permit various civil liberties to atheists, socialists, and Communists, Stouffer found the size-of-place gradient for national samples in 1954. Rural dwellers were the least tolerant (16 percent) while those living in cities of 100,000 or more were the most tolerant (40 percent), and the same relationship appeared in both the South and non-South.[8]

Many of the Stouffer items were repeated in national surveys 20 years later. Table 1, which reports the percentage of tolerant respondents toward three items dealing with Communists, indicates that tolerance of nonconformity has risen over time, although a size-of-place gradient can still be seen. The pattern in the South on all three items is clearest, with tolerance uniformly increasing with community size. In the non-South, where tolerance levels are higher, farmers are still the most conservative and large city residents the most liberal, but the rural non-farm population is not distinguishable in attitude from the urban groups. Thus, while the farmers are still the most conservative category and the size-of-place gradient seems to hold in the South, the magnitude of differences seems to have diminished since Stouffer's initial study as the overall level of tolerance has grown.

### EXTREMIST MOVEMENTS

While no farmers' group has mounted an effective electoral

---

size-of-place gradient for domestic economic welfare attitudes in Richard F. Hamilton, *Class and Politics in the United States* (New York: John Wiley & Sons, Inc., 1972), p. 250.

8. Samuel A. Stouffer, *Communism, Conformity, and Civil Liberties: A Cross-Section of the Nation Speaks Its Mind* (New York: Doubleday & Company, Inc., 1955), ch. 5.

challenge since the demise of the LaFollette progressives more than 40 years ago, two major extremist movements in recent decades have held disproportionate sway among rural Americans. Both Senator Joe McCarthy and Governor George Wallace found their brands of anti-Establishment rhetoric gaining votes from rural and small-town adherents. But the nature of their appeals indicates that, rather than seeking a radical restructuring of the social system, their supporters expressed the conservative traditions of the rural milieu.

Several liberal scholars have characterized McCarthyism as a lineal descendant of the populist/ progressive "rural utopianism." On superficial grounds, the thesis has some plausibility since McCarthy's greatest electoral support in Wisconsin came from rural counties. But Michael Rogin's painstaking analysis disclosed that McCarthy's rural appeal was widespread throughout the state, while Robert LaFollette had always been rejected by the rich southern counties. "The rural supporters of McCarthy were not reacting to specific economic conditions and constellations of power that produced agrarian radicalism."[9] McCarthy's support, never a true mass movement, was basically confined within traditional Republican party politics among voters disturbed by communism and foreign policy issues.

George Wallace's third party presidential bid in 1968 was more successful in winning popular votes nationally than any since the LaFollette progressives. Yet the core of his support was concentrated in southern "black belt" counties—the

rural areas of antebellum plantation slavery and contemporary high concentrations of blacks. These areas have a long history of repression, often violent, by whites against the blacks whose numerical strength posed a threat to white political supremacy. Southern whites living in black belt counties have historically given the highest electoral returns to candidates promising to delay or prevent black social, economic, and political advances.

The 1968 election saw non-metropolitan areas of the South giving Wallace more than 57 percent of their votes, while southern cities returned fewer than 40 percent, furnishing Richard Nixon with most of the remainder.[10] Even in the urban South, Wallace drew much of his support from first-generation farm and small-town migrants who remained attached to traditional, fundamentalist cultural values and beliefs.[11] The Wallace movement can best be seen as a classic rural conservative desire to rescind the flood of social change flowing against the rural way of life in the South (outside the South, Wallace held no special appeal for rural residents[12]). By the 1976 primaries,

9. See Rogin, *The Intellectuals and McCarthy*, p. 91.

10. Walter Dean Burnham, *Critical Elections and the Mainsprings of American Politics* (New York: W. W. Norton, and Company, Inc., 1972), p. 144. A correlation of +.38 for the percentage black and percentage vote for Wallace in 1968 for southern counties is reported in Ira M. Wasserman and David R. Segal, "Aggregation Effects in the Ecological Study of Presidential Voting," *American Journal of Political Science*, vol. 17 (February 1973), pp. 177–81.

11. Harold G. Grasmick, "Rural Culture and the Wallace Movement in the South," *Rural Sociology*, vol. 39 (Winter 1974), pp. 454–70.

12. Outside the South, rural residents were no more likely to vote for Wallace in 1968 than persons living in cities of more than one million according to table 54 in

however, the movement had crested as the South was learning to accommodate the realities of industrialization and legal desegregation. Partly on the question of his health, but largely because his issues had lost their impact, Wallace's southern supporters began to abandon him for a mainstream centrist, Jimmy Carter. On the night of the North Carolina primary, Wallace delayed his concession speech waiting in vain for the rural counties to pull him through. Even the black belt gave more votes to Carter.

## THE REAPPORTIONMENT REVOLUTION

Political scientists and politicians alike have long believed that rural and urban political interests are incompatible. Nowhere has this belief found stronger expression than in the controversy over representation in state and national legislatures. Despite a doubling of the urban population from one-third to nearly two-thirds during this century, legislative districting patterns have lagged behind the shift from rural to urban society. Malapportioned districts were ascribed all manner of anti-democratic bias:

... in most states the rural districts, constituting most of the area of the states, elected a majority of the state legislature even though they often possessed a minority of the population. ... The rural vote could thus dictate what schools and roads were to be built, how local water supply was to be allotted, and what was to be taxed. It could veto urban renewal or mass transportation programs. In short, it could maintain a minority control over legislation.[13]

The Supreme Court's 1962 order in *Baker* v. *Carr* that states reapportion districts on the basis of "one man-one vote" triggered the Reapportionment Revolution of the 1960s, which effectively redressed the rural-urban imbalance in Congress and state legislatures. But the real question is, did this standard for which metropolitan areas had fought so hard produce the changes in legislative policy outputs that its proponents sought? This natural political experiment has had sufficient time to show its effects. After an extensive review of the findings on rural and urban representation in state legislatures, Congress, and the Electoral College, our conclusion is that major change in legislation and expenditure has not materialized. The original case against rural areas' ability to block urban-oriented legislation was largely overstated. Rural and urban interests, while divergent, are by no means always inimical. And the ultimate aim of reapportionment—more equitable management of public purse and policy—has proven an elusive goal which depends upon factors other than proportional representation of the population in governmental bodies. We will document these contentions in the following paragraphs.

We can dispense with a persistent myth that rural areas tend to be dominated by one political party, typically the Democrats in the South and the Republicans in the Midwest, while urban areas are the center of competitive party politics. A massive investigation of party competition in all United States counties for the 1960 election turned up meager

Seymour Martin Lipset and Earl Raab, *The Politics of Unreason: Right-Wing Extremism in America, 1790–1970* (New York: Harper & Row, Publishers, 1970), p. 385.

13. Marjorie G. Fribourg, *The Reapportionment Crisis* (New York: Public Affairs Committee, 1967), p. 2.

support for the assumption that increased urbanization leads to greater party competition. The correlation between the percentage of a county's population living in places of more than 2,500 people and the percentage of the vote going to the majority party in the presidential contest was only −.16. None of the 74 measures of county characteristics had a sizable impact on party competition.[14] Thus, reapportionment would not have led to the diminished presence of one party in legislative bodies, since neither Democrats nor Republicans were disproportionately distributed by size of place.

## STATE LEGISLATURES

Little evidence has been produced to demonstrate that reapportionment has had significant effects on state policy and expenditures. While the ideal of equal representation is a deeply held value, the merits of this ideal do not lend themselves to easy empirical verification.[15] Indicators of the effects of malapportionment on public policy should be measured before and after redistricting in state legislatures, to ascertain how much of the change could be attributed to fairer representation. Most political theorists agree that environmental forces, including malapportionment, have some influence on legislative decisions. The difficulty lies in disentangling changes in legislative outputs due to reapportionment from those due to other environ-

mental factors.[16] Richard Hofferbert observed that in the American states, most environmental forces do not seem strong enough to account for major differences in government policies, with the exception of party competition which, as we noted above, does not coincide with the rural-urban cleavage.[17]

If characteristics of legislative districts influence the behavior of state legislatures, it most likely occurs indirectly. Thus, the lack of evidence to the effect that malapportionment has obstructed needed urban legislation may simply reflect the complexity of the process by which constituency preferences are translated into legislators' votes. One possible complicating factor is the pluralistic nature of the urban population. Geographic divisions form just one political cleavage, along with racial, ethnic, religious, occupational, and status divisions. The spectre of a monolithic urban majority or rural minority imposing its will in state legislatures is unrealistic.

The so-called urban majority is actually an aggregate of numerous and often politically antagonistic groups. Furthermore, political alliances cut across the boundaries of local units and legislative districts. Some urban groups have a closer identification with certain rural forces than with other urban interests.[18]

14. Charles M. Bonjean and Robert L. Lineberry, "The Urbanization-Party Competition Hypothesis: A Comparison of All United States Counties," *Journal of Politics*, vol. 32 (May 1970), pp. 305–21.

15. Thomas R. Dye, "Malapportionment and Public Policy in the States," *Journal of Politics*, vol. 27 (August 1965), pp. 586–601.

16. R. S. Erikson, "The Partisan Impact of State Legislative Reapportionment," *Midwest Journal of Political Science*, vol. 15 (February 1971), pp. 57–71.

17. Richard I. Hofferbert, "The Relation between Public Policy and Some Structural and Environmental Variables in the American States," *American Political Science Review*, vol. 60 (March 1966), pp. 73–82.

18. Gordon E. Baker, "One Person, One Vote: 'Fair and Effective Representation'?" in Robert A. Goldwin, ed., *Representation and Misrepresentation* (Chicago: Rand McNally & Company, 1968), p. 78.

Studies have consistently found few correlations between equal representation and public policy in the individual states. Thomas Dye's analysis for all 50 states found that the policy choices made in malapportioned legislatures were not noticeably different from those of well-apportioned legislatures. Most of the differences which occur result from socioeconomic differences among the states rather than as direct consequences of gerrymandered districts. Thus, reapportionment should not· be expected to significantly alter the performance of state governments.[19] Similarly, Glen Broach's analysis of legislative roll calls in the 50 state legislatures discovered that urban-rural dimensions occur only on idiosyncratic issues and only sporadically on problems which clearly and homogeneously divide rural from urban interests. Urban and rural legislators do not organize as consistent legislatives blocs, nor does a rural or urban constituency consistently predispose a legislator to vote in given directions on most bills.[20]

Studies of individual state legislatures have generally found no enduring anti-city coalitions among the rural legislators. More frequently, the main opposition to urban-oriented legislation comes from interests within the metropolitan districts or adjacent suburbs.[21]

In fact, one of the major consequences of the reapportionment revolution of the 1960s was an increase in the number of suburban districts in state and national legislatures at the expense of both rural and urban populations. Conflicts which superficially seem to be urban against rural interests, on closer look resolve themselves into more complex contests among social, economic, and cultural groups which are only incidentally associated with urban and rural geography. Present trends are likely to find these conflicts dissociated from the historical rural-urban dimension.

We do not mean to imply that no important differences exist between residents of the city and of the countryside. Differences of opinion, belief, and values persist as we have documented above. But the important point is that these differences are neither incompatible nor overwhelming in the actions of state legislatures. Clearly there are other social forces of greater importance which affect the outcome of political processes at the state level.

## CONGRESS AND ELECTORAL COLLEGE

Compared with the large research literature on the effects of reapportionment in state legislatures' policy outputs, evidence of the impact of "one man-one vote" on the federal House of Representatives is scanty. Proponents of reapportionment had argued that the Congress would take on a more liberal tone with regard to domestic welfare legislation once redistricting had reduced the rural imbalance in the House. Little work subsequent to the Supreme Court's decision was undertaken to determine the validity of this argument, but that which has appeared tends

19. See Dye, "Malapportionment and Public Policy," p. 599.

20. Glen T. Broach, "A Comparative Dimensional Analysis of Partisan and Urban-Rural Voting in State Legislatures," *Journal of Politics*, vol. 34 (August 1972), pp. 905–21.

21. See F. M. Bryan, "The Metamorphosis of a Rural Legislature," *Polity*, vol. 1 (1968), pp. 191–212; David R. Derge, "Metropolitan and Outstate Alignments in Illinois and Missouri Legislative Delegations," *American Political Science Review*, vol. 7 (December 1958), pp. 1051–65.

not to support it. The weighted-vote technique used by most investigators generally shows small changes in liberal legislation with more equitable population apportionment.[22]

Most of the controversy over reapportionment's effects on policy outcomes in the Congress has centered on the suburban districts rather than rural areas and inner cities whose share of the national population, and hence of representatives under the one man-one vote formula, has been shrinking to the benefit of the suburbs. The topic of suburban politics is too large to cover in a paper on the political structure of rural America, except to note the extreme diversity of political interests present in places adjacent to metropolitan areas. Milton Cummings pointed out that demographic trends will give suburban areas a plurality of House seats over metropolitan and rural areas in the near future, yet the legislative consequences will depend on "whether an issue fosters unity or division within the suburbs." On many issues pitting the suburbs against the central cities, rural congressmen may find themselves aligned with the suburbs.[23] After all, both areas have a common interest in avoiding the social and economic ills which plague the core cities. At other times, however, rural representatives may find themselves confronting an urban-suburban coalition, as in the dismantling of farm subsidies.

Presidential elections have thus far defied extension of the one man-one vote principle, despite several attempts to alter the Electoral College's winner-take-all formula in which the candidate with a state's plurality gets electoral votes equal to the number of senators and representatives. Several studies, operating from different assumptions, have tried to determine which social groups are disadvantaged under present Electoral College arrangements and what the impact of various alternatives might be. Lawrence Longley and Alan Braun, using a "voter power" method developed by John F. Banzhaf III, concluded that the most disadvantaged citizens reside in the medium-to-small states (from 4 to 14 electoral votes), while those in the eight largest states have disproportionately large influence. Specifically, suburban residents were found to be the most advantaged at 9.1 percent above the national per-citizen voter average, followed by central city residents (+8.0 percent), SMSA residents (+7.2 percent), and urban residents (+4.2 percent). Rural residents were the most disadvantaged with the rural non-farm at −8.0 percent and the rural farmers at −14.6 percent.[24]

Using a computer simulation, Seymour Spilerman and David Dickens simulated the effects of various alternatives to the Electoral College on the relative influence different population groups would have on the outcome of the presidential election. Although they were

22. Andrew Hacker, *Congressional Districting, the Issue of Equal Representation* (Washington, D.C.: The Brookings Institute, 1963).

23. Milton C. Cummings, Jr., "Reapportionment in the 1970s: Its Effect on Congress," in Nelson W. Polsby, ed., *Reapportionment in the 1970s* (Berkeley: University of California Press, 1971), pp. 209–41.

24. Lawrence D. Longley and Alan G. Braun, *The Politics of Electoral College Reform* (New Haven: Yale University Press, 1972), p. 122; see, also, John F. Banzhaf III, "One Man, 3.312 Votes: A Mathematical Analysis of the Electoral College," *Villanova Law Review*, vol. 13 (Winter 1968), pp. 303–46.

critical of the Longley and Braun and the Banzhaf approaches, Spilerman and Dickens concurred that the current arrangement greatly enhances the influence of large metropolitan centers. Other arrangements would reverse the bias in favor of the rural counties, with a district allocation of electoral votes and a proportional division of a state's electoral votes according to candidates' popular vote percentages favoring rural and small town areas even more than the adoption of a strict popular-vote rule.[25] Not surprisingly, the strongest advocates of district and proportional division reforms are interest groups with a rural origin, such as the National Grange and the American Farm Bureau. The benefits to large urban states and to ethnic minorities in their disproportionate influence on presidential elections, as Spilerman and Dickens point out, is to some unknown degree offset by the larger rural representation in the Senate and through seniority control of congressional committees.

## A LOOK FORWARD

Our review of contemporary political behavior and attitudes of the rural populace and their representatives in government leads to the conclusion that agrarian apathy and agrarian radicalism are no longer valid characterizations.[26] Agrarian

25. Seymour Spilerman and David Dickens, "Who Will Gain and Who Will Lose Influence under Different Electoral Rules," *American Journal of Sociology*, vol. 80 (September 1974), pp. 443–77.

26. An apparent instance of agrarian radicalism in recent times is Cesar Chavez's unionization of farm workers. With recent success, it has become a part of the union system, rather than a radical challenge to the economic structure.

conservatism continues to hold, although the differences between rural and non-rural groups have blurred in several instances. For the future, the shrinking farm population and the continual shift from family farms to agribusinesses portends a decreased electoral importance of that occupational group, excepting in the state politics of the Midwest where agriculture still dominates the local economy. The one issue likely to have persistent national impact is the role of the federal government in expanding export opportunities for the farm sector. Agricultural commodities will undoubtedly be a greater bargaining chip for the United States in the international political economy than they are today. Whether this importance will translate into enhanced influence in the domestic political system for the agricultural producers remains to be seen.

The key trend for the non-farm rural sector would seem to be toward greater homogenization with the urban political culture. As it has over the post-World War II period, the hinterland will continue to be exposed through mass media and interpersonal contacts to the dominant social, cultural, and political styles emanating from the metropole. Thus, we can expect the cities to further the colonization of the interior much as they have for the past 200 years. Barring some unforeseeable disruption, the end result of this trend will be to make the rural population as heterogeneous and politically diverse as the urban environment, so that all meaningful distinctions between the two will have disappeared.

Aiding this blending process is a backflow of urban dwellers to the small town and rural areas, bringing to these places the political ideas and styles of the city. Probably a more important demographic component of this change has been the centuries-long infusion of rural migrants to the cities. Acculturation has always been a slow process, sometimes taking generations to complete. Meanwhile the first-generation farm offspring have by their presence altered the mass political behavior of cities to more closely resemble the rural areas.[27] In the future, farm-reared elements will be a drastically diminished proportion of the population, but their historic role has been to reduce the political cleavage between the cities and the country.

A major example of how the political influences of historical rural and small town America continue to affect contemporary politics occurs in Congress. Samuel Huntington described congressmen as "small town boys," more likely than administrative leaders to retain the parochialism and conservatism of their upbringing even as the nation became increasingly cosmopolitan and sophisticated. Hence Capitol Hill remains a bastion of

the nineteenth century well into the present one.[28]

Much of the future course of American rural politics lies outside the scope of demographic change, whose contours are at least visible if not predictable. The actions and inactions of political elites in the decades ahead will have a more profound effect on the issues that are articulated and placed on the agenda. But it is unlikely that the major social cleavage around which future political conflicts arise will involve the rural-urban dichotomy. Issues which differentiate Americans geographically currently have a low salience for both masses and elites. Only the eruption of a major crisis, such as in food production or energy resources, might polarize the rural and urban populations. Barring such a calamity, we are unlikely to find rural politics intruding on the national consciousness much in the future.

27. David Knoke and Angela Lane, "Size of Place, Migration, and Voting Turnout," *Journal of Political and Military Sociology*, vol. 3 (Fall 1975), pp. 127–39.

28. Samuel P. Huntington, "Congressional Responses to the Twentieth Century," in David B. Truman, ed., *The Congress and America's Future* (Englewood Cliffs, N.J.: Prentice-Hall, Inc., 1965), pp. 5–31. But see reservations expressed by Leroy N. Rieselbach, "Congressmen as 'Small Town Boys': A Research Note," *Midwest Journal of Political Science*, vol. 14 (May 1970), pp. 321–30.

# Farm Labor

By Varden Fuller and Bert Mason

ABSTRACT: Farm population estimates indicate that the massive off-farm exodus is approaching its termination; during 1970–74 the rate of farm population decline fell to an average 1.2 percent per year. Estimates of farm occupations for 1974 imply that the nation's agriculture is dominantly a self-employment industry, though multiple job holding is widespread. The aggregate of persons doing some farm wagework is extremely heterogeneous and the market for hired farm labor is characterized by casual employment relationships. Farm labor in the U.S. lacks market structure and is seldom a chosen life-time occupation. Of nearly 2¾ million who did some farm work in 1974, it was the chief activity for only 693,000. Contrary to popular conception, hired farm labor is not dominated by migrants; in 1974, about 8 percent of the farm work force was migratory. Evidence on labor force participation, daily and annual earnings, and hourly wages illustrates that the hired farm labor market is dominantly a ready-access, casual market for the salvage of low opportunity cost time. Recent developments in federal policies indicate that farm workers are likely to receive federal protection equal to nonagricultural workers. Since 1967, hired workers on large farms have been covered by Fair Labor Standards Act minimum wage requirements, and agricultural minimum wages will be increased to general industry levels by 1978. Agricultural workers remain excluded from the federal unemployment insurance program and National Labor Relations Act. Farm worker unionization is prominent only on large-scale industrialized farms but will apparently continue to be exceptional nationally.

*Varden Fuller is Professor Emeritus of Agricultural Economics, University of California, Davis.*

*Bert Mason is Assistant Professor of Agricultural Economics, Cornell University. The assistance of Lois Plimpton in collecting much of the data is gratefully acknowledged.*

I N 1974, 4.4 percent of the nation's population lived on farms and 4.3 percent of its work force was engaged in agriculture. If these census estimates had been referring to the same persons, the writing of a chapter on farm labor would seemingly be simple and forthright. But, unfortunately, the near-identity of these percentages is coincidence; furthermore, both magnitudes have limited significance. American ways of living and of working have versatility and variety that are formidable to statisticians and social analysts who would define, measure, and classify. That "farm" and "rural" no longer are synonymous is quite generally understood. But that people living on farms are not necessarily engaged in agriculture or that persons who do farm work may not be "farm population" or even engaged in agriculture are facts not generally comprehended.

To be counted in "farm population," a person need only be living on a place that meets the census definition of a farm. In recent times, that definition has been 10 acres of land from which $50 worth of farm produce had been sold in the preceding 12 months or any size of unit from which $250 worth of farm products had been sold.[1] Institutional populations falling under this definition are included. So inclusive a concept of what constitutes a farm has long been in controversy; the debate thereon brought about an

agreement between the Bureau of the Census and the Department of Agriculture that in 1975 and onward minimum annual sales will be $1,000.

No less debatable and more elusive are the definitions and estimates of persons engaged in agriculture. They are based upon work performed within a specified week in April of each year. A farm operator doing any work whatever on his farm in the sample week is classified as self-employed—unless he has another job on which he spent more time in the sample week. Unpaid family farm workers must work at least 15 hours on the farm in the sample week to be counted as such, and they too may be otherwise classified if they had another job on which more time was spent. Wage workers are counted as employed if they did any work in the sample week; they are classified by principal activity. Both population and occupation estimates are based on a household sampling procedure.

Given the widespread practice by farmers and hired farm workers of multiple job holding and the fact that April is not a peak of activity in farming, it follows that this occupational estimating procedure must omit numerous persons who do some farm work. An alternative to asking people what they did in a week in April is to ask them in December what they did in the past year. With respect to hired farm workers, this approach was initiated by Louis J. Ducoff of the former Bureau of Agricultural Economics in the mid-1940s and has been continued by the successor Economic Research Service.[2] With the excep-

1. Estimates of farm population are obtained as an integral part of the annual April-based current population survey by the U.S. Bureau of the Census. Economic Research Service, USDA, participates in preparation of the farm population reports. Each annual report contains an explanatory section on definitions and procedures. *Farm Population* is Series Census-ERS, P-27; the 1974 report is No. 46.

2. This series is titled *The Hired Farm Working Force.* It is issued annually by Economic Research Service, USDA, as part of its Agricultural Economic Report series.

tion of a few missed years prior to 1956, it has provided a valuable annual statistical accounting of persons who do any farm wage work—their numbers and characteristics, their earnings and participation in the labor force. Yet another way to find out about hiring of farm workers is to inquire of employers. This has been done monthly for many years by the U.S. Department of Agriculture in connection with crop reporting work.[3] A long and useful series on wages paid as well as volume of hiring is available from this source.

## TRAVAILS OF IDENTIFICATION AND MEASUREMENT

All statistical categories about farm labor are compounds of discomfort: they depend upon recall; their definitions are arbitrary; they impose an appearance of homogeneity upon situations that are heterogeneous; they usually are derived as incidental by-products of other measurement enterprises, and then generally with a slim input of resources. Yet, even though periodic magnitudes may be dubious, their continued availability over a span of time offers a degree of solace. To know that estimated farm population in 1974 was 9,264,000 acquires more significance when we also know that (by the same estimating procedures) the comparable figure in 1960 was 15,635,000, for now we can speak of a 41 percent decline. And even if the magnitudes had been more restrictively estimated, the rate of changes would not likely have been substantially different.

Farm population estimates, which go back to 1910, quantify and expli-

cate the swift transition to an urban industrial nation. In a half century the farm population fell from 32 million to 9¼ million—from one-third of the population to less than one-twentieth. When the off-farm torrent was at its postwar crest, the draining away was five to seven times the net natural increase each year. There were signals of impending urban social chaos embedded in the figures, but few were disposed to read them.

Through the 1960s, the off-farm drain continued at around 5 percent per year. A leveling-out had to come, and it seems now to have arrived. During 1970–74 the farm population decline has fallen to an average of 1.2 percent per year. Net off-farm movement is now confined to nonwhites, which means primarily southern blacks. In 1974 estimated nonwhite farm population was 655,000, or 7 percent of national farm population; measured against their own base, the off-farm movement of nonwhites was 9 percent per year, which also cannot last long.

Of the labor force residing on farms, some are engaged exclusively in agriculture, some in nonagriculture, and in many regions multiple job holding is prominent. The off-farm drain has mainly affected those that had been entirely or principally agricultural; the nonagricultural component of the farm population has remained fairly constant. As farm population has declined, this stable nonagricultural component has risen in percentage terms, thereby generating the arithmetic foundation for one of many quasi-myths: it is said that farm people are increasing their nonfarm work, but the fact is that farm people are decreasing their farm work. A similar illusion relates to nonfarm residents engaged in agriculture: their numbers have re-

3. This series is titled *Farm Labor*, U.S. Crop Reporting Board, Statistical Reporting Service.

TABLE 1

FARM POPULATION, LABOR FORCE, OCCUPATIONS; NUMBERS IN AGRICULTURE,
BY RESIDENCE, 1960, 1965, 1970–1974

| | FARM POPULATION | | FARM RESIDENTS IN NONAGRICULTURAL OCCUPATIONS | | OCCUPIED IN AGRICULTURE | | | |
|---|---|---|---|---|---|---|---|---|
| YEAR | ALL PERSONS (000) | LABOR FORCE (000) | NUMBER (000) | PERCENT OF FARM RESIDENT LABOR FORCE | ALL PERSONS (000) | FARM RESIDENTS (000) | NONFARM RESIDENTS (000) | PERCENT, NONFARM RESIDENTS OF TOTAL |
| 1960 | 15,635 | 6,266 | 2,064 | 33 | 5,395 | 4,025 | 1,370 | 25 |
| 1965 | 12,363 | 5,175 | 1,915 | 37 | 4,719 | 3,155 | 1,564 | 33 |
| 1970 | 9,712 | 4,293 | 1,878 | 44 | 3,696 | 2,333 | 1,363 | 37 |
| 1971 | 9,425 | 4,263 | 1,864 | 44 | 3,668 | 2,291 | 1,377 | 38 |
| 1972 | 9,610 | 4,361 | 1,956 | 45 | 3,678 | 2,308 | 1,370 | 37 |
| 1973 | 9,472 | 4,454 | 2,121 | 48 | 3,729 | 2,249 | 1,480 | 40 |
| 1974 | 9,264 | 4,419 | 2,078 | 47 | 3,773 | 2,242 | 1,531 | 41 |

SOURCE: Base data are from current issues of *Current Population Reports*, Series Census—ERS, P-27, U.S. Department of Commerce, Bureau of the Census and U.S. Department of Agriculture.

mained fairly constant since 1960, but as the agricultural total has declined their percentage has risen. Again the cutting blade in the percentage computation was decline in farm occupations by farm residents. The numbers involved are summarized in table 1. One may observe therein that farm residents having nonfarm occupations exceed nonfarm residents having farm occupations.

Estimates of farm occupations for 1974 (summarized in table 2) imply that the nation's agriculture remains dominantly a self-employment industry notwithstanding the revolutionary shift to bigger farms. Most but not all farm operators and unpaid family laborers still live on farms; most but not all hired farm workers now live elsewhere, the latter in consequence of a well-defined trend. Women hold considerable prominence as unpaid family workers but little as operators. Women nonfarm residents who

do farm work are mainly in the hired category.

## WHO DOES NATION'S FARM WORK?

The greatest elusiveness about who does the nation's farm work resides in the awkward fact that a substantial fraction of it is done by persons who are not normally counted as being occupied in agriculture. These include farm residents whose chief activity is nonfarm work and numerous nonfarm residents who mainly are students, housewives, unemployed, retired, or otherwise not usually seeking work, and nonfarm workers who do some incidental farm work. The December inquiry procedure mentioned previously seeks to identify all persons in the current sample survey who did any farm wagework in the preceding year and thereby includes these various categories. In contrast to the April-based occupational approach which estimated

TABLE 2

PERSONS IN AGRICULTURAL OCCUPATIONS BY SEX AND RESIDENCE, 1974

| SEX AND CLASSIFICATION | FARM RESIDENTS (000) | NONFARM RESIDENTS (000) | TOTAL (000) |
|---|---|---|---|
| Both sexes, total | 2,242 | 1,531 | 3,773 |
| self-employed | 1,350 | 455 | 1,805 |
| wage & salary workers | 469 | 1,016 | 1,485 |
| unpaid family workers | 423 | 59 | 482 |
| Male, total | 1,832 | 1,268 | 3,100 |
| self-employed | 1,266 | 412 | 1,678 |
| wage & salary workers | 393 | 830 | 1,223 |
| unpaid family workers | 173 | 27 | 200 |
| Female, total | 410 | 262 | 672 |
| self-employed | 84 | 44 | 128 |
| wage & salary workers | 76 | 186 | 262 |
| unpaid family workers | 250 | 32 | 282 |

SOURCE: *Current Population Reports*, Series Census—ERS, P-27, No. 46, U.S. Department of Commerce, Bureau of the Census and U.S. Department of Agriculture, December 1975.

that 1,485,000 persons were agricultural wage and salary workers in 1974, the December inquiry procedure estimates that 2,737,000 did some farm wagework in 1974.[4] Of this large total, only 1,568,000 did 25 days or more of farm work. This smaller number bears a resemblance to the number that reported their April occupation. But these two numbers are only arithmetic lookalikes, not mildly divergent estimates of the same population.

Over the past 30 years, the total of persons doing some hired farm work has been estimated as high as 4⅓ million (1950) and as low as 2½ million (1970, 1971). Since 1960, the tendency has been toward decline, but inconsistently and without a strong trend. The highly casual portion doing less than 25

4. Except as otherwise indicated, the discussion that follows is based on data derived from *The Hired Farm Working Force of 1974*, Agricultural Economic Report No. 297.

days of farm work has stood in the neighborhood of two-fifths. There has been a downward tendency in numbers of persons who obtain 150 or more days of farm wagework per year and a trend toward fewer days of work per year for those in this category. The statistics therefore say that the hired work of American agriculture is not becoming less casual and seasonal as its technological revolution progresses.

Of nearly 2¾ million who did some farm work in 1974, for only 693,000 was it chief activity; only 641,000 worked at it for at least 150 days; 1,435,000 were students, housewives, and others not regularly in the labor force. One-fifth of the large total were females; just under one-fifth were nonwhites; approximately 8 percent were migratory—according to a definition to be discussed subsequently. Two-fifths of the large total in 1974 did both farm and nonfarm work—the report speaks of these persons as "farm wageworkers who also did some nonfarm wagework." But for only one-eighth of these interindustry workers was farm wagework their chief activity whereas nonfarm work was the chief activity for almost two-fifths. In these facts and in such statements about them as quoted above lies the source of another quasi-myth. It is often said that hired farm workers are not so poor as they seem because they supplement their farm earnings by working at nonfarm jobs. But the truth is that this dual-sector employment is mostly by nonfarm workers who are supplementing their incomes by doing farm work. Those principally engaged in other than farm work plus those not normally in the labor market (but employed temporarily at both farm and nonfarm work) outnumber persons who are chiefly farm workers with supplementary nonfarm employment by 7:1. The greater truth, therefore, lies on the side of saying that farming offers substantial opportunities for nonfarm people to supplement their incomes. To a limited extent, farm operators also supplement their incomes by working as hired farm laborers.

## MOST SEASONAL WORKERS ARE NOT MIGRATORY

Contrary to impressions that one may encounter, hired farm labor is not dominated by migrants. The urban tendency to speak of people doing harvest or casual farm labor as migrants or migratory workers promotes this exaggeration. In a nation of movers and high mobility, definitions that usefully distinguish migratoriness are not easily made. Nonrecurrent relocation of household is not migrancy as usually meant; nor is changing from one temporary job to another within commuting distance of a stable domicile. A signifi-

cant perception of migratoriness undoubtedly involves recurrent uplifting of household concurrent with seasonality of employment. But there are many—such as entertainers and ski instructors—that meet this test, yet are seldom regarded as migratory workers.

For the annual *Hired Farm Working Force* reports, migratory workers include "those who (1) left their homes temporarily overnight to do farm wagework in a different county within the same State or in a different State with the expectation of eventually returning home, or (2) had no usual place of residence, and did farm wagework in two or more counties during the year."[5]

Thus defined, approximately 8 percent of the estimated 2¾ million who did some farm work in 1974 were migratory (table 3). This percentage level is characteristic of the 1970s and is reduced from the range of 10–15 percent that pertained in the 1960s. Regional patterns in the West and South reflect trends toward decreasing migratoriness which are more accentuated than national aggregates.

Of the 209,000 classified migratory in 1974, about half did both farm and nonfarm work, and their work pattern—some 50 days of farm work and 120 of nonfarm—was similar to that of nonmigratory workers who worked in both sectors. But migratory workers earned more per day in both sectors. Of those doing farm work only, migratory workers gained nothing over nonmigratory in days of employment, although their earnings per day were higher. These findings challenge another quasi-myth: that by following the sun and the crop maturity cycles, migratory

5. Ibid., p. 29.

TABLE 3

MIGRATORY FARM WORKERS, 1961–74

| YEAR | NUMBER OF MIGRANT FARM WORKERS | | | MIGRANTS AS PERCENTAGE OF TOTAL U.S. HIRED FARM WORKER FORCE | MIGRANTS AS PERCENTAGE OF WEST HIRED FARM WORKER FORCE | MIGRANTS AS PERCENTAGE OF SOUTH HIRED FARM WORKER FORCE |
|---|---|---|---|---|---|---|
| | U.S. (000) | WEST (000) | SOUTH (000) | | | |
| 1961 | 395 | 108 | 226 | 11.3 | 17.4 | 11.3 |
| 1962 | 380 | 123 | 190 | 10.5 | 18.9 | 9.6 |
| 1963 | 386 | 130 | 201 | 10.7 | 18.9 | 10.1 |
| 1964 | 386 | 102 | 178 | 11.5 | 15.7 | 9.9 |
| 1965 | 466 | 144 | 188 | 14.9 | 21.4 | 11.7 |
| 1966 | 351 | 151 | 118 | 12.7 | 20.5 | 9.1 |
| 1967 | 276 | 112 | 109 | 12.2 | 13.4 | 7.7 |
| 1968 | 279 | 92 | 115 | 9.6 | 12.3 | 8.6 |
| 1969 | 257 | 102 | 70 | 10.0 | 15.5 | 6.5 |
| 1970 | 196 | 64 | 84 | 10.1 | 11.3 | 7.7 |
| 1971 | 172 | 82 | 56 | 6.7 | 14.4 | 5.1 |
| 1972 | 184 | 70 | 63 | 6.6 | 9.9 | 5.5 |
| 1973 | 203 | 89 | 60 | 7.6 | 12.1 | 6.3 |
| 1974 | 209 | 66 | 67 | 7.6 | 9.4 | 6.5 |

SOURCE: USDA, ERS, *The Hired Farm Working Force*, annual issues.

NOTE: Regions—West includes Montana, Wyoming, Idaho, Colorado, New Mexico, Utah, Arizona, Nevada, Washington, Oregon, California, Hawaii, Alaska. South includes Maryland, Delaware, District of Columbia, Virginia, West Virginia, North Carolina, South Carolina, Georgia, Florida, Kentucky, Tennessee, Alabama, Mississippi, Arkansas, Louisiana, Oklahoma, Texas.

workers are able to get nearly a full year's employment.

In further contradiction of the popular image, it was found in 1965 that three-fifths of migratory workers (as above defined) had only one farm employer; the most typical migrant was a 25-year-old white male employed mainly at a nonfarm job who traveled without minor children across a county line but less than 75 miles within his home state to work temporarily at one farm job.[6] The dramatized migratory streams of the Atlantic and Pacific coasts and the mid-continent have had at least a semblance of structure and recurrent pattern, but their relative impor-.

6. *Domestic Migratory Farmworkers*, Agricultural Economic Report No. 121, Economic Research Service, USDA, September 1967.

tance in the national farm labor scene was never equal to the prevailing image.[7]

## REWARDS OF MIGRANCY ARE MEAGER

In terms of annual earnings, as reported for 1974, the worst situation is that of nonmigrants who do farm work only; those who either became migrants or got nonfarm

7. In 1970, it was estimated that 51,000 or 24 percent of the hired labor force in 14 states of the Atlantic coast region were interstate workers and were thus involved in the Atlantic coast migrant stream. These migrants were primarily black, Puerto Rican, or Mexican-American. Source: Ward W. Bauder, *Minorities in the Hired Farm Work Force of 14 Eastern States* (Ithaca, N.Y.: unpublished manuscript, 1976).

work did better, and those who did both made the highest earnings. Here are the comparative earnings for 1974:

|  | ANNUAL EARNINGS | |
| --- | --- | --- |
|  | NONMIGRANT | MIGRANT |
| Persons doing farm work only | $1,891 | $2,476 |
| Persons 25 or more days of farm work | 3,046 | 3,102 |
| Persons doing both farm and nonfarm work | 3,200 | 3,688 |

If these earnings comparisons were to suggest inferences about rational behavior, it needs being noted that there are 2,528,000 persons in the lowest earnings category as against 107,000 in the highest, which leaves doubt that opportunities and choice prevail. Even were a choice of migrancy available, rational decision would have to go beyond weighing prospective additional costs and gains to matters of family welfare, housing, schooling, and what not. The gains in earnings to migrants are too meager to support a theory of rational choice as to migrancy—either to be or not to be.

Impressions and meager evidence concur in the prospective demise of farm labor migrancy. A settling down seems to be occurring, even in the lack of nonfarm job opportunities. Less harsh residency policies (eligibility for welfare), higher costs of being on the road, and stronger motives toward child education and family well-being seem likely to be influences.

## YOUTH IS CHARACTERISTIC OF HIRED FARM WORKERS

We have seen that the typical migrant is young, this is a characteristic shared by hired farm workers generally and is in contrast with the typically advanced age of farm operators. In 1969, the median age of U.S. farm operators was 51.2 years, whereas the median age for both males and females who did any amount of hired farm work was under 25.[8] Workers in the prime years of occupational life, 25–54, are less than one-third of the total. As table 4 further reflects, females who constituted less than one-fourth of the total, shared the tendency to be youthful. Yet, to inject a bit of humanity into cold percentages, it may be noted that the 1 percent in the females 65 years and over group includes 2,000 women who did more than 150 days of farm work in 1974.

What of others—those in prime occupational years and presumably committed? To examine this question, let us look at farm wagework participation of males in ages 35–54. In 1974, there were 316,000 of these, and they were 12 percent of all males who did any farm wagework. Almost one-fifth of these adult males were extremely casual—they worked on farms less than 25 days; at the other extreme, just over a third worked 250 days or more. The published tabulations do not permit us to know the extent of inter-sectoral employment by 35–54 year old males. But there is a tabulation which suggests that a 35-year-old may already have passed his prime earning years. Of those doing 25 or more days of farm work, males in the 25–34 age category got the most work (average 256 days) and earned the highest annual incomes (average $5,203 from farm work and nonfarm work for those that had any). The downward trend in annual earnings after the peak in age category 25–34 is sharp and

8. U.S., Department of Commerce, Bureau of the Census, 1969 Census of Agriculture, 1973, vol. 2, ch. 3.

TABLE 4

AGE-SEX COMPOSITION OF HIRED
FARM LABOR FORCE, 1974

| AGE | PERCENTAGE OF TOTAL | | |
| --- | --- | --- | --- |
| | MALE | FEMALE | TOTAL |
| 14–17 | 24 | 8 | 32 |
| 18–24 | 21 | 3 | 24 |
| 25–34 | 11 | 4 | 15 |
| 35–44 | 6 | 3 | 9 |
| 45–54 | 5 | 2 | 7 |
| 55–64 | 6 | 1 | 7 |
| 65 & over | 5 | 1 | 6 |
| Total | 78 | 22 | 100 |

SOURCE: Derived from *The Hired Farm Working Force of 1974*, Economic Research Service, U.S. Department of Agriculture, Agricultural Economic Report No. 297, July 1975.

consistent, ending with $1,614 for those 65 and over. Farm wagework may hold some rewards for schoolboys and muscular young men but not for the aging or the aged.

## WHITES AND NONWHITES

Approximately four-fifths of the large total who do some farm wagework are classified as whites. Nonwhites doing farm wagework are principally southern blacks. Nonwhites obtain about the same average days of farm work as whites but only about half as many days of nonfarm work. Earnings per day are substantially lower for nonwhites in both farm and nonfarm work. In consequence of these differences, annual earnings of nonwhites in 1974 were 32 percent below those of whites. Since wage rates are comparatively low in the South, one may be inclined to suppose that regional differences are behind this apparent ethnic difference. But this hypothesis fails, because in the southern region nonwhites earned $2.40 less per day at farm work and $5.55 less

per day at nonfarm work—and of the latter, they received an average of 30 days as against 54 for whites. In consequence, annual earnings for southern nonwhites at $1,613 were one-third below the $2,403 level of southern whites. In regions outside the South, the survey sample contains insufficient numbers of nonwhites to permit separate calculations.

## FOREIGN WORKERS

As an emergency measure in the Second World War, farm laborers were temporarily imported from Mexico, Jamaica, the Bahamas, and Canada under federal government auspices.[9] Some of this importation continued in following years. According to U.S. Immigration Service figures, approximately 8,400 contract workers were imported from Jamaica in 1975, primarily for the sugar cane harvest in the Southeast; there were no contract workers from the Bahamas during that year. Importation from Mexico was continued under quasi-government auspices until 1965, and in many years it was larger in volume than in the war emergency. Since 1964, Mexican citizens have continued to be a factor of some significance in the seasonal farm work force, especially of the southwestern region. These

9. Details of the wartime importation and the practices of early postwar years may be found in *Migratory Labor in American Agriculture*, Report of the President's Commission on Migratory Labor, 1951. The continuance of Mexican contract labor importation under the Bracero program until its termination in 1964 has been written about extensively but lacks a comprehensive reference. An instructive overview is Ellis E. Hawley, "The Politics of the Mexican Labor Issue, 1950–1965," *Agricultural History*, July 1966. Writings about illegally entered Mexican aliens are seldom informative.

are not contract workers as under the expired Bracero program but illegally entered Mexican nationals (wetbacks) and Mexicans legally entered under immigrant visa. Citizens of Mexican origin (by birth or by parental origin) are a substantial and well-known component of the farm work force of the Southwest. Contrary to attitudes that are manifested occasionally, Americans of Mexican descent are not classified as nonwhite. Information on numbers, locations, and activities of this population segment is not comprehensively available. Nor is it with respect to the illegally entered aliens from Mexico.

## IS THERE A LABOR MARKET FOR HIRED FARM WORKERS?

Economists like to visualize goods and services as flows through market places where those who have something to offer and those who want can come together, confront each other, and bargain to agreement. Countless books and articles are written about the markets for this and for that, including labor. Among the latter is a handful of items dealing with "the farm labor market." There are some markets, obviously not including the world market for grain and not likely including markets for farm labor, that have institutional structure, procedural regimen, and predictable modes of operation. In farm labor, the nexus of hiring and of subsequent employer-employee relationships is not much burdened by the paraphernalia that are supposed to characterize labor markets or the bargained outcomes that are supposed to emerge from them. There are undeniably particular situations—localities of specialization such as dairying, poultry, nurseries—that have mar-

ket-like practices for the acquisition of labor. But for the great bulk of farm work, procedures of job-getting and hiring are as miscellaneous as the labor force is heterogeneous.

That farm labor in the United States is lacking in market structure reflects the fact that it is seldom a chosen, life-time occupation. We have seen that few (only 13 percent) of those doing farm work in 1974 were at it at least 250 days. These few might be regarded as the "professional" corps—persons committed to farm wagework and doing well enough at it to remain for the time being. This corps performs half of the nation's hired farm work. For the large remainder, farm wagework is a salvage opportunity—an easy-entry chance to earn something for time that otherwise has little or no value. The validity of this view is most clearly seen in the instance of students and housewives. But most of those who worked at both farm and nonfarm work (there were 1,138,000 of them) were salvaging time. The person who was chiefly not a farm worker and earning $23.55 per day at nonfarm work is not likely to forego days at that level of earning in order to do farm work at $15.20 per day. He and the other 437,999 similarly situated nonfarm workers in 1974 were utilizing the opportunity to work on farms when they otherwise might not have been employed. Their relation to farm employment was basically not different from that of students, housewives, retirees, or those whose chief activity was unemployment. Viewed in this manner, the ratio of "salvagers" to "professionals" in farm labor is almost 8:1. The earning rates of these participants in farm wagework reflect their varying degree of attachment to the industry. In 1974, those whose chief activity was farm wage-

## TABLE 5

### HOURLY FARM WAGE RATES WITHOUT BOARD OR ROOM, BY REGION[10]

| | CENSUS DIVISIONS | | | | | | | | | | AGRICULTURAL AS A PERCENT OF INDUSTRIAL |
|---|---|---|---|---|---|---|---|---|---|---|---|
| YEAR | NE | MA | ENC | WNC | SA | ESC | WSC | M | P | US | WAGE RATES* |
| 1955 | 1.03 | 0.98 | 1.01 | 0.99 | 0.62 | 0.54 | 0.68 | 0.95 | 1.09 | 0.82 | 48 |
| 1960 | 1.16 | 1.11 | 1.08 | 1.08 | 0.72 | 0.62 | 0.76 | 1.06 | 1.23 | 0.97 | 46 |
| 1965 | 1.33 | 1.26 | 1.21 | 1.22 | 0.87 | 0.79 | 0.93 | 1.22 | 1.41 | 1.14 | 47 |
| 1970 | 1.83 | 1.74 | 1.72 | 1.66 | 1.38 | 1.36 | 1.37 | 1.59 | 1.90 | 1.64 | 51 |
| 1971 | 1.91 | 1.82 | 1.81 | 1.77 | 1.43 | 1.43 | 1.47 | 1.68 | 1.96 | 1.73 | 50 |
| 1972 | 2.02 | 1.90 | 1.90 | 1.87 | 1.53 | 1.56 | 1.56 | 1.80 | 2.06 | 1.84 | 50 |

| | STANDARD FEDERAL REGIONS | | | | | | | | | | | AGRICULTURAL AS A PERCENT OF INDUSTRIAL |
|---|---|---|---|---|---|---|---|---|---|---|---|---|
| YEAR | I | II | III | IV | V | VI | VII | VIII | IX | X | US | WAGE RATES* |
| 1973 | 2.11 | 2.04 | 1.73 | 1.56 | 1.99 | 1.61 | 1.97 | 2.02 | 1.98 | 2.07 | 1.90 | 48 |
| 1974† | 2.30 | 2.45 | 2.39 | 1.99 | 2.24 | 2.00 | 2.36 | 2.36 | 2.56 | 2.41 | 2.32 | 55 |
| 1975† | 2.51 | 2.62 | 2.43 | 2.18 | 2.48 | 2.08 | 2.37 | 2.46 | 2.71 | 2.72 | 2.45 | 54 |

SOURCE: U.S. Crop Reporting Board, Statistical Reporting Service, *Farm Labor*; U.S. Bureau of Labor Statistics, *Handbook of Labor Statistics* and *Monthly Labor Review*.

\* Production workers on private nonagricultural payrolls.

† 1974 and 1975 data are "workers paid by hour receiving cash wages only."

work earned an average of $18 per day at farm work; those who were chiefly nonfarm workers earned an average of $15.25 at farm work; those chiefly not in the labor force earned an average of $12.75 per day in farm work.

## HOURLY WAGE RATES FOR HIRED FARM WORKERS

Hourly wage rates for hired farm workers (table 5) further reflect the salvage nature of the farm labor

10. In 1973, the Statistical Reporting Service changed the organization of reported regions from census divisions to standard federal regions. The regions are as follows: *Census Divisions* — N.E. (*New England*): Maine, New Hampshire, Vermont, Massachusetts, Rhode Island, Connecticut; M.A. (*Middle Atlantic*): New York, New Jersey, Pennsylvania; E.N.C. (*East North Central*): Ohio, Indiana, Illinois, Michigan, Wisconsin; W.N.C. (*West North Central*): Minnesota, Iowa, Kansas, Missouri, Nebraska, North

market. During the 1955–75 period, hourly wage rates for hired farm workers averaged about one-half of U.S. industrial wage rates. In the

Dakota, South Dakota; S.A. (*South Atlantic*): Delaware, Maryland, Virginia, West Virginia, North Carolina, South Carolina, Georgia, Florida; E.S.C. (*East South Central*): Kentucky, Tennessee, Alabama, Mississippi; W.S.C. (*West South Central*): Arkansas, Louisiana, Oklahoma, Texas; M. (*Mountain*): Colorado, Montana, Utah, Wyoming, New Mexico, Arizona, Nevada, Idaho; P. (*Pacific*): Washington, Oregon, California.

*Standard Federal Regions* — I: Maine, New Hampshire, Vermont, Massachusetts, Rhode Island, Connecticut; II: New York, New Jersey; III: Pennsylvania, Delaware, Maryland, Virginia, West Virginia; IV: North Carolina, South Carolina, Georgia, Florida; V: Ohio, Indiana, Illinois, Michigan, Wisconsin, Minnesota; VI: Arkansas, Louisiana, Oklahoma, Texas, New Mexico; VII: Kansas, Missouri, Nebraska; VIII: North Dakota, South Dakota, Colorado, Montana, Utah, Wyoming; IX: Arizona, California, Nevada; X: Washington, Oregon, Idaho.

prosperous agricultural years of 1974 and 1975, farm wage rates gained in relation to nonfarm wages, but still were only 55 and 54 percent, respectively, of average industrial rates. Evidence on labor force participation, daily and annual earnings, and hourly wage rates all link to illustrate the dominant characteristic of the hired farm labor market; it is an open access, casual market for the salvage of low opportunity cost time. If neoclassical economic theory is at all applicable to farm labor markets, then hired farm labor must also be low-productivity effort.

As indicated by data presented in table 5, there is considerable regional variation in hourly wage rates for hired farm workers. Traditionally, wages in the southern United States have been relatively low while those in the western regions have been at the top. In 1975, hourly wage rates for hired farm workers in the West were almost one-third above the average in the South. This differential reflects regional divergences in the structure and organization of commercial agriculture as well as the composition and functioning of markets for hired farm labor.

Although the southern region has remained at the bottom in terms of wage rates for hired farm workers, the gap between southern states and the rest of the nation has declined during the last two decades. California farm wage rates have been the highest in the continental United States, but the differential between California and U.S. averages has decreased from 32 percent in 1955 to 11 percent in 1975. Factors contributing to narrowing regional differentials might include rapid economic growth in the South, increased productivity of farm workers nationwide, minimum wage legislation, and movements toward federally-standardized income support programs.

## MINIMUM WAGE LEGISLATION AND FARM LABOR

Governmental determination of minimum wage rates through the Fair Labor Standards Act (FLSA) has had a prominent role in the history of American industrial relations. But agricultural employees were excluded from coverage under FLSA until 1967, although a few states included hired farm workers under state minimim wage statutes. Under the 1966 amendments to FLSA, minimum wage protection was extended to previously exempt irrigation workers and to some previously exempt hired farm workers. Minimum hourly wage rates for covered farm workers were $1.00 in 1967, $1.15 in 1968, and $1.30 in 1969.

In 1974, FLSA was amended to bring agricultural minimum wages up to general industry levels by 1978. These rates are as follows (table 6).

Federal minimum wage legislation applies only to larger farms, most of which already pay in excess of the applicable minimum. Agricultural employees who work for employers who used more than 500 man-days of agricultural labor during any calendar quarter of the preceding year are covered. Certain categories of farm workers, such as the employer's family and some piece-rate workers, are exempt from coverage even if they are employed on farms that meet the 500 man-day requirement. Full-time students can be paid no less than 85 percent of the minimum wage rate otherwise applicable.

## TABLE 6

### FEDERAL MINIMUM HOURLY WAGE RATES

| | EFFECTIVE DATE | | | | |
|---|---|---|---|---|---|
| MINIMUM WAGE RATES ($) | MAY 1 1974 | JAN. 1 1975 | JAN. 1 1976 | JAN. 1 1977 | JAN. 1 1978 |
| General agricultural | 1.60 | 1.80 | 2.00 | 2.20 | 2.30 |
| Full-time student, agricultural | 1.36 | 1.53 | 1.70 | 1.87 | 1.96 |
| General industry | 2.00 | 2.10 | 2.30 | 2.30 | 2.30 |

According to special studies conducted for the Department of Labor by the U.S. Department of Agriculture (USDA) Enumerative Survey, approximately 2 percent of all farms met this man-day requirement in 1967 and 1968.[11] These covered farms employed 35 percent of all hired farm workers in 1967 and 45 percent of all hired farm workers in 1968. Trends toward increasing farm size have probably resulted in higher proportions of covered farms and farm workers since the 1968 survey.

Several states have minimum wage coverage of hired farm workers. In most of these states, minimum wages are the same as specified by FLSA. The major effect of these state statutes is that many extend coverage to hired farm workers who work for employers not meeting the federal 500 man-day criterion. For example, California law specifies that farms having 5 or more hired farm workers at any time during the calendar year qualify for coverage.

Economic theory predicts that minimum wage rates will reduce employment, and workers who remain employed in affected markets will receive increased wages. Several attempts have been made to estimate the impact of minimum wage legislation on agricultural wage rates and employment. There is considerable divergence in the conclusions of these impact studies. For example, the previously-mentioned Department of Labor study concluded that the $1.00 minimum first applied in 1967 caused wages to rise without noticeably accelerating the decline in agricultural employment. In a later econometric study, Bruce Gardner concurred with the Department of Labor on wage effects, but disagreed on employment impact: "[P]oint estimates of the minimum wage variables imply that the 1967 extended minimum wage coverage raised the farm wage rate about 13 percent and that hired farm employment was reduced by about 18 percent from what it would otherwise have been."[12]

Limited research evidence available suggests that minimum wage legislation has probably exerted the dual effects of raising wages for some low-wage farm workers, while causing some low-productivity workers

11. *Hired Farmworkers, a Study of the Effects of the $1.15 Minimum Wage under the Fair Labor Standards Act* (Washington, D.C: U.S., Department of Labor, Wage and Hour and Public Contracts Division, 1969).

12. Bruce Gardner, "Minimum Wages and the Farm Labor Market," *American Journal of Agricultural Economics*, vol. 54, no. 3 (August 1972), p. 475.

to be displaced from farm employment. The precise magnitude and significance of these impacts remain moot issues.

At present and future levels of minimum wages for farm labor, it is clear that the major effect of FLSA will be in the low-wage areas of the nation, particularly the southern states. By comparing regional hourly wage rates for hired farm workers (table 5) with legislated minimum wage levels, it is clear that the *average* farm wage level is above the present statutory minimum in all regions.

In regions with low wages, most workers are employed on small farms and therefore will not be covered. The Department of Labor estimated in 1968 that only one-third of the farmworkers in the South were employed on farms that were large enough to be covered by FLSA minimum wage provisions. Conversely, 55 percent of all covered workers in 1968 were in the West, where average wage rates were and continue to be considerably higher than legislated minima. For example, California farming operations tend toward large-scale and therefore experience a high percentage of FLSA coverage, but average wage rates in 1975 were $.43 above the legal minimum established for 1978. Consequently, the impact of present federal legislation upon farm wages is not likely to be great, although it may have significant effects in limited instances of low-wage workers employed on large farms where state laws do not apply.

UNEMPLOYMENT INSURANCE FOR FARM WORKERS

The Federal Unemployment Insurance Law of 1935 excluded farm work on the avowed grounds that it was not administratively feasible to apply the tax to farm employment and that seasonality of agricultural employment would threaten solvency. During the last 20 years, several unsuccessful attempts have been made to bring farm workers into the program. The Senate approved such a change in 1970, but the Senate-House Conference rejected it. In 1973, the Nixon administration proposed that coverage be extended to agricultural employers with four or more workers in each of 20 or more weeks or a $5,000 payroll in any calendar quarter. The House Subcommittee on Unemployment Compensation in 1975 held extensive hearings on several coverage proposals. These hearings eventually produced H. R. 10210, sponsored by Corman (D-Calif.), Steiger (R-Wis.), and others. The Ways and Means Committee reported this bill to the House in December 1975. At the time of this writing (May 1976), House consideration of H. R. 10210 is underway.

In a related development on the federal scene, the 93rd Congress approved a bill providing special unemployment insurance benefits at no cost to the states through December 31, 1975, to many workers not previously covered, including farm workers, domestics, and employees of state and local governments. This recession-generated program, called Special Unemployment Insurance, was later extended through March 1977. A few agricultural workers have been among the 900,000 recipients under this program.

Farm workers are covered under state unemployment compensation in Hawaii, Minnesota, Puerto Rico, District of Columbia, and California (since January 1, 1976). Other states have generally left agricultural employment uncovered, although several allow voluntary participation by employers.

## IMPACT OF EXTENDING UNEMPLOYMENT INSURANCE TO FARM WORKERS

After the failure in 1970 to extend unemployment insurance coverage to agricultural employees, Congress mandated the Department of Labor to undertake a study on the effect and impact of extending unemployment insurance to farm workers. The result was a regional research project in 12 northeastern states plus Ohio, Florida, and Texas.[13] Three additional studies were conducted by the state employment security agencies of Washington, Minnesota, and California.

These studies sampled worker and employer payroll experience and were based upon the 4-worker/20-week criterion mentioned previously. Highlight findings are summarized in table 7. Column 1 indicates that the largest number of covered employees would be in California, Florida, and Texas. Percentages of total farm employment covered (column 2) would vary from 93 to 33. Column 3 shows the benefits which covered farm workers would receive as a percentage of the wages on which farm employers would pay taxes. All states have ceilings on maximum tax rates to be paid by an employer, listed in column 4. Finally, column 5 indicates that farm employment is a small part of total employment and therefore would have only a minor effect on the state average tax rate.

This study sheds light on a major concern about extending unemployment insurance to farm workers. This concern is high benefit costs and high taxes. As shown in column 3, table 7, in most of the states studied, average farm cost was below the state's maximum tax. For the 48 contiguous states, average cost rates were estimated in a later study to be 3.3 percent of total agricultural payrolls.[14] These results indicate that, from the viewpoint of cost, it should be feasible to extend unemployment insurance to agriculture. Although the average benefit cost rate for agriculture is high in most states, it is not as high as for other seasonal industries such as construction.

Evidence available suggests that unemployment insurance for farm workers would not be prohibitively costly nor would it effect major disruptions in labor markets. Benefit cost levels for agriculture would be relatively high, but no worse than many presently-covered industries. Some workers would choose unemployment benefits over farm work and particular crops or geographic regions might be adversely affected, but in the aggregate a significant decline in farm labor supply is unlikely.

There appears to be little justification for continued exclusion of agricultural employees from unemployment insurance and the income security it guarantees other workers.

13. W. W. Bauder et al., *Impact of Extension of Unemployment Insurance to Agriculture* (Washington, D.C.: Report submitted to the U.S. Department of Labor, 1972). The 15 states included in this report were: Connecticut, Delaware, Florida, Maine, Maryland, Massachusetts, New Hampshire, New Jersey, New York, Ohio, Pennsylvania, Rhode Island, Texas, Vermont, and West Virginia.

14. Joachim Elterich and Richard Bieker, "Cost Rates of Extending Unemployment Insurance to Agricultural Employment," *American Journal of Agricultural Economics*, vol. 57, no. 2 (May 1975).

TABLE 7

ESTIMATED IMPACT OF EXTENSION OF UNEMPLOYMENT INSURANCE COVERAGE
TO FARM WORKERS, CALENDAR YEAR 1969*

| STATE | COVERED EMPLOYMENT | | FARM COST RATE† (3) | MAXIMUM U.I. TAX RATE‡ (4) | TAXABLE FARM WAGES AS A PERCENT OF ALL TAXABLE WAGES§ (5) |
| | NUMBER (1) | PERCENT OF TOTAL FARM EMPLOYMENT (2) | | | |
|---|---|---|---|---|---|
| California | 216,000 | 86 | 7.6 | 3.7 | 1.6 |
| Connecticut | 5,916 | 83 | 7.4 | 2.7 | .3 |
| Delaware | 1,718 | 73 | 4.2 | 4.5 | .5 |
| Florida | 58,667 | 93 | 3.1 | 4.5 | 2.4 |
| Maine | 4,123 | 67 | 2.3 | 3.7 | 1.1 |
| Maryland | 4,122 | 56 | 2.5 | 4.2 | .3 |
| Massachusetts | 3,951 | 76 | 3.0 | 4.1 | .1 |
| Minnesota | 3,600 | 34 | 2.4 | 4.5 | .2 |
| New Hampshire | 761 | 57 | 3.2 | 4.3 | .2 |
| New Jersey | 8,967 | 82 | 6.9 | 4.2 | .2 |
| New York | 15,626 | 60 | 1.9 | 4.2 | .1 |
| Ohio | 10,712 | 61 | 3.4 | 4.7 | .2 |
| Pennsylvania | 13,387 | 63 | 2.2 | 4.0 | .2 |
| Rhode Island | 366 | 71 | 8.4 | 4.0 | .1 |
| Texas | 36,427 | 53 | 3.8 | 2.7 | 2.4 |
| Vermont | 852 | 33 | 1.0 | 4.4 | .4 |
| Washington | 19,437 | 72 | 4.3 | 2.7 | .8 |
| West Virginia | 1,657 | 52 | 1.2 | 3.3 | .2 |

SOURCE: W. W. Bauder et al., *Impact of Extension of Unemployment Insurance to Agriculture*, Report submitted to the U.S. Department of Labor (Washington, D.C.: U.S. Department of Labor, 1972), and special studies conducted by the state unemployment insurance agencies of California, Minnesota, and Washington.

* Farms with four or more workers in each of 20 weeks or with a quarterly payroll of $5,000.
† Cost rate = benefit payments as percent of taxable payrolls.
‡ The tax rate in effect at the time of the study.
§ Estimates based on coverage of four workers or more in 20 weeks, but without the additional provision of $5,000 in quarterly wages.

A corollary benefit of extending unemployment insurance to farm workers would be to put them in touch with other available but often unknown forms of aid and employment. An unemployed farm worker who files for benefits will have better access to programs and opportunities of which he might otherwise be unaware.

## UNIONIZATION AND COLLECTIVE BARGAINING

"Agricultural laborers," not defined, were excluded from the National Labor Relations Act (1935, NLRA). In the Senate committee, their exclusion was said to be for "administrative" reasons; in the House committee, it was described as being only temporary. However described or excused, the legislative record was sparse on this point and did not establish that exclusion, as a class, was other than arbitrary, discriminatory, possibly unconstitutional, and a political casualty. Whatever else, it was unequal treatment under the law.

In following decades, attempts were made occasionally to amend

NLRA and strike out this exclusion. In the absence of effective organizations of farm laborers, these efforts were carried vicariously—by sympathetic churchmen, liberal civic groups, the AFL-CIO and unaffiliated national unions, and a few pro-labor legislators, the latter beginning with Senator Robert LaFollette. Whenever such efforts seemed to be getting serious, they were opposed by organized farmers, but not including National Farmers Union and National Farm Organization.

Collective bargaining by hired farm workers is rare. Although there have been several short-lived efforts elsewhere to unionize farm workers, many involving strikes, only on the large industrialized farms of California and Hawaii has the movement attained prominence and endurance. These states are exceptional in that they have labor-management relations laws covering farm workers. That farm unionization and labor laws are coincidental in these two states does not mean that if laws are enacted to protect it, unionization will follow. In both states, some degree of power to organize pre-existed, and legislative reactions were more concerned with monitoring exercise of power than with conferring it. Neither state governments nor the federal are noted for conferring power upon the powerless in the name of justice and equity. Governmental intervention into this area holds protections for both employers and workers. Hence it is only when union power emerges or threatens that employers withdraw opposition to such legislation sufficiently to allow it minimum political support.

Unionization does not normally occur unless cohesiveness and articulation are already developed or show promise of development. These attributes, in turn, depend upon a broadly shared community of continuing interests and channels for their communication. Among nonprofessional workers, the development of these attributes does not readily occur without physical compaction at the work site. Even though the requisite conditions come into being, the recent history of unionization does not suggest that indigenously initiated organization is likely; rather, with favorable conditions in place, outside organizers may become impressed with their possibilities. Accordingly, unionization of farm workers in California and Hawaii depended heavily upon nonfarm union initiative, including, among others, the longshore and teamster unions as well as AFL-CIO. Rational decision-making by established labor organizations as to where to allocate organizational resources does not much more rest on sentiment than does assessment of product markets by business corporations.

Viewed through these perspectives, the unlikelihood of broad-scale unionization of American hired farm workers seems apparent. The bulk of them lack the shared interests, the long-range attachments, the compactness, and opportunities for communication that offer a rewarding field for organizational investment. Without radical and unforeseen changes in enterprise structure, collective determination in agricultural employment will apparently continue to be more exceptional than dominant. Nevertheless, if unionization attains strength and endurance in the exceptional locations that are favorable to it, the terms and conditions established there through collective bargaining are likely to have propensity for proliferation into non-bargaining regions. Moreover, an organized component—even though a small fraction of the total—could well become politically influential in respect to laws and programs affecting all farm workers.

## CHANGING ATTITUDES TOWARD FARM LABOR

Although agriculture is moving from a structure of traditional family farming toward an industrial enterprise system (particularly in the West), the farm labor market has not developed structure and regimen similar to that observed in nonfarm labor markets. The aggregate of all persons who do some farm wagework is extremely heterogeneous, and the market for hired farm labor is characterized by casual employment relationships. Recent evidence suggests that the farm labor force has become somewhat more stable in composition and residence, but farm employment continues to be dominated by uncertain employer-employee relations and part-time workers seeking salvage of low opportunity cost time.

Recent developments, such as extension of the Occupational Health and Safety Act of 1970 to agriculture and movements to include farm work under employment insurance reflect a shift in attitude toward agriculture and that farm workers are likely to receive increasing federal protection on a basis equal to that afforded nonfarm workers. While minimum wage legislation is unlikely to exert major economic impact, the fact that statutory rates for agriculture will be the same under FLSA as for general industry by 1978 holds important implications for public policy. This move toward standardized treatment indicates that agriculture is losing its special and exempt status under federal legislation. Continuation and amplification of this shift in posture hold important considerations for other policy matters, such as collective bargaining, fair labor practices, and workmen's compensation.

# The Rural Aged

## By E. GRANT YOUMANS

ABSTRACT: Available data suggest that the rural aged, compared with urban older people, have substantially smaller incomes, are restricted in mobility because of inadequate transportation facilities, report poorer physical health, and reveal a more negative outlook on life. Evidence suggests that the industrialization of rural communities may have a negative impact upon the rural elderly. Periodic longitudinal studies of rural older persons in strategic locations of the nation are needed to provide guidance for programs and services.

---

*E. Grant Youmans is a Sociologist with the Economic Development Division, Economic Research Service, U.S. Department of Agriculture, and Adjunct Professor of Sociology at the University of Kentucky, Lexington. He earned his Ph.D. in Sociology at Michigan State University and is a Fellow in the Gerontological Society and the American Sociological Association. Formerly he was a Research Sociologist with the National Institute of Mental Health and served on the Kentucky Commission on Aging and the Kentucky Council on Aging. In 1969 he was awarded the Certificate of Merit by the U.S. Department of Agriculture for contributions to research on aging. He edited* Older Rural Americans *and has written more than 60 research papers and review articles, most of them dealing with the social psychological aspects of aging.*

Acknowledgement for advice and assistance is made to J. S. Brown, T. A. Carlin, A. L. Coleman, A. Gabbard, B. Green, D. Larson, W. F. Kenkel, and N. LeRay.

IN RECENT decades, public attention has been directed to the conditions of life of older people in American society. Awareness of these conditions has been augmented by the increasing number and proportion of the aged in the population and their consequent greater visibility to the rest of society. In 1850 about 3 percent of the population was aged 65 and over; 100 years later, it was 8 percent; and in 1975 persons aged 65 and over constituted 10 percent of the population, representing 9.2 million men and 13.1 million women. It is estimated that the present percentage will increase slightly during the remainder of this century, but the absolute numbers of persons aged 65 and over will increase to 40.6 million by the year 2000. Slight improvements in mortality are anticipated. Average life expectancy at birth is predicted to increase to 69.9 for men and 78.0 for women by the year 2020.[1]

The U.S. Bureau of the Census reported 5,431,906 persons aged 65 and over as living in rural areas of the nation in 1970. Of these, 4,533,714 were rural nonfarm and 898,192 lived on farms. In the rural nonfarm population, the females exceeded the males in number, but in the rural-farm population there were more older men than older women.[2] Demographic data indicate a growing concentration of aged persons in small towns of the United States. This increase is partially explained by the out-migration of young people and the in-migration of retired farmers from the open country and elderly people from urban centers.[3]

The growing attention to problems of the elderly has been accompanied by an enormous volume of literature about aging. During the first half of the century (1900–1948), about 18,000 publications on aging were reported,[4] but in the 12 years following, over 34,000 publications appeared.[5] It is reasonable to assume that research on a topic of such vital concern as human aging will continue to expand.

In such a rapidly growing research field, there has been a notable defect—the limited number of studies of older persons living in rural environments in the United States. Yet such a deficiency is not too surprising. It is characteristic of American society that new fields of inquiry emerge in urban centers and then gradually spread to rural areas. Social gerontology, a late arrival to the disciplines concerned with aging, has followed this pattern. Almost all social gerontologists are urban dwellers, and their research efforts have been directed mainly to studies of human aging in city environments.

The objective of this chapter is to present information on the objective

1. *Interchange*, vol. 1, no. 1 (Washington, D.C.: Population Reference Bureau, Inc., January 1976).

2. U.S. Bureau of the Census, *Census of Population 1970: Detailed Characteristics*, Final Report PC(1)-D1, United States Summary (Washington, D.C.: Government Printing Office, 1973), table 199.

3. Donald O. Cowgill, "The Demography of Aging in the Midwest," in Arnold M. Rose and Warren A. Peterson, eds., *Older People and Their Social World* (Philadelphia: F.A. Davis, 1965).

4. Nathan W. Shock, *A Classified Bibliography of Gerontology and Geriatrics* (Stanford, Calif.: Stanford University Press, 1951).

5. Nathan W. Shock, *A Classified Bibliography of Gerontology and Geriatrics, Supplement One, 1949–1955* (Stanford, Calif.: Stanford University Press, 1957); and *A Classified Bibliography of Gerontology and Geriatrics, Supplement Two, 1956–1961* (Stanford, Calif.: Stanford University Press, 1963).

and subjective conditions of life of the sizable number of older persons who live in rural areas of the United States. It is recognized that standards for assessing the life of the rural elderly do not exist in either the objective or subjective domain. In the absence of such criteria, it is assumed that comparisons of data on the rural aged with data on the urban aged will be useful.

The observations that follow are organized around selected questions that are assumed to have an important bearing on the lives of the rural aged in the United States. What is the nature of "rurality" in the United States: What are the income levels of the rural aged? Does industrialization of rural areas benefit older people? What is the nature of the social life of the rural elderly? What is the health status of older persons living in rural areas? How adequate is the subjective life of the rural aged? What are the implications of the answers to these questions for older rural Americans?

## RURALITY

The status and well-being of any large category of persons is inextricably interrelated with the social, economic, and cultural conditions of the society in which they live. The term "rural" suggests an agricultural economic base, low population density, and relative isolation from large population centers.[6] As a social psychological concept, "rurality" suggests a continuum. At one extreme is a complex of behavior and mental outlook characteristic of what

anthropologists call a folk[7] or *gemeinschaft*[8] society. At the other end of the continuum are found the orientations characteristic of contemporary large urban centers. Both types of orientation obtain in any given region, area, village, town, or city, and the degrees of commitment to one or the other pose important problems for the inhabitants.

The traditional or folk type of society and culture places strong emphasis on conventional behavior and conformity to traditions and customs and values strong adherence to kinship control of behavior. Persons living in societies predominantly of the folk type tend to have few interpersonal contacts and such contacts tend to be primary in nature and of long duration and limited to a small geographic area. Sacred and religious beliefs play an important role in the orientations of people in the folk type of society.

In contrast, the modern orientations of contemporary urban life emphasize more individualistic behavior, a rejection of custom and tradition, and weakened kinship control. The typical urbanite engages in many social contacts of a secondary nature and of short duration. In the urban centers, one finds strong adherence to secular values and beliefs and a tendency to reject sacred and religious orientations.

In recent decades, most rural areas in the United States have undergone substantial changes. There has been a notable shift from the older folkway of life to a more modern and technologically advanced type of

---

6. Robert C. Atchley, *Contemporary Conceptions of "Rural"* (Oxford, Ohio: Scripps Foundation at Miami University, prepublication manuscript, 1976), pp. 1–14.

7. Robert Redfield, "The Folk Society," *American Journal of Sociology*, vol. 52 (1947), pp. 293–308.

8. Charles P. Loomis and J. Allan Beegle, *Rural Social Systems* (New York: Prentice-Hall, Inc., 1950), p. 784.

society. Trends toward modernization in most rural areas are reflected in increased productivity, fewer farms, and more part-time farming; in more specialized and increasingly efficient agricultural businesses; in more complex social organizations, such as schools, churches, and business enterprises; in improved transportation and communication facilities; and in greater movements of rural people from place to place.[9]

The conflicts between allegiance to the folk or to the modern urbanized type of culture and society pose critical problems for many older Americans who live in small cities, towns, villages, and the open country, or on farms. The older population in these areas, most of whom were born before 1910, undoubtedly internalized orientations toward life that are characteristic of a folk type of society. The young adults, born mostly in the 1950s, tended to adopt a way of life more typical of an industrialized type of society.

The intergenerational differences that ensue are acutely painful for many olders persons. The differences in outlook, the variances in behavior, and the conflicts are especially troublesome to older people who are members of minority groups. These older persons, such as rural black Americans, rural American Indians, and rural Spanish-speaking people, experience the trauma of witnessing the disappearance of the cultural ways that gave meaning and significance to their lives.[10] Rejected, lonely, and out-of-touch with contemporary values and behavior, many of them have little to look forward to and little to live for. They tend to be the forgotten and neglected people passed by in the modernization process.

## INCOME

An adequate annual income is probably the most important indicator of the economic well-being of persons at any stage of the life cycle. It is assumed that annual incomes received by men and women living in urban centers of the United States reflect the economic rewards derived from an industrialized society and that such incomes may be used as a standard of comparison.

Data on annual incomes in the United States by age, sex, and place of residence are provided by the U.S. Bureau of the Census for 1959 and 1969. An examination of these income figures indicates the economic position of various rural age groups in the nation relative to that of urban persons age 14 and over for that decade.

Table 1 places in salient perspective the disadvantaged economic position of the rural aged males relative to that of other male age groups in the nation in 1959 and 1969. Throughout the decade, the annual median incomes of the rural aged males were markedly less than those of all urban males age 14 and over, substantially less than those of all rural nonfarm and farm males age 14 and over, and less than those of urban males age 65 and over.

The relative economic position of

9. Everett M. Rogers and Rabel J. Burdge, *Social Change in Rural Societies* (New York: Appleton-Century-Crofts, 1972).

10. Jerold E. Levy, "The Older American Indian," Olen E. Leonard, "The Older Rural Spanish People of the Southwest," and Stanley H. Smith, "The Older Rural Negro," in E. G. Youmans, ed., *Older Rural Americans* (Lexington: University of Kentucky Press, 1967).

TABLE 1

ANNUAL MEDIAN INCOME BY SEX, AGE GROUP, AND PLACE OF RESIDENCE
IN THE UNITED STATES, 1959 AND 1969

| | MALE | | | |
| | 1959 | | 1969 | |
| AGE GROUP AND RESIDENCE | ($) | % | ($) | % |
|---|---|---|---|---|
| Urban age 14 and over | 4,559 | 100 | 6,860 | 100 |
| Rural nonfarm age 14 and over | 3,330 | 73 | 5,591 | 82 |
| Rural farm age 14 and over | 2,105 | 46 | 4,509 | 66 |
| Urban age 65 and over | 1,961 | 43 | 3,188 | 46 |
| Rural nonfarm age 65 and over | 1,351 | 30 | 2,205 | 32 |
| Rural farm age 65 and over | 1,417 | 31 | 2,514 | 37 |

| | FEMALE | | | |
|---|---|---|---|---|
| Urban age 14 and over | 1,606 | 100 | 2,514 | 100 |
| Rural nonfarm age 14 and over | 951 | 59 | 1,838 | 73 |
| Rural farm age 14 and over | 823 | 51 | 1,534 | 61 |
| Urban age 65 and over | 844 | 53 | 1,562 | 62 |
| Rural nonfarm age 65 and over | 662 | 41 | 1,104 | 44 |
| Rural farm age 65 and over | 632 | 39 | 887 | 35 |

SOURCE: Computed from U.S. Bureau of the Census, *Census of Population, 1960 and 1970: Detailed Characteristics*, Final Reports PC(1)-D1 and PC(1)-D1, United States Summary (Washington, D.C.: Government Printing Office, 1962 and 1973), tables 219 and 245.

the rural aged males was fairly constant over the decade. In 1959 and 1969, the respective annual median incomes of rural nonfarm males age 65 and over were $1,351 and $2,205, only 30 and 32 percent, respectively, of that of all urban males age 14 and over. For the rural-farm males age 65 and over, the respective annual median incomes were $1,417 and $2,514, only 31 and 37 percent, respectively, of that of all urban males age 14 and over. The disparity for the urban aged over the decade was not as great; respective annual incomes were $1,961 and $3,188, or 43 and 46 percent of that of all urban males age 14 and over.

The annual median incomes of female age groups in the nation showed trends similar to those for the men from 1959 to 1969. Over the decade, the annual median incomes of the rural aged females were substantially less than those of all urban females age 14 and over, much less than those of all rural nonfarm and farm females age 14 and over, and less than those of urban females age 65 and over (table 1).

The relative economic position of the rural aged women, like that of the rural aged men, was fairly constant over the 10-year period. In 1959 and 1969, the respective annual median incomes of rural nonfarm females age 65 and over were $662 and $1,104, only 41 and 44 percent, respectively, of that of all urban females age 14 and over. For rural farm females age 65 and over, the respective annual median incomes were $632 and $887, only 39 and 35 percent, respectively, of that of all urban females age 14 and over. Again, the income of elderly urban females compared more favorably ($844 and $1,562; 53 and 62 percent respectively) than did that for rural females (table 1).

## RURAL DEVELOPMENT

Many rural communities in the United States, while retaining characteristics of traditional and folk societies, have undergone considerable industrialization. The Rural Development Act of 1972 was designed to encourage and accelerate economic growth in rural areas of the nation. Implementation of the act involved developing strategies whereby rural communities could attract industrial enterprises. It was assumed that such enterprises, if established in rural areas, would increase employment and services, increase incomes, inject new money into the community, and, in general, improve the quality of life.

Many rural communities have painfully discovered that the expected benefits from industrialization have not been achieved. Preliminary evidence suggests that the process of industrialization in many rural areas of the nation has had a differential impact upon various categories of persons. Some groups in the communities have benefited while other groups have experienced detrimental effects.[11]

A five-year longitudinal study in rural Illinois offers evidence of the negative impact of industrialization upon the economic well-being of the elderly in the area studied.[12] The hypothesis examined in the study was that the "industrial development of small communities is directly associated with a decline in the relative economic status of the elderly residents of the communities." The hypothesis was subjected to empirical tests in what the authors called a "natural experiment." Two communities of comparable social, demographic, and economic characteristics were selected. One community, designated the "experimental" area, had witnessed the construction of a heavily capitalized, ultra-modern cold rolling mill in the five-year period. The second community, used as a "control" area, had not experienced industrial development.

The findings in the study suggest that neither the economically active rural aged nor the retired rural residents of the experimental area benefited from industrial development. The study did not attempt to assess the impact of industrial development upon other aspects of life of the older residents, such as the cost of living, mental and physical health, local tax structure, and community facilities and services.

## SOCIAL LIFE

An important indicator of well-being is the freedom and opportunity to interact with persons and groups of one's choice. Many older rural persons are limited in their social activities and an important factor in these restrictions appears to be the lack of adequate transportation facilities.[13] Older rural women apparently are more restricted in social life than older rural men.[14] A

11. Mary Jo Grinstead, Bernal L. Green, and J. Martin Redfern, *Rural Development and Labor Adjustment in the Mississippi Delta and Ozarks of Arkansas* (Fayetteville, Ark.: Agricultural Experiment Station, Bulletin 795, 1975).

12. Frank Clemente and Gene F. Summers, "Industrial Development and the Elderly: A Longitudinal Analysis," *Journal of Gerontology*, vol. 28 (1973), pp. 479–83.

13. Ira Kaye, "Transportation Problems of the Older American" in J. B. Cull and R. E. Hardy, eds., *The Neglected Older American* (Springfield, Ill.: Charles C. Thomas, Publisher, 1973).

14. Carl V. Patton, "Age Groupings and Travel in a Rural Area," *Rural Sociology*, vol. 40 (1975), pp. 55–63.

low socioeconomic level and retirement are salient factors in the reduced social participation of many older rural men.[15] Further, according to Walter McKain, the present generation of older rural people grew to maturity when the family provided the dominant form of social life.[16] Today, the traditional social function of the family has almost disappeared in many rural areas of the nation, and no satisfactory social organization has been developed to replace it.

A comparative study of older persons living in an urban and a rural environment provides some detailed data on their family relationships, their community participation, and their leisure-time hobbies and pastimes.[17] In both rural and urban areas, proximity was an important factor in the frequency of visits between the older person and his or her children and siblings. The children and siblings of the urban aged were somewhat more widely dispersed than those of the rural elderly; despite this distance factor, urban older persons visited with their children and their siblings more often than did the rural older persons. In addition, the rural older people said they depended more on their children and siblings to initiate visits than did the urban aged. These rural-urban differences in family

visiting patterns probably reflected the more limited financial resources of the rural elderly as well as the poorer transportation facilities available in the rural area.

Slight differences were found between older rural and urban persons in the average number of reported community activities (rural 1.5 and urban 1.7). In both areas the most popular community activity was church related, and for the great majority this was the only activity reported. A greater proportion of the urban than rural aged took part in service and welfare organizations, in social clubs and lodges, and in Golden Age clubs. As might be expected, a larger proportion of the rural aged were members of farm organizations. Informal social activities played a slightly more important role in the lives of the older rural persons and a greater proportion of the rural than of the urban elderly said they knew people in the community well, offered help to their friends and neighbors, and visited with friends and neighbors.[18]

Older rural persons engaged in slightly fewer hobbies and pastimes than did the older urban persons (average number 2.5 and 2.7, respectively). A slightly larger proportion of rural older persons engaged in fishing and hunting, while a larger proportion of urban aged engaged in playing cards, woodwork and crafts, dancing, and collecting. More than one-fourth of the persons in the study said they would like to take part in more activities, but there was little difference between the rural and the urban older persons in this desire. A slightly larger proportion of the rural than urban aged said that their lives could be more useful and that time was a burden.[19]

15. Philip Taietz and Olaf F. Larson, "Social Participation and Old Age," *Rural Sociology*, vol. 21 (1956), pp. 229–38.

16. Walter C. McKain, Jr., "Community Roles and Activities of Older Rural Persons," in E. G. Youmans, ed., *Older Rural Americans* (Lexington: University of Kentucky Press, 1967).

17. E. Grant Youmans, *Aging Patterns in a Rural and an Urban Area of Kentucky* (Lexington, Ky.: Agricultural Experiment Station Bulletin 681, 1963). In 1959, data were collected from 1,236 men and women age 60 and over, half of whom lived in a metropolitan center and half in a rural county of Kentucky.

18. Ibid.
19. Ibid.

## HEALTH

It is commonly believed that rural living in the United States offers distinct health benefits to older people. It is alleged that the rural elderly enjoy the advantages of abundant fresh air and sunshine, out-of-doors activities, a slower-paced lifestyle, and strong emotional support of close family and friends. It appears that such an idyllic picture of rural America is the product of popular writers. Careful studies do not substantiate the pastoral fantasy that glorifies rural communities as a paradise for older persons.[20]

Two studies in Kentucky offer systematic data on the comparative health status of rural and urban older persons. In both studies, each person interviewed was asked if he or she had any ailments or health conditions that bothered the respondent either all the time or periodically. Those who answered "yes" were then asked to name the ailments or health conditions. In the 1959 study, 74 percent of the rural aged reported one or more ailments, compared with 61 percent for the urban aged; the rural older persons reported a higher prevalence of arthritis and rheumatism, high blood pressure, urological difficulties, and ailments of the respiratory system.[21]

In the 1971 study, responses to the question on physical health were placed in eight substantive categories.[22] On seven of these categories, the older rural men and women reported a greater proportion of ailments than did the urban aged; the rural elderly reported double the proportion of persons afflicted with cardiovascular difficulties and slightly greater proportions having respiratory, sense organs, endocrine, urinary, and psychiatric problems.

Available data on self-reported health ratings provide some clues about the health of rural and urban older men. Rural older men consistently rated their health as poorer than did the older urban men. Only 15 percent of the rural elderly men rated their health as "good," compared with 47 percent for the older urban men. Of the rural aged men, 75 percent said their health was worse than at age 50, compared with only 51 percent of the urban older men; 56 percent of the aged rural men said they had serious health problems, but only 24 percent of the urban aged men made such a statement; and 76 percent of the rural aged men compared with only 40 percent of the urban older men reported that their health conditions had obliged them to cut down on their activities.[23]

The comparatively poorer health of older rural persons undoubtedly reflects a variety of social and economic conditions. Among these are the characteristically lower economic and educational levels of the rural people which inhibits their benefiting from health programs and knowledge. In addition, in the United States, the distribution of medical and health care services has favored urban locations, as is evidenced by the concentration of

20. Walter C. McKain, Jr., "Aging and Rural Life," in W. Donahue and C. Tibbits, eds., The New Frontiers of Aging (Ann Arbor: University of Michigan Press, 1957).

21. E. Grant Youmans, Aging Patterns in a Rural and an Urban Area of Kentucky.

22. E. Grant Youmans, "Age Group, Health, and Attitudes," The Gerontologist, vol. 14 (1974), pp. 249–54. The older persons studied were age 60 and over.

23. E. Grant Youmans, "Health Orientations of Older Rural and Urban Men," Geriatrics, vol. 22 (1967), pp. 139–47. The younger men were age 60 to 64 and the older men age 75 and over.

research centers, clinics, medical specialists, dentists, and various ancillary medical personnel in the more populated areas of the nation.[24]

## SUBJECTIVE LIFE

For most persons, old age brings limitations of one kind or another. The cumulative effect of these decrements tends to have a negative impact upon the subjective life of many older persons. Each person has within his life-span a potential for developing a positive outlook, depending on a variety of biological, psychological, and sociological forces influencing his behavior. Available evidence suggests that rural environments have less potential than urban settings for producing a favorable mental outlook among older people.

A study of value orientations offers some clues about the subjective life of older rural and urban persons.[25] In a Kentucky study, nine scales were used to assess orientations toward selected values in American society, such as authoritarianism, religion, achievement, dependency, and pessimism. Respondents in the rural and urban samples agreed or disagreed with three statements on each scale. Responses to the statements indicated that the rural older people tended to have a more negative outlook on life than did the urban older people. The rural aged were also more authoritarian in viewpoint, more fundamentalistic in

religious outlook, less motivated toward achievement, evidenced a greater dependency on government, and revealed greater hopelessness and despair.

An attitudinal study of rural and urban older persons revealed findings similar to the previous report on values.[26] In this study each person in the rural and urban samples responded to 72 agree-disagree statements constituting 24 attitude scales about economic well-being, self-image, morale, community life, family relationships, and general outlook. Comparison of mean scores on the 24 attitude scales yielded 17 statistically significant differences between the older rural and urban persons studied; of these, the urban aged scored more favorably than the rural elderly on 12, and the rural aged scored more favorably than urban older persons on 5, resulting in an overall ratio favoring the urban aged of 2.4 to 1.

The findings of the study indicated that the rural elderly, compared with the urban aged, worried more about their financial conditions, revealed less satisfaction with their housing, and maintained they had greater need for more money; revealed a more negative view of themselves and a poorer self-evaluation of their health; found their lives more dreary and were more concerned about their inability to lead useful lives; rated their communities less favorably in terms of visiting patterns, neighborliness, and gen-

24. Bert L. Ellenbogen, "Health Status of the Rural Aged," in E. G. Youmans, ed., *Older Rural Americans* (Lexington: University of Kentucky Press, 1967).

25. E. Grant Youmans, "Perspectives on the Older American in a Rural Setting," in J. B. Cull and R. E. Hardy, eds., *The Neglected Older American* (Springfield, Ill.: Charles C. Thomas, Publisher, 1973).

26. These findings are based on a survey this author conducted in 1971 of 803 persons age 20 and over living in a metropolitan center and a rural county of Kentucky. Aged persons were age 60 and over. The study was carried out jointly by the Economic Development Division, Economic Research Service, U.S. Department of Agriculture, and the Kentucky Agricultural Experiment Station, Lexington, Ky.

eral benefits; and reported greater alienation and more worry.[27]

In contrast, the rural aged, compared with the urban aged, revealed a greater sense of general happiness, greater family pride, stronger family support, and stronger feelings of personal gratification, as well as giving more favorable ratings to their neighborhoods as places in which to live.[28]

## IMPLICATIONS

The disadvantaged position of older persons in urban environments in the United States has been previously documented.[29] Older persons in rural environments of the nation appear to be even more disadvantaged. Available information suggests that many rural older persons have extremely small incomes, inadequate means of transportation, a restricted social life, and poor physical and mental health. Many suffer from triple jeopardy: they are old, poor, and isolated in communities lacking organizations to serve the aged.[30]

The conditions of life of rural older persons in the United States strongly suggest the need for research and

application in nonmetropolitan gerontology. Reliable information is needed on all aspects of life of older persons living in smaller cities, towns, villages, the open country, and on farms. Of special importance is the need for regional comparisons and for careful longitudinal studies conducted at strategic locations. Periodic assessments at these locations could provide public and private agencies with reliable data on demographic and migratory trends; on income, employment, housing, taxation, transportation facilities, and the industrialization process; on physical and mental health and nutritional levels; and on public safety, crime, social welfare, family and community life, and recreational and leisure-time facilities.

A feasible organizational structure to serve the interests of the rural and nonmetro aged is the concept of the Area Agency on Aging as outlined in the 1973 amendments to the Older Americans Act.[31] Such a client-centered agency could serve as an advocate of the interests of older persons, as a planner and coordinator of services for the aged without actually providing services, and as a catalyst and innovator in finding and pooling untapped resources and information needed for comprehensive programs and services for the older people.

27. Ibid.
28. Ibid.
29. Mathilda W. Riley and Anne Foner, *Aging and Society*, vol. 1: *An Inventory of Research Findings* (New York: Russell Sage Foundation, 1968).
30. *Triple Jeopardy: Myth or Reality* (Washington, D.C.: National Council on the Aging, 1972).

31. U.S. Bureau of the Census, Social Statistics for the Elderly, Area Level System, Stage 1, Omaha (Washington, D.C., 1975).

ANNALS, AAPSS, **429**, Jan. 1977

# Farmer Cooperatives

## By RANDALL E. TORGERSON

ABSTRACT: Farmer cooperatives are voluntarily owned business organizations controlled by their member patrons and operated for and by them on a nonprofit or cost basis. These organizations are an integral part of the economic organization of agriculture. They are organizational tools that enable farm families to have access to markets and achieve a degree of marketing power so that farmers can compete and survive in an increasingly concentrated food and fiber economy. Cooperatives also represent an alternative organizational form to carry out business activities and are distinguished from other types of businesses because they represent economic democracy in action. Growth in their use, as a dimension of market structure, has been limited by the prevailing school of thought on cooperation in the U.S. A conflict exists between cooperatives' perceived role in this school and the hard realities of fundamental changes in market structure. Expanded use of cooperatives is also influenced by the external environment, such as the legal climate for growth, sources of finance, and public attitude toward collective action by farmers in an era of a close balance between supply and demand for food and relatively higher food prices. The ultimate measure of cooperative success, however, is performance in enhancing the economic well-being of members and rural communities.

---

*Randall E. Torgerson is serving as Administrator of the Farmer Cooperative Service, U.S. Department of Agriculture, while on leave from the Department of Agricultural Economics, University of Missouri-Columbia. He received his agricultural economics education at the University of Minnesota, B.S. in 1962; attended the first Swedish Seminar for Cooperative Development in 1962–63; was Fulbright Graduate Fellow at the Agriculture College of Norway, 1965–66; and completed his M.S. and Ph.D. at the University of Wisconsin-Madison in 1966 and 1968. He is author of* Producer Power *at the Bargaining Table and* Farm Bargaining. *He served as Staff Economist to the Agricultural Marketing Service, USDA, in 1974 and 1975.*

COOPERATIVES are, in practice and theory, an off-farm extension of the farm firm, an integral part of the farming enterprise that allows farm operators to extend themselves vertically to one or more stages in the marketing channel. The premise for cooperation lies primarily in the structural relationship of farm operators, characteristically atomistic in nature (many in number and relatively small in size), compared to those with whom they buy and sell (few in number and relatively large in size). Without ability to organize, farmers are powerless to deal with firms that are increasingly characterized by fewer numbers, larger market shares, more diversification in product lines, and greater vertical integration of operations. The changing market structure of agriculture, a prime motivator in early organizing efforts associated with the emergence of commercial agriculture, remains today the underlying rationale for cooperative efforts by farm operators.

Farmers also organized because services were not available to them in their rural communities or because those services were not available at reasonable costs. A broader social purpose was embraced in early organizing efforts—popularly called the "cooperative movement" —to improve one's individual position, community, and the competitiveness of the capitalistic economic order through self-help organizational activity based on democratic principles. Each of these ingredients is very much a part of the fabric of cooperative organizations today and can be expected to continue in the future.

## STRUCTURAL CHANGES AFFECTING COOPERATIVES

As concentration continues in the industrial organization that comprises our political economy, the food and fiber production sector finds itself affected by and engulfed in some of the same forces that are leading to structural change in nonfarm industry. Vertical coordination, for example, has proceeded to such an extent in some commodity sectors that farmers without a contract or cooperative through which to market simply have no market outlet, especially in years of heavy production. Farmers in California, for example, are often motivated more by simply having a home for their production—through their cooperatives—than by a primary concern with price.

Changing marketing patterns, furthermore, have eroded the viability of traditional pricing mechanisms for raw farm products. Open assembly markets for farmers in some commodities have even ceased to exist. This situation prevails in most processed fruit and vegetable markets and in dairy, poultry, and livestock subsectors in certain parts of the country. Creditors, an important determinant of direction in the economic organization of agriculture, are typically reluctant to extend production credit unless producers have a guaranteed market for their products. The net result of vertical arrangements has been a more fragmented marketplace in which value determination and price discovery are complicated by a variety of direct sales arrangements and formulas.

Like vertical coordination, horizontal growth in the food industry—motivated by economies of size and new technological advances in processing, handling, and transportation—has expanded trade territory and supply requirements of food and fiber firms. In order to meet these large supply demands, farmers have had to organize more broadly, primarily through merger of local cooperatives, acquisition, and internal growth, on a market-wide scale. Organization on a regional basis by dairy farmers to supply the requirements of 500,000 quarts-per-day distribution plants serving a multi-state area typifies this development.

Similarly, noncooperative firms have organized on a conglomerate basis through a merger explosion in the 1950s–1970s. This typically involves firms in several industries and has given them more stabilized earnings potential as well as tremendous strength derived from their diversified character. Earnings from one business endeavor can easily be plowed into expanded growth in another industry. Or assets of an acquired company can be stripped and the company sold in a financially deteriorated state. To compete with diversified agribusiness firms, cooperatives have felt some compulsion to diversify themselves rather than risk the trauma of low earnings in one commodity or supply field due to an off year. However, cooperatives by their nature, as well as by public policy constraints, are limited to engagement in only member-related activities. Diversified growth, to the extent that it has occurred among cooperatives, has therefore been limited to combinations of various product marketing or service functions which were oriented to needs of members.

The gravity of these currents of changing market structure weigh heavily upon farmers, especially in assessing the adequacy of their marketing tools to fend for them. Similarly, it is generally important to the public that an appropriate power balance is maintained between agricultural producers and processor-handlers in a time when increasing contracting and other means of internalized vertical coordination are replacing open markets as a means of establishing prices and other terms of trade. Balanced marketing power is highly important to the preservation of a competitive framework for agricultural transactions, as well as for the retention of a dispersed form of ownership in agricultural production.

Farm operators have met these challenges by developing countervailing power through strongly financed and well-structured cooperatives and bargaining associations that have been able to meet competition on a more nearly equal basis. Strong local associations have been developed that meet farmers' needs along with a system of regional cooperatives that support the local associations. Cooperatives have come of age in the past decade in their capacity to serve farmers' and ranchers' needs for farm supplies, credit, marketing, and related services. Capability to meet these needs was not possible until cooperatives developed into large-scale efficient operations with a high degree of sophistication.

Despite organizational adjustments by producers, the pace of structural change in the nonfarm sector is proceeding at a rate that challenges, and sometimes exceeds, farmers' willingness and financial ability to organize in an effort to countervail it.

## MEMBERSHIP, BUSINESS VOLUME, AND MARKET SHARE TRENDS

Since the close of World War II, cooperatives have made slight gains in their share of marketing and purchasing activity. Aggregate memberships have decreased about 1 million since 1950, along with a diminishing total farm population from which to draw membership. Business volume

TABLE 1

COOPERATIVE MEMBERSHIP, BUSINESS VOLUME, AND MARKET SHARE
STATISTICS FOR SELECT YEARS[1]

| YEAR | AGGREGATE MEMBERSHIPS (MILLION) | AGGREGATE BUSINESS VOLUME NET (BILLION $) | AGGREGATE MARKET SHARE, MKTG. & SUPP. (%) |
|---|---|---|---|
| 1950 | 7.1 | 8.1 | 20.9 |
| 1955 | 7.7 | 9.8 | 23.9 |
| 1960 | 7.2 | 12.4 | 26.0 |
| 1965 | 6.8 | 15.6 | 28.3 |
| 1970 | 6.2 | 20.6 | 26.8 |
| 1975 (est.) | 6.1 | 37.8 | 30.1 |

has increased over 400 percent in the same time period to nearly $38 billion in net volume as shown in table 1. This figure is put in perspective when one considers that the combined net business volume of the 7,800 farmer cooperatives in the U.S.A. in 1975 was not even equal to the $44 billion business volume in 1975 of Exxon, the country's largest industrial corporation.

The aggregate market share of net cooperative business, before adjustments for value added, increased from almost 21 percent in 1950 to 30 percent in 1975. The volume of farm marketings handled by cooperatives experienced the most rapid growth from 23 to 34 percent in this time period, as shown in table 2.

TABLE 2

MARKET SHARES REPRESENTED BY
COOPERATIVES OF TOTAL FARM
MARKETING AND FARM SUPPLY
ACQUISITIONS FOR SELECTED
YEARS (%)

| YEAR | MARKET SHARE (MARKETING) | MARKET SHARE (FARM SUPPLY) |
|---|---|---|
| 1950 | 22.7 | 16.0 |
| 1955 | 26.1 | 17.9 |
| 1960 | 29.1 | 18.3 |
| 1965 | 31.8 | 19.5 |
| 1970 | 30.6 | 18.5 |
| 1975 (est.) | 34.1 | 20.8 |

Farm supply business, in contrast, increased from 16 to 20 percent from 1950 to 1975.

While these aggregate figures suggest progress by cooperatives, individual commodity statistics provide a rather sobering picture. In those subsectors representing the major value of off-farm sales, such as grain, poultry, and livestock, cooperatives have been just holding their own or have experienced decreasing market shares. In contrast, farmers have increased their use of cooperatives in the dairy and specialty crop subsectors over the same time period. The importance of these developments must be evaluated against the backdrop of nonfarm entry into farm production and vertically coordinated arrangements used by food marketing firms that tend to displace farmers and limit their marketing opportunities. In short, there are many farm commodity subsectors and areas of the country in which cooperatives are not well organized and suffer from low market shares and weak market penetration. To the extent that vertical organization continues in agriculture, farm operators will face problems of access to markets and

1. Farmer Cooperative Service, "Statistics of Farmer Cooperatives," Select Research Reports from 1950–1975.

parity of marketing power that demands fuller use of cooperatives as their organizational tools.

Limitations to the expanded use of cooperatives are conditioned by (1) farmers' individualistic and fatalistic notions that preclude effective group action; (2) a prevailing normative school of thought on cooperation that conflicts with more vigorous initiatives; and (3) by an external environment, found in public sentiment and our economic and political institutions, that has been hostile to group action by farmers, particularly in times of shortages and relatively higher food prices.

### INFLUENCE OF SCHOOLS OF THOUGHT ON EXPANDED USE OF COOPERATIVES

The genesis of the cooperative movement has given rise to several distinct schools of thought. Historically, six of these at one time or another, have had a particular impact on the development of cooperatives on the North American continent. To the extent that at least one of these has a current constraining influence upon the extent of cooperative development in the United States, it is worth summarizing the evolution of these distinct schools.

The first school of thought originating in the United States was known as the "Sapiro school" of thought, named after Aaron Sapiro, who, as a bright young California lawyer, was active as an organizer of cooperative marketing organizations in the early 1920s. Sapiro advocated a form of orderly commodity marketing that was at that time unique to organizational efforts within the United States and which had several distinct features. Included among the features of Sapiro's school were association on a commodity basis; long-term legally binding contracts with grower members; a centralized organization structure; pooling of products according to grade; controlling a large enough proportion of the crop to be a dominant market factor; democratic control of cooperatives by members; use of professional experts in management and other technical positions within the cooperative; and limitation of membership to growers.[2]

As such, the Sapiro school advocated a specific organizational structure as well as a plan of action on the part of cooperatives so that they would become a major factor in the agricultural community. Sapiro's organizing capability carried his particular brand of cooperation throughout the United States as well as Canada and left an indelible mark on U.S. agricultural cooperation, particularly on the Pacific coast. The advocacy of Sapiro led to a wave of organizational activity that had as one of its goals a legal monopoly for cooperatives engaged in agricultural marketing.

Sapiro's goal or objective was to organize countervailing monopoly power for farmers through strong commodity cooperatives which maintained long-term supply and production contracts as necessary. Contracts were designed to be a production-marketing coordinating device so that cooperatives could provide a predictable quantity of products for sale. This type of aggressive and top-down organizational philosophy was subsequently challenged by another distinctly American school of cooperative thought advocated by E. G. Nourse.

The school of thought advocated

2. Grace C. Larsen and Henry E. Erdman, "Aaron Sapiro: Genius of Farmer Cooperative Promotion," *Mississippi Valley Historical Review*, September 1962, p. 242–68.

by Nourse became known as the "competitive yardstick school." Cooperatives were viewed, as in the Sapiro school, as being part and parcel of the existing capitalistic system and a legitimate form of business activity. But they were viewed as serving to restrain the capitalistic system and to modify excesses that were associated with it. Stated in other words, cooperatives were viewed as being a yardstick by which cooperators could measure the performance of the capitalistic system, at levels where they felt exploited, and of the conduct of the firms in it. Cooperatives were also viewed as correcting many evils of capitalism and performing a balance wheel or checkpoint function that improved the competitive performance of the economic system itself.[3] Cooperatives were thus viewed as being supplementary to capitalist enterprise, a view held in common with a German school of thought in the late 1800s led by Herman Schulze-Delitzsch.[4]

The competitive yardstick school attributed to cooperatives a broader societal function in the political economy than was ever endorsed or conceived by the Sapiro school. To successfully perform this normative function, it was believed that cooperatives need handle as a goal only about 15 to 30 percent of the particular commodity in question. As is easily discerned, this perspective was substantially different from the goal embraced by the Sapiro school. A

3. E. G. Nourse, "From Dogma to Science in Cooperative Thinking," *Agricultural Cooperation—1946* (Washington, D.C.: American Institute of Cooperation, p. 8).

4. Paul Lambert, *Studies in the Social Philosophy of Cooperation*, Cooperative League of the USA, 1963, p. 96. See, also, G. Fauquet, *The Cooperative Sector* (Manchester: Cooperation Union Ltd., 1951), pp. 11–14.

cooperative's major attribute, according to Nourse and subsequent followers, was enhancing competition and perfecting the capitalistic system compared to a system performing without the cooperative alternative.

A third school of thought that has influenced cooperative development on the North American continent, particularly in Canada, is known as the "cooperative sector" school. In essence, the cooperative sector school developed following the philosophy of Fauquet, a French scholar who conceptualized cooperatives as basically separate and distinct from both capitalism and public enterprise, and thereby affording a "middle way" between them. Four distinct sectors could be distinguished in an economy according to Fauquet: (1) the public sector; (2) the capitalist sector; (3) the private sector proper that includes noncapitalist units and activities of households, farms, and crafts; and (4) the cooperative sector.[5] The difference in the cooperative sector was in the fact that ownership, control, and use of the particular enterprise involves the same group of people, namely owner-users, as members of the cooperative. The cooperative sector of the economy, being separate, required a distinct set of laws and supporting institutions.

A fourth school is known as the "cooperative systems" school. As identified by Torgerson in 1967, this school views "cooperative systems" as being national organizations in the geographic sense, such as cooperatives, professional associations, and political parties that are in a specific relationship by reason of cooperation of people for at least one

5. Ibid, p. 106.

definite end.[6] Since farmers have supported both cooperatives and professional interest organizations (general farm and single commodity types) as instruments for goal attainment, it is deemed necessary to examine the functional unity of structural forms in the study of decision making and representation by farm operators.

This school views analysis of the total bundle of organized farm activity as essential to understanding how farmers divide organizational tasks structurally and functionally in pursuing their improved farm income goals. The activities of these organizations are viewed as being mutually supportive and complementary with any conflicts ultimately resulting from the farmer's multidimensional role as manager, laborer, investor, and landowner. This school, which finds support in earlier theoretical works by Robert Liefman[7] and Ivan Emelianoff,[8] establishes coordinated cooperative systems as necessary for accomplishing the division of labor and specialization between cooperatives and professional associations needed to accomplish specific functional tasks to achieve optimum marketing strength for farmers.

The fifth school of thought—also the most radical because of its departure from basic cooperative fundamentals—might be appropriately called the "management manipulation" school. In essence, this school, originated from the Harvard Agribusiness Management complex, advocates the use of cooperative-corporate combinations.[9] Cooperatives are viewed as a means of enhancing management strategy of private firms that desire an assured source of continuous supplies of farm products and a means of avoiding major capital expenditures. A linkage is made between a group of farmers organized through a cooperative and the corporate firm—often called a joint venture. In many instances, this arrangement also involves certain types of management contracts between the initiating corporate firm and the farmer-owned processing facility. In other situations, a joint processing operation may be undertaken by the cooperative, which serves an assembly function, and the corporation. While strongly advocated in recent times on the North American continent and abroad, this particular school of thought originates more as a management device for the benefit of the corporate sector than for the benefit of farmer-members as users of cooperatives.

A sixth school, the "cooperative commonwealth" school of thought, originated outside the United States but has strongly influenced cooperative development in this country and throughout the world. The cooperative commonwealth arrangement, which is found in many European countries, places no limitation on the possibilities that cooperatives have of expanding into many fields of business activity. Ultimately, cooperatives can even achieve dominance in any particular commodity or service activity in a country and would thereby improve and help to develop a fuller cooperative and

6. Randall E. Torgerson, "The Cooperative Systems Approach to Improving Farm Incomes" (Ph.D. diss., University of Wisconsin, 1967).

7. D. Robert Liefman, *Cartels, Concerns and Trusts* (London: Methuen and Co. Ltd., 1932).

8. Ivan V. Emelianoff, *Economic Theory of Cooperation* (Ann Arbor, Mich.: Edwards Brothers, Inc., 1942).

9. Ray A. Goldberg, "Profitable Partnerships: Industry and Farmer Co-ops," *Harvard Business Review*, March 1972, pp. 108–21.

economic social order. In many respects, the Rochdale weavers, widely known for packaging the "principles of cooperation," had this as one of their goals and objectives when they originated their cooperative activities in 1844 in England. This school is found today among the highly developed and successful consumer cooperatives in England and the farmer cooperatives in the Scandinavian countries.

The commonwealth school in most respects is grounded in pragmatism. An economy is envisioned in which producers and consumers undertake joint activity to enable them to succeed as viable units. If this involves such a high degree of organization that cooperatives become the dominant economic institution, then so be it. Profit-seeking enterprises continue to exist but maintain a secondary role, just the opposite of what is found on the North American continent today. Since the cooperative is simply an organizational tool in behalf of owner-users, it is viewed as a higher order economic institution because it embraces equitable treatment of members economically and higher social ideals through democratic processes than does the conventional profit-seeking firm. Implicit in this school is the notion of strong control and leadership from members originating at the local level and succeeding, through federation, to regional, national, and even international levels of organization.

Of the schools of thought identified, the first two have had the initial as well as the most significant impact to date upon cooperative development in the United States. An obvious conflict exists between the Sapiro and the competitive yardstick schools concerning the cooperative's role and just how dynamic

these organizations should be in fulfilling their member-oriented and societal objectives. The Sapiro school is directed primarily toward internalized benefits and advocates a fuller organizational development of marketing power in behalf of members, approaching that advocated by the commonwealth school. Its strongest following is found among the fruit and vegetable and other specialty crop cooperatives and bargaining associations on the Pacific coast and more recently among the direct membership regional dairy cooperatives that have emerged in the Midwest and South since the late 1960s.

The competitive yardstick school, in contrast, advocates pro-competitive external benefits derived from cooperative activity as well as internal market correcting benefits to members. The chief difference is that cooperatives accomplish their role in the yardstick school with only a limited aggregative market share and seek nothing more; that is, they play a secondary role to the profit-seeking firms that dominate the capitalistic system. In fact, E. G. Nourse argued that cooperative objectives were not to supersede other forms of business, but were to see that they (other business forms) were kept truly competitive.[10]

Of the two schools of thought, the competitive yardstick school has had the most prevailing acceptance and influence, particularly in the Midwest where most of the cooperatives are found and where the concept originated. Similarly, it is the school that has met with the widest support from public policy makers. Interestingly, it is the precise level that cooperatives in the aggregate have

10. Joseph G. Knapp, *Great American Cooperators* (Washington, D.C.: American Institute of Cooperation, 1967), pp. 372–78.

occupied in all of the post World War II era. Whether this rather limited scope of cooperative activity, as envisioned by early thinkers of the competitive yardstick school, is adequate in today's structural environment represents a major question.

Clearly there are new dimensions to the environment in which farm operators and their cooperatives must operate today. A power struggle is underway for the control of agriculture. A realization is developing in the farming community that a mere 15 to 30 percent of the farm credit, purchasing, and farm marketing activity offers no assurances that farm operators have the organizational tools to adequately represent their best economic interests and to keep them in business in the future. Greater organizational efforts are being called for to increase market shares, secure market outlets through obtaining a consumer's franchise for cooperative branded products, obtain fair prices, and assure access to reliable sources of farm inputs at reasonable prices.

If a new school of cooperative thought is emerging to replace the competitive yardstick school, it is in the formative stages at this time. In all likelihood, it will embrace some of the positive features of the yardstick school insofar as stimulus to competition is concerned, but will also embrace more of the cooperative systems, commonwealth, and Sapiro schools in terms of substance and goals. The extent of this development will be largely conditioned by the external environment.

## THE CHANGING EXTERNAL ENVIRONMENT TOWARD COOPERATIVES

The external environment that establishes the climate for group action by farm operators has undergone an element of change in the mid-1970s. The basis for this change can be found in the basic supply and demand balance for food and fiber items, the rise of populism, and associated concern with size of institutions, financial constraints on younger farmers entering farming, and the prevailing enforcement of antitrust laws and other governmental regulations relating to group action by farmers.

When availability of foods at cheap prices was affected by worldwide shortages beginning in 1972 and food prices vacillated widely in tune with our current market-oriented policy, the climate toward cooperatives and other forms of group action by farmers appears to have changed. Cooperatives, much to the surprise of their members, came under a barrage of attacks, each suggesting that they were the sources of higher food prices, that is the food price villains. The attitude toward group action in agriculture therefore appears to be conditioned in part by the relative supply and demand balance of food and fiber items. So long as food was in abundance and farmers suffered from the traditional depressed markets, public sentiment appears to have been strongly supportive of their efforts to organize for fairer prices. In the food-short environment, however, it appears that public sentiment toward policies and action encouraging group action turned hostile.

Many farm operators questioned how farmer cooperatives, as the instrument of farmers' marketing efforts, could have become villains simply by virtue of the turnaround in traditional supply and demand relationships. The thought to producer patrons was astonishing—as well as revolting. What were cooperatives doing differently that could have brought on such a shower of wrath? If cooperatives played the role envisioned in the competitive yardstick school of thought, and were in fact competition enhancing instruments in the marketplace, why would the political environment turn so hostile toward them with regard to farmers' rights to organize and market collectively through their organizations?

In attempting to answer these questions, farm leaders have been forced to rethink many of the basics of organization, their legislative underpinnings, and the type of activity and external climate which is going to be necessary to keep farmers in business and to keep farmer cooperatives viable as effective instruments in behalf of members. Of paramount importance is the realization that the nature of the cooperative has not changed significantly from the past. Production decisions continue to be made individually by farm operators in response to market signals. Cooperatives are generally obliged to accept all of the products that farmers deliver to them. Since farm production is not as yet an industrialized production process in which production control decisions are centralized, cooperatives are clearly operating in a market-oriented fashion in which the public interest is protected by the self-regulating market mechanism. Cooperative leaders are aware of the need to more effectively communicate their public interest and competition-enhancing role, irrespective of size of market share, to the public at large.

One of the characteristic features of the political economy in the mid-1970s has been the rise of populist sentiments on the part of many people. This is manifested in the form of mistrust of large-scale institutions like corporations, labor unions, and government. People express a desire for more direct access to government and the economic activity that envelopes their lives. It is also manifest in talks by many political candidates who, in this Bicentennial and presidential election year, have picked up the cry for a return of power to the citizenry and for more control over big business, whose growing presence ostensibly stifles competition.

Cooperatives appear to have been cast into the lot with other big businesses. Since several cooperatives appear in "Fortune's 500" list of largest industrial businesses in America and since a few cooperatives in this category have annual sales exceeding $1 billion, cooperatives appear to be viewed as "just another business" and are not distinguishable in the public's mind's eye. A question that is frequently asked is whether cooperatives, like other large-scale voluntary organizations, are responsive to members' needs as they grow in size. Are they subject to member control and influence? Or are cooperatives tending to fall into the trappings of other large-scale voluntary groups in which only a small minority are active participants and therefore more influence in decision making is shifted to the sophisticated managers who have been hired to operate these organizations on a day-to-day basis? The answer is that a cooperative business, even when big, is fundamentally different from big business in two respects: (1) it is oriented to the needs of users, not investors; and (2) it has two goals in view. One is an economic goal of improving the well-being of members and the other the social goal which is aimed at elevating the position of members upward through a bootstrap organizational process based on self-help principles and democratic organizational processes. Clearly this is a problem which is not going to go away. Cooperative leaders must continually work to structure their organizations for effective representation and control by owner-users.

Another influence from the external environment concerns the availability of credit for expanded growth of cooperatives. One of the biggest challenges cooperatives continually face is keeping ownership in the hands of current users. Farmers typically must balance financing of their off-farm businesses —their cooperatives—with on-farm capital and equipment investments. During inflationary times, these investment decisions become critical because plant replacement costs are very high. Furthermore, young people entering into farming are faced with high land values and frequently have a low equity base. Traditional lenders are hesitant to grant long-term loans without government guarantees. At the same time, many cooperative financial experts advance management strategy for building permanent capital in cooperatives. This gives management more flexibility to do what it wants to do—a potential threat to members if management, uncontrolled, adopts the philosophy that control follows money, not member-users. New institutional reform, such as permanent debt financing or long-term lease of farms, will likely help alleviate these problems. In the meantime, capital availability will serve as a major constraint on expanded cooperative marketing efforts.

The other major area in which

concern has been expressed and which continues to condition the environment in which cooperatives operate is the attitude toward enforcement of the nation's antitrust laws. Careful scrutiny of regulatory activity in all industries including the food industry has followed the advent of higher food prices. This has focused much attention on cooperatives' leeway under the antitrust laws and on federal marketing orders, which embrace the Sapiro concept of "orderly commodity marketing" and have helped to operationalize it. It also manifests itself in concerns by public interest and consumer groups about whether the marketing institutions and government programs established in times of food surpluses and depressed farm incomes are now appropriate in times of food shortages, such as those experienced in recent years. Agencies, such as the Department of Justice and the Federal Trade Commission, which have responsibility for enforcement of antitrust laws have traditionally viewed cooperatives with a jaundiced eye. Consumer concern over higher food prices led to stricter enforcement and to advocacy of changes in basic enabling legislation for cooperatives, such as the Capper-Volstead Act of 1922.

Areas of concern expressed by the regulatory agencies are focused on such things as corporate membership in cooperatives, market shares held by farmers through their cooperatives, and the ability of cooperatives under the law to make use of federations and agencies-in-common to establish prices and to effect other marketing arrangements over broad regional areas. Cooperatives growth opportunity in the future will be largely evaluated in terms of cooperative performance. A lesson learned from the recent scrutiny is that cooperatives cannot succeed organizationally in behalf of members by simply emulating a corporate model. Instead, cooperatives need to maximize their uniqueness and their distinctive owner-user features as an alternative form of business organization. New legislation to enable farmers to develop effective pricing mechanisms and allow greater latitude for organizational activities at higher levels will be necessary to fully develop this alternative.

In summary, cooperatives have an underlying strength in serving our national interest by providing an avenue for farmers to participate in an increasingly concentrated business economy. By their very nature, cooperatives interject a degree of market competition that pushes the market nearer to the competitive norm. As is true with experiences in development of the cooperative movement to date, a basic underlying requirement is the role for education concerning cooperative techniques, organization structure, practices, and principles to the various publics including cooperative members, employees, the public at large, Congress, and other branches of government. In order to survive and to make their continuing contribution, cooperatives need to emphasize their uniqueness and stick to their organizational basics. In the final analysis, however, cooperatives' contributions will be measured by the economic survival and well-being of members.

Annals, AAPSS, **429**, Jan. 1977

# The Rural Church and Rural Religion: Analysis of Data from Children and Youth

By Hart M. Nelsen and Raymond H. Potvin

ABSTRACT: The heyday of studies of the rural church was the 1920s–1940s. Even then researchers noted that structural rather than ecological characteristics were especially important in understanding it. A more recent focus has been on rural-urban differences in religiosity. Research done in the 1960s and 1970s indicated differences only on the ideological (belief) dimension. Data from two 1975 studies—one involving children in Minnesota and the other adolescents in a national sample—are reported, showing continuing rural-urban-metropolitan differences in religious belief. There are higher rates of fundamentalism for Protestants in the first two residential categories. For the first sample, the relationship between SES and fundamentalism virtually disappears in the rural area. The importance of residential (and church) propinquity of social classes is suggested as an important intervening variable, and this brings the focus full circle in terms of ecological versus structural and organizational characteristics. Finally, the future of the rural (small) church is discussed. Negative effects of inflation and the overall decline in national church membership and participation and the positive effect of church decentralization as they impinge upon the rural church are discussed.

---

Hart M. Nelsen is Professor and Chair of Sociology and member of the Boys Town Center for the Study of Youth Development of the Catholic University of America, Washington, D.C. He is coauthor of Black Church in the Sixties and coeditor of The Black Church in America.

Raymond H. Potvin is Professor of Sociology and member of the Boys Town Center. He is the coauthor of College Women and Fertility Values, Seminarians of the Sixties, and Vocational Challenge and Seminary Response.

PARALLEL with the changing perspective from religious sociology to the sociology of religion has been the decline of locality-based, descriptive studies and the emergence of broader, theoretical interests in the overall relationship between religion and society. The older orientation had more to say about the rural church, while the newer approach addresses more general questions about religion, whether urban or rural. However, because of an apparent decline in religious practice, renewed interest in religious organizations, at both the local and national levels, as well as an increase in denomination-based research may well be forthcoming. It appears that the churches are now ripe for organizational analysis; if so, some of that interest will surely center on the rural religious institution.

This article will review the literature on the rural church and on the religious orientations of rural residents. We will then present current data on differences between religious orientation of rural and urban children and adolescents, focusing on the relative importance of residence and class membership in explaining these differences. In a concluding section, we will speculate on the future of the rural church as well as on the impact of interclass contact within residential areas and local religious organizations upon religious orientation. We suggest a considerable gain in insight when ecological and structural perspectives are linked in the study of rural religion.

## THE RURAL CHURCH

The period of the 1920s through the 1940s was replete with studies of rural and urban churches. Research conducted under the auspices of the Institute of Social and Religious Research, funded with Rockefeller money during 1920–1934, contributed to this heyday of parish sociology. A perspective held by some, including H. Paul Douglass,[1] was that "the city church is an evolved rural church." Benson Y. Landis commented that "there is some evidence that organized religion is of more importance in the rural than in the urban community."[2] In a general, sociological description of religion in America some four decades ago, C. Luther Fry commented on the membership differences by residence:

It is widely believed that country people belong to church in relatively greater numbers than city people. As a matter of fact the proportion of people who belong to church is higher in cities than in rural areas. This . . . seems to reflect differences in opportunity arising from the fact that many sparsely settled areas have few churches.[3]

The close relationship between population size and religious mem-

1. Harlan Paul Douglass, 1000 City Churches (New York: George H. Doran, 1926), p. 83. For an introduction to the early works, see Frederick A. Shippey, "The Variety of City Churches," Review of Religious Research, vol. 2 (Summer 1960), pp. 8–19. See, also, C. Joseph Nuesse and Thomas J. Harte, eds., The Sociology of the Parish (Milwaukee: Bruce Publishing Co., 1951).

2. Benson Y. Landis, "The Church and Religious Activity," American Journal of Sociology, vol. 40 (May 1935), pp. 780–87.

3. C. Luther Fry, with the assistance of Mary Frost Jessup, "Changes in Religious Organizations," President's Research Committee on Social Trends, Recent Social Trends in the United States (New York: McGraw-Hill, 1933), pp. 1021–22. For a comparable, recent overview, see N. J. Demerath III, "Trends and Anti-Trends in Religious Change," in Eleanor Bernert Sheldon and Wilbert E. Moore, eds., Indicators of Social Change (New York: Russell Sage Foundation, 1968), pp. 349–445.

bership and attendance was documented by Edmund DeS. Brunner.[4] These studies seemed to document that while there were too few churches for a given geographical area, there were too many for the size of population supporting them.[5] With population shift, many of these small churches would continue to close or curtail their programs. As Charles P. Loomis and J. Allan Beegle noted, "as the trade-center churches grow at the expense of those in the rural neighborhoods, the wealthier farmers tend to withdraw to the town churches, leaving other farmers without adequate church facilities."[6]

In his bibliography on the church in rural areas, W. Seward Salisbury[7] observed that the most extensive study of the rural church was that directed by Lawrence Hepple.[8] Luckily, that study of the church in rural Missouri was replicated in 1967, some 15 years later. It was noted that while there was a slight net loss in the number of congregations in the area surveyed at the two points in time, the loss was more among church- than sect-type groups. Furthermore, Edward Hassinger and John Holik, who redid the

study, noted that the loss was not due to merger but that "in the vast majority of the cases, it is clear that the demise of a church resulted from failure to maintain a membership sufficient to provide a minimal program—that is, to function as an organized group."[9] Churches were more likely to close in the open country and villages with less than 200 population.[10]

From his study of the rural Missouri churches, Hepple had concluded that "it appears that it would be more advantageous to study churches in terms of size . . . than in terms of location."[11] This comment returns us to the work of the pioneers in denominational research, especially the comment by Douglass and Brunner that

the real difference is not between the church in the small city and in the large, but between churches of different sizes; for larger churches everywhere strongly tend to have more complicated organization, to employ staffs of paid workers instead of the single pastor, and to undertake more varied programs.[12]

9. Edward W. Hassinger and John S. Holik, "Changes in the Number of Rural Churches in Missouri, 1952–1967," *Rural Sociology*, vol. 35 (September 1970), p. 359.

10. Edward W. Hassinger, J. Kenneth Benson, and John S. Holik, "Changes in Program and Suborganization of Rural Churches in Missouri in a Fifteen-Year Period," *Rural Sociology*, vol. 37 (September 1972), pp. 428–35. Another outstanding restudy was that undertaken in Southern Appalachia by Earl D. C. Brewer. See his "Religion and the Churches," pp. 201–18 in Thomas R. Ford, ed., *The Southern Appalachian Region: A Survey* (Lexington: University of Kentucky Press, 1962). The earlier Southern Appalachian study was by Elizabeth R. Hooker, *Religion in the Highlands* (New York: Home Missions Council, 1933).

11. Lawrence M. Hepple, *The Church in Rural Missouri: Part V, Rural-Urban Churches Compared*, Research Bulletin 633E (Columbia: Missouri Agriculture Experiment Station, July 1959), p. 296.

12. Harlan Paul Douglass and Edmund DeS. Brunner, *The Protestant Church as a*

4. Edmund DeS. Brunner, "Sociological Significance of Recent Rural Religious Surveys," *American Journal of Sociology*, vol. 29 (November 1923), pp. 325–37.

5. Robert L. Skrabanek, "The Rural Church: Characteristics and Problems," in Alvin L. Bertrand, ed., *Rural Sociology* (New York: McGraw-Hill, 1958), p. 244.

6. Charles P. Loomis and J. Allan Beegle, *Rural Social Systems* (Englewood Cliffs, N.J.: Prentice-Hall, Inc., 1950), p. 454.

7. W. Seward Salisbury, *Religion in American Culture* (Homewood, Ill.: The Dorsey Press, 1964), pp. 511–12. In chapter 16, "Religion in Representative Subcultures," Salisbury addresses the rural church (see pp. 430–39).

8. Lawrence M. Hepple et al., *The Church in Rural Missouri*, Research Bulletins 633A-G (Columbia: Missouri Agriculture Experiment Station, September 1957–February 1961).

After all their work based on a model of the city church as "the rural church evolved," that comment seemingly guts the rural-urban perspective.[13] It appeared that an organizational rather than ecological perspective would have more payoff. Indeed, the old "Town and Country" units within the denominations were changed to focus instead on the problems of the small church.[14]

## RURAL RELIGION

This conclusion does not negate the possibility that rural-urban dif-

ferences in religious orientation do, indeed, exist. While Hart Nelsen and Stuart Storey observed that the literature of the 1950s and 1960s claimed that rural-urban attitudinal differences were greatly diminished, if not eliminated, because of increasing rural-urban contact, they presented evidence to document continued differences in at least one attitudinal area and suggested the need for continued research.[15] Additional evidence for (even an increase of) differences was presented by Fern Willits, Robert Bealer, and Donald Crider.[16]

Prior to this work, Norval Glenn and Jon Alston subjected poll data to secondary analysis. They found that ruralites were more traditional and fundamentalist in religious beliefs and more likely to attend religious services and to listen to or watch services on the radio or television. However, they were lowest in church membership and the authors commented that "we doubt that church membership is a good index of religious interest or devoutness."[17]

From secondary analysis of four sets of Gallup data gathered between 1954 and 1968, Hart Nelsen, Raytha Yokley, and Thomas Madron ex-

*Social Institution* (New York: Harper & Row, Publishers, 1935), p. 87. For a comparable, more recent study, see David O. Moberg, *The Church as a Social Institution* (Englewood Cliffs, N.J.: Prentice-Hall, Inc., 1962).

13. For an analysis assessing the independent effects of church size and residential location, see Hart M. Nelsen and Robert F. Everett, "Impact of Church Size on Clergy Role and Career," *Review of Religious Research*, vol. 17 (Fall 1976), pp. 62–73. In general, clergy serving small congregations were more likely to consider career changes than those serving larger ones. Ministers serving the smaller rural congregations seem more satisfied with their ministries than their counterparts elsewhere. Church size was a more important variable than church location.

14. A United Presbyterian committee at the synod level noted that "small churches are facing the issues of survival at the present time, in part because of financial burdens, in part because of the unavailability of pastoral leadership, in part because of a sense of hopelessness, in part because other avenues of ministry have yet to be explored and their full implications realized." This committee discussed the "viable church" not by location but in terms of size; and they noted that although 350 is sometimes used, they adopted 250 members or less as the definition of the small church. See: Task Force on the Small Church, Synod of Lakes and Prairies, United Presbyterian Church, U.S.A., "The Small Church" (Bloomington, Minn.: Office of Communication, Synod of Lakes and Prairies, UPCUSA, 1975), pp. 9, 1. For working papers used at a symposium on the small church, see Jackson W. Carroll,

ed., *The Small Congregation: A Search for New Possibilities* (Hartford, Conn.: Hartford Seminary Foundation, 1976).

15. Hart M. Nelsen and Stuart E. Storey, "Personality Adjustment of Rural and Urban Youth: The Formation of a Rural Disadvantaged Subculture," *Rural Sociology*, vol. 34 (March 1969), pp. 43–55.

16. Fern K. Willits, Robert C. Bealer, and Donald M. Crider, "Level of Attitudes in Mass Society: Rurality and Traditional Morality in America," *Rural Sociology*, vol. 38 (Spring 1973), pp. 36–45.

17. Norval D. Glenn and Jon P. Alston, "Rural-Urban Differences in Reported Attitudes and Behavior," *The Southwestern Social Science Quarterly*, vol. 47 (March 1967), pp. 381–400.

amined residential differences on four dimensions of religiosity — ideological, intellectual, experiential, and ritualistic.[18] The authors divided the last dimension into two subdimensions — prayer and attendance. Significant differences were found on the ideological dimension, with ruralites being more conservative than urban dwellers. The data were presented controlling separately for sex, education, age, region, and religious identification (Protestant-Catholic). The writers noted that "residential differences were greater for less-educated, older, Southern, and Protestant respondents, suggesting that residential differences may, indeed, be diminishing over the course of time." It was also concluded that one could not claim that the rural dwellers were more religious; it could be said, however, that they were more conservative in ideology.[19]

Two final studies need review. Claude Fischer analyzed 1957 Gallup and 1968 SRC poll data on religion, controlling "as many individual-level and confounding attributes as were available, meaningful, and practical in order to isolate a contextual effect of community." The relationship between residence and the Gallup religiosity scale (heavily centered on the ideological dimension) persisted, while there was little relationship between resi-

dence and church attendance, consistent with the finding by Nelsen et al. One exception was that metropolitan suburbanites with children were especially likely to be church attenders. Fischer concluded that "though the associations are, as we expected, quite small, there is some indication that urbanism has an independent effect on traditionalism as reflected in religiosity. . . ."[20]

From an analysis of data from a sample of North Carolina Episcopalians, W. Clark Roof conceptualized localism-cosmopolitanism as explaining the effect of size of city on religious orientation, or "the local-cosmopolitan distinction aids in interpreting the psychological process by which urban experiences shape religious commitments." On the relationship between community size and orthodoxy, he found, however, that the direct effects were stronger than the indirect effects. Overall, "local community attachments undergird both socio-religious group participation and personal beliefs and practices."[21]

## ANALYSIS OF NEW DATA

Not only are many of the data used for the studies we have reviewed somewhat out-of-date, but they are also from adults, some of whom received their socialization as children

18. On dimensions of religiosity, see Charles Y. Glock and Rodney Stark, *Religion and Society in Tension* (Chicago: Rand McNally, 1965), pp. 18–38; but see, also, Richard R. Clayton and James W. Gladden, "The Five Dimensions of Religiosity: Toward Demythologizing a Sacred Artifact," *Journal for the Scientific Study of Religion*, vol. 13 (June 1974), pp. 135–43.

19. Hart M. Nelsen, Raytha L. Yokley, and Thomas W. Madron, "Rural-Urban Differences in Religiosity," *Rural Sociology*, vol. 36 (September 1971), pp. 389–96.

20. Claude S. Fischer, "The Effect of Urban Life on Traditional Values," *Social Forces*, vol. 53 (March 1975), pp. 420–32. See, also, Hugh P. Whitt and Hart M. Nelsen, "Residence, Moral Traditionalism, and Tolerance of Atheists," *Social Forces*, vol. 54 (December 1975), pp. 328–40.

21. Wade Clark Roof, "Traditional Religion in Contemporary Society: A Theory of Local-Cosmopolitan Plausibility," *American Sociological Review*, vol. 41 (April 1976), pp. 195–208; see, also, his "The Local-Cosmopolitan Orientation and Traditional Religious Commitment," *Sociological Analysis*, vol. 33 (Spring 1972), pp. 1–15.

in rural areas but later migrated to the urban area. If we speculate that the more personal elements of religious orientation, such as religious belief and experiential religion including prayer, might be less likely to change upon migration, the expectation of residential differences on the ideological dimension of religiosity is considerably reduced, since the presence of urban dwellers with rural backgrounds would mute these differences. On the other hand, migration patterns have changed, religious beliefs supposedly are on the wane, and so forth. However, such speculation does lead to the importance of studying rural and urban children and adolescents or of controlling for residential background in using adult data. In this article we opt for the former.

The religious beliefs and practices of rural people are directly linked with life as they experience it.[22] Consequently, religion can be seen as an expression of worldview. Earlier, in describing an especially rural subculture, we noted that fundamentalistic, episodic religion provides Southern Appalachians

with a general model they have of life and the world as experienced.[23] The concept of a wrathful and punishing God is related to sectarianism.[24] Such a belief and orientation stem from social conditions related to a simplistic and fatalistic worldview of life. Of course, we are describing very isolated and not simply rural locations and subcultures when we write in this vein.[25]

Nonetheless, we would expect to find traces of fundamentalism in the

22. Roof's orientation—with a "conception of traditional religion essentially as a subculture rather than as the normative basis of modern society"—is central here. We might wish that he had a better measure than that of local-cosmopolitan. See Roof, "Traditional Religion in Contemporary Society," p. 206. Nelsen attempted to get at much the same concept which he called "religion as world view"; but he utilized class, residence, and reading level. See Hart M. Nelsen, "Sectarianism, World View, and Anomie," Social Forces, vol. 51 (December 1972), pp. 226–33. For an acculturation model of religious change for black Americans as they moved from participation in the rural church to residence in the metropolitan environment, see Hart M. Nelsen and Anne K. Nelsen, Black Church in the Sixties (Lexington: University Press of Kentucky, 1975), pp. 1, 58–81.

23. Hart M. Nelsen and Raymond H. Potvin, "Appalachian Religion Transplanted," Paper given at the Conference on Appalachians in Urban Areas, Columbus, Ohio, the Academy for Contemporary Problems, March 28, 1974. On religion and worldview, see Clifford Geertz, "Religion: Anthropological Study," in David L. Sills, ed., International Encyclopedia of the Social Sciences, vol. 13 (New York: Macmillan and Company, 1968), pp. 398–406; and Robert Bellah, "The Sociology of Religion," in International Encyclopedia of the Social Sciences, vol. 13, pp. 406–14.

24. See Brewer, "Religion and the Churches"; Hart M. Nelsen, Thomas W. Madron, and Karen Stewart, "Image of God and Religious Ideology and Involvement: A Partial Test of Hill's Southern Culture-Religion Thesis," Review of Religious Research, vol. 15 (Fall 1973), pp. 37–44; Charles Hudson, "The Structure of a Fundamentalist Christian Belief System," pp. 122–42, in Samuel S. Hill, Jr., et al., eds., Religion and the Solid South (Nashville, Tenn.: Abingdon Press, 1972).

25. It is in these "more rural" areas where the churches must accommodate to familism and the emotional orientations of the residents. Consequently, these churches tend to be small, kinship-oriented, and fundamentalistic. Revivalism is central, and there is considerable backsliding. It is in this setting where religious membership is probably less frequent, in comparison to the less rural areas and to the city. Organized church programs play a less important role in the Southern Appalachians and similar areas. See Hart M. Nelsen, "Attitudes toward Religious Education in Appalachia," Religious Education, vol. 65 (January–February 1970), pp. 50–5. See, also, Hassinger, Benson, and Holik, "Changes in Program and Suborganization of Rural Churches in Missouri

rural area. The findings already cited in this article (that rural dwellers are more likely than urbanites to subscribe to conservative religious ideology) support this. To this end, we analyzed two sets of data collected from children and youth. Studying these age groups means that a significant part of the possible rural to urban migration effect previously discussed is avoided. Presumably, we will measure more closely possible subcultural, that is, residential differences in religiosity.

The first set of data, collected by Hart Nelsen, is from school children residing in the "Valley of the Jolly Green Giant," from the area around LeSueur to Minneapolis, Minnesota. Schools were selected in order that both working- and middle-class children would be represented in rural, urban, and metropolitan categories. In our tables, as well as in the study, rural meant under 2,500 population, urban 2,500 through 49,999, and metropolitan 50,000 and larger (including Standard Metropolitan Statistical Area—SMSA). For this set of data, residence is determined by location of the school. Students enrolled in grades four through eight (about ages 10 through 14) attending public and Catholic parochial schools completed in the classroom an extended questionnaire taking between one-half and one hour. A total of 3,085 children cooperated; but of these, 85 did not

respond to one-third or more of the questionnaire, generally because they did not complete it. These 85 were deleted, leaving a sample of 3,000. The data were collected in 1975. In our analysis, we use only the public school data.

The second set of data, collected by Raymond Potvin, is from a national probability sample of youth —young men and women 13 to 18 years of age living in households in the continental United States in April 1975. The sample was selected and questionnaires administered by the Gallup Organization for the Boys Town Center at Catholic University. The response rate was 70.3 percent, a fairly high rate for studies of this kind and with this target population. The data was gathered by means of a self-administered questionnaire in the home, with the interviewer present to guarantee the respondent privacy and confidentiality. The number of respondents totaled 1,121. For these youth, residence is determined by their own place of residence.

Our focus is on religious ideology, particularly fundamentalism. In line with previous findings, our expectation is that children and youth from the rural areas will be more conservative in religious ideology. However, some of this relationship may be due to social class. Therefore, we will examine residential differences in ideology holding constant social class.

In assessing residential propinquity between high and low status persons by race, Brigitte Erbe has written that "differences in the socioeconomic composition of the immediate neighborhood in which blacks and whites of the same socioeconomic status live may account for some of these [racial] differences [even though class is

in a Fifteen-Year Period"; William G. Mather, Jr., *The Rural Churches of Allegany County*, Bulletin No. 587 (Ithaca, N.Y.: Cornell University Agricultural Experiment Station, March 1934); Louis Bultena, "Rural Churches and Community Integration," *Rural Sociology*, vol. 9 (September 1944), pp. 257–64; and John A. Hostetler and William G. Mather, "Participation in the Rural Church," Paper No. 1762 (State College: Pennsylvania State College School of Agriculture and Agricultural Experiment Station, October 1952).

held constant]."[26] The same might be said for residence. Even though social class is controlled, residential differences might remain because in some localities and churches middle-class ruralites might well have a greater chance to interact with working-class individuals, thus eliminating the class differences and increasing the residence differentials in some contexts. For example, since the smaller, rural Protestant churches are more class-inclusive than their counterparts in the urban areas,[27] one might expect class differences to be reduced because of middle-class interactions with lower classes in these areas. Also, one might expect the residence differential to be greater among the middle classes because of this middle-class interaction with lower classes in the rural and small town churches. On the other hand, Catholic parishes are territorial (with the exception of some ethnic-constituted parishes) in both rural and city areas and thus are generally more class-inclusive than Protestant churches. Therefore, one might not expect the same effect (lack of class interaction in the city); and residential differences, if any, should be slight.

## THE FINDINGS

For measuring fundamentalism on the part of the children, we utilized one item from Nelsen's measure of sectarian religious ideology: "Do you believe that God sends bad luck and sickness on people as punishment when they do wrong?"[28]

Residential differences on this item are found in table 1. There was a low negative relationship on the part of Protestant children and a negligible negative relationship for Catholic children. Among Protestants, the value of the partial gamma (controlling socioeconomic status—SES) was somewhat lower than the value of the zero-order gamma ($-.17$ compared to $-.20$). Parenthetically, the zero-order gamma for Protestants for the relationship between SES and fundamentalism was $-.23$ ($P < .001$); children whose fathers held white-collar jobs were less likely to believe that God sends bad luck and sickness on people as punishment when they do wrong.

For the national sample of adolescents, a fundamentalism scale was devised,[29] consisting of four Likert-

---

that God sends misfortune and illness on people as punishment for sins?"; see Nelsen, "Sectarianism, World View, and Anomie," p. 229. The analysis reported in this article uses collapsed responses, counting the "I don't know" response together with belief that God does send misfortune and illness. Two other analyses were completed: leaving the response out (which gives two categories—disbelief and belief) and making it a middle category. All three methods gave essentially the same results. "No responses," however, were deleted from the analyses utilizing the children data (the nonresponse rate here was low).

29. Using a principal component factor analysis and a varimax orthogonal rotation, the responses to 13 religious questions were reduced to four factors: (1) personal-experiential religion, emphasizing, for example, closeness of God, prayer, and the importance of religion; (2) assent to authority, or believing one's faith should be accepted without question; (3) religious practice, focusing on formal religious participation; and (4) fundamentalism.

The four fundamentalism items given in the text had loadings ranging from .51 through .84 on this fourth factor. Parenthetically, let us note that of the three variables other than fundamentalism, both the personal-experiential and the religious practice factors

---

26. Brigitte Mach Erbe, "Race and Socioeconomic Segregation," *American Sociological Review*, vol. 40 (December 1975), pp. 801–12.

27. For example, see Mather, *The Rural Churches of Allegany County*, p. 26.

28. The item was slightly reworded from the original, which read: "Do you believe

TABLE 1

PERCENT FUNDAMENTALISTIC BY RESIDENCE (ZERO-ORDER AND PARTIAL RELATIONSHIPS)

| SAMPLE AND DENOMINATION | PERCENT FUNDAMENTALISTIC BY AREA OF RESIDENCE | | | GAMMA | |
|---|---|---|---|---|---|
| | RURAL | URBAN | METROPOLITAN | ZERO-ORDER | PARTIAL* |
| Children | | | | | |
| Protestant | 53.2 (188) | 53.3 (270) | 40.2 (388) | −.20† | −.17 |
| Catholic | 41.1 (202) | 46.8 (77) | 38.4 (255) | −.05 | −.05 |
| Adolescents | | | | | |
| Protestant | 62.4 (258) | 63.5 (96) | 49.8 (297) | −.21‡ | −.16 |
| Catholic | 46.4 (69) | 58.1 (62) | 50.8 (199) | .01 | −.01 |

* SES is controlled.
† P < .001.
‡ P < .01.
NOTE: For all other relationships, P > .10. Here and elsewhere in the article, significance was tested through the use of Chi-square.

type items: God punishes people who sin, the Bible is God's word and must be obeyed, the church or religious authorities represent God in this world, and God controls everything that happens everywhere.[30] Note the similarity of the first item to the measure used in analyzing the children data; it had the highest factor loading (.84) on fundamentalism of these four items. As in the case of the children data, there was a low negative association between residence and fundamentalism on the part of Protestant

but not Catholic adolescents. The data appear in table 1. Again, the partial gamma had a value somewhat reduced from the zero-order gamma (−.16 and −.21, respectively). Parenthetically, the relationship between educational level of the fathers and fundamentalism of the Protestant youth was low and inverse (gamma = −.21, with P < .01). It is interesting to note that even within the Protestant samples the relationship between residence and fundamentalism is not linear. While the lowest percentages are found in the metropolitan areas, urban areas appear as fundamentalist as and sometimes more so than rural areas. We shall return to this fact in our discussion. Since Catholic youth showed no significant residential differences, as hypothesized previously, they were dropped from further analysis.

Table 2 presents the same relationship among Protestants specifying for SES level. For the children, occupational level of the father was used for the measure of SES, since this measure was more reliable with younger children (only 6 percent of

were inversely related to residence in the case of Protestant but not Catholic adolescents (the values of gamma were −.16 and −.20, respectively). Rural adolescents were most and metropolitan youth least religious here. Our focus in this article is on the ideological dimension, here being fundamentalism, and thus we give no additional data on these other factors.

30. Points were assigned to the responses to these four items as follows: 1—strongly disagree; 2—disagree; 3—don't know and no response; 4—agree; and 5—strongly agree. (similarly, no response on education will be assigned to education's middle category.) The summated scores were dichotomized as low fundamentalism—scores 4–14; and high fundamentalism—scores 15–20.

TABLE 2

PERCENT FUNDAMENTALISTIC BY RESIDENCE AND SES
(CONDITIONAL RELATIONSHIPS—PROTESTANT ONLY)

| SAMPLE AND SES (PROTESTANTS) | PERCENT FUNDAMENTALISTIC BY AREA OF RESIDENCE | | | CONDITIONAL GAMMA* |
|---|---|---|---|---|
| | RURAL | URBAN | METROPOLITAN | |
| Children | | | | |
| blue-collar | 53.1 (98) | 61.4 (145) | 46.0 (124) | −.11§ |
| white-collar | 53.3 (90) | 44.0 (125) | 37.5 (264) | −.21§ |
| conditional gamma† | .01 | −.34‡ | −.17 | |
| Adolescents | | | | |
| low education | 68.3 (104) | 72.0 (25) | 53.6 (69) | −.23** |
| medium education | 60.6 (104) | 66.7 (36) | 55.5 (119) | −.09 |
| high education | 54.0 (50) | 54.3 (35) | 41.3 (109) | −.21 |
| conditional gamma† | −.19 | −.25 | −.18 | |

\* Strength of the relationship between residence and fundamentalism at each level of SES.
† Strength of the relationship between SES and fundamentalism for each area of residence.
‡ P < .01.
§ P < .05.
** P < .10.
NOTE: For all other relationships, P > .10.

the respondents under analysis did not know or respond to this question, while the comparable rate for father's education was 29 percent). For adolescents, education was employed; and it was collapsed as low (did not graduate from high school), medium (high school graduate), and high (some college or more).

An examination of both tables indicates again that urbanites are as apt to be fundamentalistic (if not more likely) as rural dwellers, while those in the metropolitan areas are less likely to be fundamentalistic. The exception consists of the white-collar urbanite children who are midway between children from the rural and metropolitan areas in terms of percent fundamentalistic (see table 2). Within this group alone do we find a unilinear relationship between residence and fundamentalism.

In the rural areas there are no SES differences for children, while in the urban and metropolitan areas children with white-collar fathers are less likely than those from blue-collar backgrounds to be fundamentalistic. These differences are especially pronounced among urban children. Metropolitan adolescents with fathers who have either a low or a medium level of education tend to be alike in terms of percent fundamentalistic, while youth of high education backgrounds are less likely to be fundamentalistic. Education and fundamentalism are inversely related, but not significantly so, for rural and urban adolescents.

## CONCLUSIONS

Let us sum up the model of rural religiosity and organized religion in the rural areas implicit in the main part of the text. In isolated rural areas (more applicable in the past), residents were less likely to belong to and regularly attend church services; but, in part because of low education levels and because of revivals which occasionally oc- curred, these same individuals were as likely or perhaps more likely to believe in God. Frequently this was a punishing God; and the religious ideology was one of fundamentalism. As urbanization occurred and with the building of hard-surfaced roads and the increase in levels of educa- tion, rural residents became as likely to participate in organized religion as their city cousins.[31]

Research done on the rural church indicates the importance of con- sidering it not from an ecological but an organizational perspective. It is not the place of residence but the size of the church that is important in determining the program, whether there is a minister (and how well trained he or she is), and, most important of all, its fate—whether it continues or closes its doors. With out-migration from the rural areas, many small churches did, in fact, cease, while many continue a precarious existence. Of those that have continued, many are sectarian and often utilize lay preachers. Of the mainline small churches that continue, many are "yoked" in twos or threes so as to have sufficient budget for more viable programs. With inflation, as well as a current decline in membership on the part of many mainline denominations, there is no reason to expect the decline of the rural (small) church to abate. Though the rural areas are probably less affected by the overall decline in membership and partici- pation, still the national head- quarters of the denominations are harder pressed for monies, meaning

that there are fewer subsidies for the small churches.

On the positive side for the small church is the movement toward decentralization on the part of at least one major denomination (United Presbyterian), with regional units taking more incentive instead of leaving programs in the hands of the national body or its larger units. This might spur parishioner interest and involvement; and that, of course, is central in the life of the small church.

Can any change be expected in rural religious orientations? Pre- vious findings indicated that rural residents are more likely than urban- ites to hold conservative religious beliefs. Using two sets of data— from children and adolescents—we found some evidence for such differences continuing with the younger generation. Metropolitan dwellers score lowest on funda- mentalism, but a shift seems to be taking place between rural and urban dwellers (but not at the high educational or white-collar levels), the latter generally scoring some- what higher. Is the simplistic and fatalistic worldview of life which characterized rural dwellers in years past now becoming a charac- teristic of small urban areas, thus explaining the greater percentage scoring high on fundamentalism in those areas?

Furthermore, the interaction be- tween social class and residence is important in explaining funda- mentalism. Earlier we noted that middle-class ruralites and small- town dwellers are more likely to be in contact with working-class in- dividuals than, presumably, are city or suburban dwellers. Protestant churches especially tend to be more class-inclusive in the rural areas and small towns. This should tend to

31. Indeed, rural Protestant adolescents were most likely to engage in religious practices and to score high on the personal- experiential factor of religiosity. See the previous footnote.

increase residential differences among middle-class Protestants but reduce SES differences among rural and small-town Protestants.[32] This is, in fact, what we generally discovered with one important exception—the "medium education group" among adolescents showed the lowest relationship between residence and fundamentalism. This may be due to measurement error, since "no response to father's education" was classified in this middle group. Catholic parishes are more class-inclusive than Protestant churches in the metropolitan areas; and, as expected, while Protestants revealed significant residential differences, the Catholics did not.

Remaining to be tested is our suggestion of the importance of class integration. We had no items to operationalize directly that concept in our studies; and, therefore, we can only note that our findings gave some support to the promise of residential (and church) propinquity of social classes as an intervening variable. We have come full circle in our discussion of rural religiosity in turning from ecological effects on belief to the structural or organizational perspective recommended by earlier researchers of the rural church.

32. We suggest research on the effects of class-integration on the part of both children and teachers in the religious education programs.

ANNALS, AAPSS, **429**, Jan. 1977

# The Quality of Life in Rural America

By Don A. Dillman and Kenneth R. Tremblay, Jr.

ABSTRACT: Attempts to measure quality of life (QOL) in rural America have gone through three stages, focusing first on economic well-being, later on a broad array of so-called objective indicators, and finally on subjective evaluations. All remain important to gaining a comprehensive understanding of the QOL in rural America. An analysis of objective conditions points to several areas of deprivation among rural people, especially economic well-being and the receipt of institutional services, but suggests they are better off than urban Americans with respect to their material and social environment. Rural people's subjective assessments are strikingly consistent with the objective conditions of their environment. However, they evaluate their overall QOL more positively than do urban Americans, possibly because they give greater weight to the relatively intangible aspects of their environment. A cautious look at the future suggests the current population turnaround and prospects of resource scarcity are critical factors likely to affect the QOL enjoyed by rural Americans.

---

Don A. Dillman is Associate Professor of Sociology and Chairman of the Department of Rural Sociology at Washington State University where he formerly directed the Social Research Center's Public Opinion Laboratory. Educated at Iowa State University, he is author of articles on public values, population distribution policy, and survey methods in various scholarly journals.

Kenneth R. Tremblay, Jr., is Research Assistant in the Department of Rural Sociology at Washington State University.

Work on this paper was supported under Project 0106 of the College of Agriculture Research Center, Washington State University, Scientific Paper #4647.

OPINIONS on the quality of life (QOL) being experienced by rural Americans are far from unanimous. There are those who view rural life as one of considerable deprivation, with major human needs going unmet. Rural residents are described by them as the "people left behind," a characterization that refers to far more than the massive rural exodus that has left well over 200 counties in America with less than one-half the number of residents that once lived there and hundreds more with greatly reduced populations. The phrase also depicts the conditions under which large numbers of rural people are seen as living, that is, fewer jobs, lower incomes, fewer educational facilities, poorer health care services, less adequate fire protection, and basically too little of most important services. Population decline in rural areas is viewed as having brought about the weakening of the tax base of rural communities and the deterioration of social institutions. This has resulted in a lack of financial resources and leadership which drastically limits the ability of these rural communities to deal with the critical problems affecting their residents. Thus it is concluded that the QOL in rural America is neither high nor adequate.

Even if rural areas were similar to the rest of the country on the conditions just described, and they are not, a strong case could be made that being rural inherently means being deprived. Both rural and urban America have changed radically since Benjamin Franklin justified his preference for cities by noting that it was only there he could find "the satisfaction of pursuing whatever plan is most agreeable, without being known or looked at." But the role constraints and more regularized lifestyles enforced by the smallness of the rural community remain, and

have been something from which many feel the need to escape. In addition, rural communities have a deserved reputation for being harbingers of social injustice. They have been among the last to accept tenets of equality and individualism which have been defined as progressive by the dominant society. Neither are rural areas known for their support of the cultural arts. Size alone makes it impossible for them to provide their residents with cultural facilities—from operas to museums to professional sports—which come close to equaling those found in large cities.

This negative evaluation of rural America is countered by one that focuses on the current social ills afflicting cities and sees rural life as possessing the natural cure. People flocked to the cities in search of opportunity. While many found it, many more found themselves confronted by a complete inventory of society's worst problems—crime, traffic jams, polluted air and water, noise, and racial tension. To live in a large city has meant for many of these people a life that is unsettled and filled with conflict. Ironically, rural America has become viewed by a growing number of Americans as having a higher QOL not because of what it has, but rather because of what it does not have!

Rural life has been idealized ever since Thomas Jefferson's dream of a society of free farmers. Thoughts about a slower pace of life, neighborliness, open spaces, and clean air have exhibited the same magnetic attraction to some people that skyscrapers and symphony orchestras have for confirmed urbanites. Existence of a strong desire for a more rural life has recently become more prevalent among Americans, as indicated by polls and surveys which have repeatedly, and to our knowledge without exception, shown the general population to have a strong distaste for life in large cities.[1] In addition, the current reversal of the rural to urban migration trend suggests that these preferences of at least some Americans for rural life is not an idle pipedream. People are beginning to act on their preferences in ways that would suggest they are looking to rural America as a way of improving their QOL. Thus, for this group of Americans, rural America is seen as the place where the good things in life can be found, something like living a contemporary version of the "Waltons" for yourself.

The two views we have stated above, one maintaining that the QOL is lower and the second that it is higher in rural as opposed to urban America, both have some basis of justification. Clearly, there are advantages as well as detriments associated with rural life. Reconciling these viewpoints is made difficult less by different interpretations of the same data than it is by disagreement on what constitutes QOL.

## WHAT IS QUALITY OF LIFE?

Efforts to define and measure QOL have gone through three stages. The first, which prevailed for most of this century, tended to equate QOL with economic well-

1. See, for example, Don A. Dillman, *Population Distribution Policy and People's Attitudes: Current Knowledge and Needed Research*, Paper prepared for the Urban Land Institute under a grant from the U.S. Department of Housing and Urban Development, 1973, pp. 27–68; James L. Sundquist, *Dispersing Population: What America Can Learn from Europe* (Washington, D.C.: The Brookings Institute, 1975), pp. 24–6; Duane Elgin et al., *City Size and the Quality of Life* (Washington, D.C.: U.S. Government Printing Office, 1974), pp. 27–38.

being; not an unreasonable thing to do considering the times. Rapid economic growth had put substantially greater purchasing power into the hands of most Americans, thus giving them the ability to acquire more of the material goods and services they desired. There were few doubts in anyone's mind, whether scholar or laborer, that the public was far better off and closer to realization of its dreams, and therefore a high QOL, than at any time in our history. This view prevailed until shortly after the middle of the present century.

Ironically, economic prosperity was largely responsible for the emergence of dissatisfaction with its adequacy as a singular indicator of QOL. One reason why this occurred has to do with man's seemingly insatiable appetite for improving his life situation. When certain wants are satisfied, other wants seem always to surface. Efforts to achieve a satisfactory QOL thus take on the aura of a never-ending search for which the object is not a single tangible item, but rather improvement over one's current situation. The economic progress of this century might well be described, in Maslowian terms, as having met lower level needs (such as physiological, safety, and security) to such an extent that people's energies became free to focus on higher level needs (such as belongingness, esteem, and self-actualization). The search for satisfaction thus switched from concrete goals, whose relationship to specific needs was generally clear (and realizable by economic means), to more abstract goals, whose relationship to needs was often vague even to those in pursuit of them.

A second way in which economic prosperity hastened its own demise as an accurate indicator of QOL stemmed from its interference with the achievement of non-economic wants. For example, the drive for economic wealth treated the environment with wanton disregard. Resources that might have been spent on minimizing the effects of effluents on air and water became wages and profits instead of costs of production. A clean environment became a much desired goal partly because our affluence allowed us to afford it. Yet, a reason for prosperity and the material goods it brought us was our willingness to accept a dirty environment. Economic progress also brought about fundamental changes in the organization and location of industrial activity which extracted severe human costs. Cities, for quite understandable reasons, became centers for a much larger share of the productive enterprise. One reason for this phenomenon was that economic activity had become footloose—by 1971 only about 7 percent of the labor force needed to be located close to natural resources as opposed to 30 percent some 30 years earlier.[2] The phenomenal rise in per capita productivity in agriculture, enabling the farm labor force to shrink while continuing to meet national demand for farm products, was an important component of this change. A second reason for urban growth was the emergence of new sets of locational constraints, which, in general, rural communities could not provide (for example, well-developed utility systems, a full range of transportation facilities, and financial institutions). Large cities thus became the spawning ground and natural place of growth for new industries, the kind best able

to pay premium wages and make high profits. As a result of these changes, migration to the cities was inevitable. There is little doubt that these migrants were better off economically than they had been previously. But for many, migration meant breaking family ties and leaving behind cherished lifestyles. It also meant adapting to the kinds of places that polls show people do not want to live. That this adaptation was not entirely successful is suggested by the research finding that the people who most want to move from cities to rural areas are those who once lived there.[3]

The situation seemed almost paradoxical. On the one hand, the attractiveness of economic well-being was so powerful that no other forces could arrest the drive toward it. But once attained, and perhaps taken for granted, people turned to how they might satisfy other wants, including some which had previously been given up for financial gain. Unfortunately, some of these wants, such as clean air and water, had become the victims of economic progress and were no longer readily available. Economic well-being, considered by most to be the original solution to mankind's woes, had itself become the problem, bringing with it the need to rethink the meaning of QOL.

The second stage in development of the QOL concept consisted of its expansion into many areas of life. Emphasis was placed on identifying ways of objectively measuring educational achievement, health services, political participation, leisure time, crime rates, and a seemingly

2. Niles M. Hansen, *Intermediate-Size Cities as Growth Centers* (New York: Praeger Publishers, 1971), p. 13.

3. Don A. Dillman and Russell P. Dobash, *Preferences for Community Living and Their Implication for Population Redistribution* (Pullman: Washington Agricultural Experiment Station, 1972), pp. 13–21.

indeterminate number of other conditions that somehow express mankind's wants. Near statistical madness prevailed as researchers rushed to count acres of parks, ratios of people to libraries, and how many suspended particulates were in the air. The development of these so-called objective indicators of well-being raised a new set of issues which could not be satisfactorily answered, however. When one's focus was on economic well-being, more always seemed better. But for many of the new QOL indicators, the question was open as to what goals contributed to a high QOL. For example, are more years of schooling necessarily a good thing? Is there not some point beyond which educational attainment becomes superfluous? And if so, what is that point? These questions might conceivably be given tentative answers except that the expansion to multiple indicators of well-being meant that interconnections among them had to be taken into account. Somehow we must be able to ascertain whether societal resources might be better spent on achieving additional increments of education or equally costly increments of health services or perhaps trading off crime rates against pollution levels.

For some of the objective indicators, the question also arose concerning which direction for change was most desirable. Consider, for example, the divorce rate. Some would consider a rise in the divorce rate as indicative of an increase in family instability and therefore a decline in the QOL. Others could argue that such an increase reflects greater individual freedom and a decline of societal pressures for holding together marriages that were less than satisfying to those involved in them. The essential weakness of the objective indicators movement, then, is the lack of "a commonly accepted social welfare function or value system whose existence is a necessary condition of an efficient indicator of quality of life, meaningful to all people in the nation."[4] Thus, even though this second stage in the development of the QOL concept succeeded in focusing attention on the great need for multidimensional measurement, it fell short of describing exactly what those measures should be and whether specific changes in indicators reflect improvement or decline. It is for this reason that the third and most controversial stage of the QOL concept—the subjective approach—emerged.

Subjective measurement of QOL is based on the seemingly simple assumption that society exists to meet the needs of people in it, and to find out whether those needs are being met we should simply go out and ask them. The focus of concern is on such terms as happiness, satisfaction, sense of well-being, aspirations, and the like. This suggests that to measure QOL in an area such as health services, we should use survey techniques to ask people whether they think their medical needs are being met. Further, we can ask them questions such as whether it is more important to increase certain health services or to expend the same resources on improving educational opportunities. The subjective approach is seen as compatible, and even essential, to the objective indicators movement previously discussed. Without it, we run the risk of concluding that our QOL has been objectively improved, but in

4. Ben-Chieh Liu, "Quality of Life Indicators: A Preliminary Investigation," *Social Indicators Research*, vol. 1 (1974), p. 188.

ways for which we haven't the slightest desire.

Strong arguments have been put forward concerning the limitations of employing subjective indicators to measure QOL as well. One shortcoming of the subjective approach is that major differences may exist between what people perceive to be true and objective reality. A person may honestly believe that his drinking water is of the highest quality, while a bacterial analysis could show that the same water is quite unfit to drink. It is similarly the case that people's perceptions are often individually focused and unrealistic. For example, a resident of a large city might express keen dissatisfaction with any detectable amounts of air pollution and have a strenuous desire to restore previous pristine qualities. Yet, accomplishment of such a goal is most likely unpractical and would result in detrimental effects on economic activity and draw from expenditures allocated to other concerns, such as health and education. Thus, acting on this preference may make little sense. Finally, we might note that expansion of people's frustrations often stems as much from socially based relative deprivation as from absolute deprivation. A physician earning $40,000 per year may be just as dissatisfied as a store clerk earning $2.50 per hour if he perceives his income as being lower relative to other doctors. Such a phenomenon as dissatisfaction, then, cannot be adequately measured simply by using subjective indicators.

It is far from clear what weight should be accorded to subjective indicators of QOL. However, the difficulties involved in making such a decision reflect the reality of the world in which we live as well as the inherent difficulties of assessing the QOL that a nation provides its people. In defense of employing the subjective approach in measuring QOL, Frank M. Andrews points out that there are "some reasons to believe that 'subjective' indicators provide at least as objective measures of what they intend to assess as do the 'objective' indicators of what *they* try to assess."[5] But the fact that subjective indicators are just as adequate as objective indicators in assessing QOL gives us little comfort, for each fails to measure certain aspects of QOL. We have attempted to make clear the notion that each stage in the development of the QOL concept has introduced concerns not adequately handled by the others, and that each has its limitations. The earlier stages discussed are thus by no means obsolete, as concern with objective indicators and economic well-being remains high. The conclusion we reach is that QOL assessment needs to consider the concerns of all three dimensions of QOL, as we shall endeavor to do in this paper.

## WHAT IS RURAL?

We cannot ignore the need to specify what is meant by "rural," a term which conjures up different connotations to different people. Some consider all people residing outside a metropolitan (metro) area (that is, a county or group of contiguous counties in which there is at least one city, or twin cities, with a population of 50,000 or more) as being rural. Others accept the traditional U.S. census definition of rural (that is, residents of open country

5. Frank M. Andrews, "Social Indicators of Perceived Life Quality," *Social Indicators Research*, vol. 1 (1974), pp. 281–82.

and towns of less than 2,500), regardless of the metro distinction. A third way of thinking about the meaning of rural, and one which we prefer, is along the lines of a range of ruralness, as set forth by Fred K. Hines and his associates. On the basis of this method, a range of ruralness can be inferred (for example, from least to most rural) by population size of either counties or cities. A flexible definition of rural is advantageous, even necessary in this paper, inasmuch as data relevant to examining the QOL in rural America have been collected using a variety of definitions, sometimes allowing for gradations in ruralness but in most instances only a dichotomous distinction between rural and urban.[6]

## OBJECTIVE INDICATORS OF QOL

Selecting areas of concern on which to base an assessment of objective QOL requires some degree of arbitrariness, as there is no agreed upon list of what constitutes an adequate set of topics. Our selection has been guided by the results of community problem surveys and the QOL literature in general. Both suggest a number of topics which are areas of high concern for most Americans, and thus important components of QOL.

*Economic well-being.* If it were necessary to pick just one indicator to evaluate QOL, there is good reason for making it an economic one. An indicator such as "family income" is a general measure of the resources that a family has at its

6. For a brief overview of the uses of "rural," see Fred K. Hines, David L. Brown, and John M. Zimmer, *Social and Economic Characteristics of the Population in Metro and Nonmetro Counties, 1970* (Washington, D.C.: Economic Research Service, U.S. Department of Agriculture, 1975), pp. 3–6.

disposal for meeting its various needs, whatever they might be. This aspect of convertibility consistent with one's subjective preferences makes such a measure qualitatively different from most other measures, such as housing and education, which indicate levels of achievement that require expenditures of one's resources.

No matter which indicators of economic well-being are used to assess the QOL of rural Americans, the conclusion is basically the same—rural areas are worse off than urban ones, and the more rural the area the greater the discrepancy. In 1969 the median family income for the United States was $9,590. Nonmetro residents earned only $7,615, less than three-fourths of the $10,406 earned by metro residents. People living in the most rural areas (for example, counties not adjacent to metro areas with no towns greater than 2,500) earned only $6,142, or 59 percent of the income of metro area residents. It should be mentioned that the effect of these differences on people's lives is somewhat less than might be imagined inasmuch as the cost of living in rural areas is somewhat lower. Unfortunately, data are not available for making precise comparisons, but those which exist suggest that cost of living differences make up for less than half the differences in actual income. As one might expect based on the data just presented, rural areas have more of the nation's poor. About 20 percent of all nonmetro residents, as compared to 11 percent of metro residents, are considered to be living below the poverty level. In the most rural counties more than one out of every four persons are classified as living in poverty.

Overall, the 1960s saw a somewhat greater improvement in the economic well-being of rural Americans than among their urban counterparts. As a share of the total population of the United States, the proportion of low income nonmetro persons declined from 22 percent to 14 percent. Incomes of all nonmetro residents increased by 79 percent during the same time, compared to a 68 percent gain for metro residents. However, it is important to recognize that in terms of absolute dollars of income, the gap widened to some degree, with metro family incomes increasing an average of $4,195 while nonmetro family incomes went up $3,337.[7] Thus, differences between rural and urban incomes remain, and seem likely to continue.

*Education.* Formal education is widely accepted as one of the most important indicators of QOL. The vast majority of all occupational positions in American society have certain minimum educational requirements which must be met. To gain entry into the most desirable occupations and professions requires even higher levels of educational achievement. Furthermore, simply living and participating in our increasingly complex society demands skills which our system of formal education seeks to impart.

It can be safely suggested that rural residents have less formal education than their urban counterparts. In 1970 the median number of school years completed by people living in metro areas was 12.2 versus 11.2 for all nonmetro residents. In the most rural counties, educational attainment drops to only 9.9 years. It is disturbing to note that the high school drop-out rate is also higher in rural areas. The percent of 16- to 17-year-old children not enrolled in school is 9.5 in metro counties and 13.6 in nonmetro counties. Consistent with previously discussed patterns, the most rural counties have the highest proportion (15.2 percent) of children in this age group not enrolled in school.[8] This suggests that the disadvantageous position of rural people is likely to persist into the future. Contributing to the difficulties of improving educational attainment in rural areas is the lack of vocational training and other post-high school opportunities made unavailable by low population densities and inadequate tax bases. Rural residents who seek such opportunities must often commute long distances or move to a larger place. In the past, most of the young people who have opted in this direction for greater education have, in effect, bought a one-way ticket to the larger cities, the only places where their newly acquired job skills could be profitably applied.

*Health care.* One of the most pressing and difficult to resolve problems of rural Americans may well be that of health care. It is a problem comprised of several dimensions, of which the availability of medical personnel is one of the most important. In 1970 there were twice as many physicians per 100,000 people in metro places as there were in nonmetro places. It was also true that the more rural the area the greater was the lack of physicians—counties of less than 10,000 people had an average of one physician for every 2,103 persons compared to 700 for the nation as a whole and 450 for the largest cities.[9]

8. Ibid., pp. 23–8.

9. For a discussion of physician shortages in rural America, see, for example, American

7. Ibid., pp. 44–60.

Particularly missing in rural areas are the highly trained specialists which form the foundation of modern medicine. In addition, rural doctors are older, generally work more hours, and are less up to date on medical advances than their urban counterparts. The situation of rural physicians applies to other realms of the medical enterprise as well, as rural areas are characterized by shortages of pharmacists, nurses, dentists, and other medical personnel.[10]

Perhaps the unavailability of health services in rural areas is reflected best by the fact that such services are used less frequently by rural people. For example, nonmetro residents average 4.1 trips to the doctor per year while metro residents average 4.8 visits.[11] And this difference can hardly be due to a lower need for medical attention on the part of rural Americans. In fact, rural areas exhibit a higher incidence of chronic disease, more days lost from work due to illness, and a greater rate of work-related injuries. The most rural areas also experience morbidity and infant mortality rates far in excess of the general population.[12]

The pattern that these data suggest is of a chain that is difficult to break—fewer medical personnel, contributing to the practice of less preventive medicine, and as a result a greater need for medical services. The difficulty of attacking health problems is accentuated by the seemingly insurmountable barrier of low population density, which is often much less than the minimum needed to support medical specialists and their even more specialized and expensive life-saving equipment. Although considerable effort is being expended by both state and federal government to improve health services in rural areas, the situation may even worsen before it becomes better. One indication of this speculation becoming reality is that the older doctors practicing in rural places are dying or retiring and not being replaced. In fact, between 1963 and 1970 the number of rural counties with no physician at all increased from 98 to 132.[13]

*Housing.* The quality of housing is of interest to us for several reasons. To a vast majority of Americans, housing represents more than just shelter. As the most immediate aspect of one's community living experience, it shapes people's lives. At the same time it is the frequent object for expression of people's drive for improvement, and thus reflects well-being in other dimensions of life. Further, money spent on one's home is, for most families, the largest single consumer expenditure they make.

In general, rural housing does not compare well with that found in urban places. Although there is a higher incidence of home ownership by nonmetro residents (70

Medical Association, *Distribution of Physicians in the U.S., 1970* (Chicago: American Medical Association, 1971).

10. Edward D. Martin, "The Federal Initiative in Rural Health," *Public Health Reports*, vol. 90 (July–August 1975), pp. 292–94.

11. U.S. Department of Health, Education and Welfare, *Health Characteristics by Geographic Region, Large Metropolitan Areas, and Other Places of Residence, U.S., July, 1963–June, 1965* (Washington, D.C.: National Center for Health Statistics, 1967); cited in Peter A. Morrison et al., *Review of Federal Programs to Alleviate Rural Deprivation* (Santa Monica, Calif.: Rand, 1974), p. 53.

12. M. H. Ross, "Rural Health Care: Is Prepayment a Solution?" *Public Health Reports*, vol. 90 (July–August 1975), p. 298.

13. Morrison et al., *Programs to Alleviate Rural Deprivation*, pp. 53–4.

percent versus 60 percent for metro residents), the median property value of that housing was only $12,200 in 1970 while that for metro areas was $19,000. Those people living in nonmetro housing were also more likely to live in relatively crowded conditions, as there was an average of 3.32 persons per household compared to 3.04 in metro housing in 1970. Of housing without adequate plumbing, about one-third are located in metro areas and about two-thirds in nonmetro areas.[14] Finally, the quality of drinking water delivered to rural homes is lower than that received by urban homes, partially a result of their reliance on individual wells while urban homes are serviced by processing plants which ensure the purification of water.[15] These discrepancies between rural and urban housing reflect far more than differences in what people can afford. The averages we have reported are greatly influenced by the fact that the vast majority of new homes have been built where population growth has been greatest—namely, in urban areas. The absence of building codes and a shortage of credit in rural areas are other important factors limiting rural housing. Essentially, it can be suggested that in rural America the building of homes has often been viewed as an expenditure likely to depreciate, whereas in fast growing metro areas it has been an investment from which sizable returns were likely to be achieved.

*Crime.* During the last decade,

14. U.S. Bureau of the Census, *1970 Census of Population and Housing* (Washington, D.C.: U.S. Government Printing Office, 1971).

15. Commission on Rural Water, *A Program for the Future—Water and Sewer in Rural America* (Washington, D.C.: Commission on Rural Water, 1974), p. 6.

fear of crime has consistently appeared near the top of the list of concerns expressed by Americans. At the same time, it is generally recognized as one of the advantages of life in rural areas. A sizable and persuasive quantity of data exists to support this view. For example, while metro areas reported a murder rate of 11 victims per 100,000 residents in 1974, it was only 8 in nonmetro areas. The incidence of aggravated assault was more than twice as high in metro areas (243 versus 112 per 100,000), and robbery was more than 13 times as high (274 versus 20 per 100,000). Similar results are found for the occurrence of property crimes, as urban areas reported greater rates of burglary, larceny-theft, and motor vehicle theft. These differences may be even more striking if we consider that criminals in urban places go unnoticed to a greater extent than is the case in rural areas. In addition, rural police are slightly more successful than their urban counterparts in solving criminal offenses — clearing 24 percent of all crimes compared to 21 percent in metro areas.[16] Greater safety from crime and violence appears to represent a clear advantage of rural life.

*Environmental quality.* The environment came into its own as a major dimension of QOL in the late 1960s, largely a result of people's growing awareness of the environment around them and the tell-tale signs of environmental deterioration—air pollution, water pollution, high noise levels, and the like. Objective data confirm people's intuition that cities are noisier, the air dirtier, and the water more polluted than rural areas. And the

16. Federal Bureau of Investigation, *Uniform Crime Reports, 1974* (Washington, D.C.: U.S. Government Printing Office, 1975).

larger the city, the worse the environmental conditions get, reaching hazardous levels in some instances.[17] For example, urban residents have a greater chance of being exposed to "unacceptable" noise levels as well as breathing air that can help lead to emphysema, asthma, and similar respiratory disorders.[18] In some places, large-scale urbanism also creates conditions contributing to a poorer climatic situation, that is, less sunshine, more rain, and higher temperatures.[19] Finally, scenic beauty is most likely lower in urban areas. Generally, there are more trees, open spaces, and natural recreational sites in a rural location. Obviously this higher level of environmental quality found in rural areas is partially a result of low population density, precisely the factor contributing to a low QOL on previously discussed dimensions.

*Recreational activity.* Increasing amounts of people's time are spent in some form of recreational activity, making it an important dimension of QOL. Generally, rural people participate in recreational activity to a somewhat lesser degree than do urban people. For example, the number of activity days per person is lower among rural residents — 91 days versus 97 days per year for urbanites. The types of activities engaged in differ significantly between rural and urban residents as well, with rural people participating more in outdoor-oriented activities (for example, fishing, hunting, and camping) and urban people

engaging more in activities requiring developed facilities.[20] These results are not surprising. Low population density and the scarcity of funds severely limit the ability of rural areas to build and support tennis courts, movie theaters, bowling alleys, and similar facilities. However, this lack is compensated to a considerable degree by the availability of outdoor activities that often cannot be provided in cities, at any price.

*In general.* One of the greatest difficulties of evaluating objective measures of QOL is that no satisfactory means exists for adding them up into an overall index. And even though we have done little more than scratch the surface with the above seven dimensions, albeit important ones, we believe some general conclusions are justified. The overall picture is mixed, with rural Americans scoring well on some conditions of life but not on others. Deprivation is most likely to be experienced in material well-being and the receipt of institutional services. The lack of educational and health services we have noted can be extended to the availability of legal aid, counseling services, and other specialized activities of all sorts. Some of the same conditions (for example, low population density) making it difficult for such services in rural America to be on a par with those of urban America also make it possible to maintain a high quality material and social environment. However, this leaves us with a question that cannot be resolved by objective evaluation alone—namely, which conditions are most important to rural people?

17. See, for example, Council on Environmental Quality, *Environmental Quality —1975* (Washington, D.C.: U.S. Government Printing Office, 1975); Alfred Van Tassel, ed., *Our Environment: The Outlook for 1980* (Lexington, Mass.: Lexington Books, 1973).

18. Elgin et al., *City Size*, pp. 97–100.

19. Ibid., pp. 102–4; see citation, p. 104.

20. U.S. Bureau of Outdoor Recreation, *1970 Survey of Outdoor Recreation Activities* (Washington, D.C.: U.S. Government Printing Office, 1972).

This is an issue which can only be addressed by turning to the realm of subjective indicators.

## SUBJECTIVE INDICATORS OF QOL

Researchers have only recently begun systematic inquiry into the subjective aspects of QOL. Those studies which have been done tend to differ in a fundamental way from those which have examined objective conditions of QOL. Whereas the latter have focused individually on each domain of life, inquiries into the subjective realm have given primary attention to generalized feelings of well-being. That the starting place for subjective evaluation of QOL has been on measures which transcend and find a balance among all life conditions is rather ironic, inasmuch as overall measures summarizing objective conditions remain a much sought but yet-to-be-realized goal. This does not mean that subjective measurement is any easier. Researchers have not yet agreed on the best method for measuring QOL; to date, a variety of approaches have been used—from asking people's "satisfaction" and "happiness," to having them select from lists of words those which best describe their life. The verdict has yet to be reached on which method or methods provide the most valid measures of people's subjective perceptions.

Although relatively few studies have been done, most of which allow only gross rural-urban comparisons and lack comparability with one another, a fairly clear image of the QOL rural Americans think they are experiencing is beginning to emerge. In the most ambitious study yet undertaken, a sense of well-being scale was carefully developed using responses to several ques-

tions. Results from this recent national study by Angus Campbell and his associates show that people's sense of well-being increases consistently as one moves from large cities to rural places.[21] Rural-urban differences persisted even when the influence of income, the strongest single predictor of well-being, was controlled. The findings are given increased strength by the discovery that strong correlations existed between a generalized measure of well-being and life satisfaction in 17 life domains (such as housing, health, and education). Perhaps most important is the authors' conclusion that reports of a global sense of well-being that can be meaningfully viewed as a composite of feelings of satisfaction and dissatisfaction with a variety of more specific domains of life.

Differences in sense of well-being reported above need to be interpreted in the context of overall levels of well-being. People throughout America report high, nearly overwhelming, satisfaction with their lives. In response to a direct question about their overall satisfaction with life, one component of the well-being scale, only 7 percent indicated a sense of dissatisfaction. The proportion of people dissatisfied with specific life conditions averaged about the same as that for overall satisfaction, with the exceptions of educational attainment and savings where dissatisfaction was somewhat higher. We conclude, then, that although the subjective sense of well-being increases with ruralness, the differ-

21. Angus Campbell, Philip E. Converse, and Willard L. Rodgers, *The Quality of American Life: Perceptions, Evaluations, and Satisfactions* (New York: Russell Sage Foundation, 1976); see, especially, pp. 51–3 and 222–37.

ence between urban and rural places most certainly is not the difference between whether or not people are generally satisfied with their lives.

A second approach to examining the subjective aspects of QOL has relied on the concept of "community" satisfaction. Focusing on people's evaluations of their community is appropriate in that it is the arena in which jobs are normally provided and institutional services offered, both of which greatly influence QOL. Angus Campbell and his colleagues found that suburbs, small cities, and towns were usually rated best on specific community attributes. While rural areas ranked lower, though still ahead of the larger cities, on the items of garbage collection, public schools, police-community relations, police-protection, public transportation, and streets and roads; they were ranked best by their residents on the attributes of levels of local taxes, climate, and parks and playgrounds. Somewhat surprising in light of the foregoing was the finding that people's overall sense of community satisfaction ascends sharply and consistently with decreases in urbanization and is decidedly higher for rural places. While urban residents tended to be less satisfied with the whole than among any of the parts, rural people were more satisfied with the whole than any one of the parts. This finding is supported by a number of state-wide surveys which have found that although rural people rated access to certain services (particularly medical care) lower than their urban counterparts, their overall community satisfaction was higher.[22]

One plausible explanation for the higher overall rating of rural communities is suggested by those same state surveys—rural people rate their communities higher on nonservice items, some of which are of an intangible nature. And, in the final evaluation, these qualities are given more weight than is the lack of certain services. For example, in one survey metro residents rated their communities as best on all income and service items (such as availability of good paying jobs, streets and roads, and education), whereas nonmetro residents, and particularly those from the most rural counties, rated their communities highest on air quality, safety from crime and violence, and desirability as a place to raise children.[23] In another state, it was reported that ruralites felt that access to the outdoors, open spaces, and friendliness of people were advantages that offset service inadequacies.[24] Similarly, a recent national survey of the elderly, a subpopulation of special interest because of their greater need for local provision of services, showed that those who lived in rural communities were more than twice as likely

22. See, for example, Anne S. Williams, Russell C. Youmans, and Donald M. Sorenson, *Providing Rural Public Services* (Corvallis: Oregon State University Agricultural Experiment Station, 1975); Don A. Dillman, Annabel Kirschner-Cook, and Richard Fernandez, *Community Satisfaction and Population Redistribution Policies* (Pullman: Washington State Agricultural Research Center, in process); James A. Christenson, *Through Our Eyes: Community Preferences and Population Distribution* (Raleigh: North Carolina Agricultural Extension Service, 1974); James A. Christenson, *North Carolina Today and Tomorrow: People's Views on Community Services* (Raleigh: North Carolina Agricultural Extension Service, 1976).

23. See Dillman, Kirschner-Cook, and Fernandez, *Community Satisfaction.*

24. See Stan Albrecht, *Rural Development: Its Dimensions and Focus* (Logan: Department of Sociology, Utah State University, 1974).

(50 percent versus 23 percent) to be satisfied with their community than were those living in cities of over 250,000 people.[25] Thus, substantial support exists for the notion that the inadequacy of certain services is off-set by the presence of other qualities in rural places.

A different indicator of community satisfaction is found in the numerous community-size preference surveys which have been done.[26] Without exception, these surveys have shown large city residents more interested in moving to rural places than are rural residents in moving to cities. Whereas surveys show that only 4 out of 10 urban residents want to remain in the city, fully 9 out of 10 rural residents want to stay just where they are.[27] Virtually none of those living in the smallest communities prefer trading their life situation for that found in the large cities. Finally, it might be noted that in recent years rural residents have been much more likely to think that their communities were getting better as places to live than were residents of cities and suburbs.[28]

The picture that begins to emerge of people's perceptions of QOL is now somewhat clearer. Overall, satisfaction among all Americans is high. Even so, differences in generalized feelings of well-being do exist between rural and urban Americans and tend to favor living in rural areas. Rural people are well aware of the shortcomings of their communities, especially the inadequacy of important services. In fact, their perceptions in this regard are remarkably consistent with the objective evaluations we discussed earlier. However, these inadequacies are balanced by the more positive evaluations of other community qualities by rural people, some of which are of a relatively intangible nature and are often omitted from objective evaluations of QOL.

## THOUGHTS ABOUT THE FUTURE

Recollections of how quickly out-migration from rural America turned to in-migration and cheap plentiful energy disappeared during the first half of the present decade compel us to be cautious in making any predictions of the future QOL of rural Americans. While the safest methods of prediction have long involved extrapolation from the past, the possibility that we are exiting from an age of economic bounty and entering a new period of resource scarcity calls our past assumptions of the world into question. We are now only beginning to grope for the correct assumptions to make about the future. Thus a discussion of possibilities rather than probabilities seems most prudent.

One factor which must be considered as having a high potential for substantially changing the QOL of rural people is the current population turnaround, if it continues. Increased economic activity and higher population densities resulting from this turnaround are likely to do more to improve educational opportunities, medical care, and other institutional services than artificial stimuli could ever hope to

25. Lawrence M. Hynson, Jr., "Rural-Urban Differences in Satisfaction among the Elderly," *Rural Sociology*, vol. 40 (Spring 1975), p. 65.

26. See, for example, Elgin et al., *City Size*; Dillman and Dobash, *Preferences for Community Living*; Glenn V. Fuguitt and James J. Zuiches, "Residential Preferences and Population Distribution," *Demography*, vol. 12 (August 1975).

27. William Watts and Lloyd Free, eds., *State of the Nation* (New York: Universe Books, 1973), p. 81.

28. Elgin et al., *City Size*, p. 36.

accomplish. Rural population growth will not be an unmixed blessing, however. Even modest increases for communities long on the decline, and now populated predominantly by homogeneous long-term residents, are likely to have dramatic impacts. New residents with city-bred beliefs are likely to question the values of long-term residents and even their cherished ways of getting things done. Conflict may well be the result of sudden increases in heterogeneity. Further, those objective aspects of QOL on which rural America scores high (such as environmental quality and crime) are partially a result of low population density. An increase in population may decrease the ability of rural areas to provide these advantages. Even though we can expect services to improve as a result of population growth, its contribution to the QOL of rural areas may be offset by a decline in the more intangible qualities that have made rural communities rank so high on subjective evaluations of QOL.

For years we have been reminded of the inextricable link of urban and rural America which closely ties the fortunes of one to the other. It is becoming increasingly clear that the future of rural areas is similarly linked to the affairs of the world as a whole. Now that the capability of creating energy and other crucial resource shortages rests in foreign capitals, "uncertain" is the word that seems to come closest to describing future hopes. Another round of energy shortages, resulting in substantially higher prices, would likely create special difficulties for rural residents. For many of these people, the fact that a city is only an hour or two away from their garage door, behind which sits their own private car, has done more than anything else to make rural America not only livable, but the most desirable place to be. Should energy shortages threaten individualized travel, people in sparsely populated areas, where mass transport is least feasible, will likely suffer the most. Further, any shortages of material goods would seem most deleterious to rural people, inasmuch as they are at the ends of the distribution lines, the usual place where cutbacks are made first.

Perhaps the most significant concern which looms ever more boldly on the horizon is a reversal in our material standard of living. If it occurs, this could shift the whole QOL issue from how to improve it to how to hang on to what we already have. Past changes in QOL give us little idea of what such a transformation would be like. In any event, the uncertainty that clouds our view of the future suggests the need for increased monitoring of QOL and more efforts to increase our understanding of it, fundamental necessities for policy decisions aimed at providing the best that is possible.

# Population Redistribution, Migration, and Residential Preferences

By GORDON F. DE JONG AND RALPH R. SELL

ABSTRACT: Census Bureau population estimates for metropolitan and nonmetropolitan areas in the 1970s reveal, for the first time in over 50 years, higher population growth and net in-migration for nonmetropolitan areas than metropolitan areas. This dramatic and largely unanticipated reversal in the traditional population growth pattern is not limited to nonmetropolitan areas adjacent to metropolitan centers, but is also happening in many of the remote nonmetropolitan counties. In this article, the impact of residential preferences on population dispersal migration behavior is analyzed by means of data from a longitudinal migration survey. The widespread preference for small cities, villages, and the countryside identified in public opinion polls is not the significant factor in nonmetropolitan migration. Rather, population dispersal migrants are characterized by the willingness and apparently better ability to give up the urban-based conveniences to shopping, work, and public transportation to live in nonmetropolitan environments. Barring the crippling effect of an energy crisis, the medium-range prospect for continued nonmetropolitan population growth appears plausible.

---

Gordon F. De Jong is Professor of Sociology and former Director, Population Issues Research Office, the Pennsylvania State University. He is author or co-author of Appalachian Fertility Decline, Social Demography, and numerous other book chapters, articles, and research papers pertaining to population change and migration. He is currently principal investigator on a study of residential preferences and migration behavior.

Ralph R. Sell is a doctoral candidate in the Department of Sociology at the Pennsylvania State University where he is also associated with the Population Issues Research Office. He was a Research Assistant on a study of Population Change and Redistribution in Nonmetropolitan Pennsylvania and is completing a dissertation on motivational models of migrant decision making.

The research in this paper was supported by the Center for Population Research, National Institute of Child Health and Human Development, Contract No. NIH-NICHD-27-2743. Views expressed are the authors' and not necessarily shared by the sponsoring agency.

THE dominant trend in population distribution and internal migration in the United States during the twentieth century has been an increase in the urban and a decline in the rural population, due primarily to an almost continuous flow of rural to urban migrants. However, recent data from the Census Bureau indicate that the rural to urban pattern of population change may have halted or even been reversed. The first indications came with the estimate that during the 1970–73 period, nonmetropolitan area population increase was 4.2 percent compared to 2.7 percent for metropolitan areas.[1] What has been the historical setting for the recent evidence concerning population redistribution? What are some of the explanations for the changing pattern of population distribution? Specifically, is the metropolitan-to-nonmetropolitan pattern of population distribution in part explained by attitude preferences for the qualities of life or lifestyle of nonmetropolitan areas? We explore these questions and some possible factors influencing future metropolitan-nonmetropolitan population distribution patterns in the United States.

## POPULATION DISTRIBUTION 1900 TO 1970

Throughout the twentieth century, the United States has been characterized by the dual dimensions of moderately rapid overall population growth and the redistribution of this growth through large-scale migration of people from rural farming areas to towns and cities. The broad

outlines of these two population phenomena are presented in table 1 which highlights the basic shifts in United States population distribution over the last 70 years. During this time, the total population of the United States increased 2.7 times over the 1900 figure. But the population within Standard Metropolitan Statistical Areas (as defined by 1960 SMSA boundaries) increased 4.4 times, while the population outside SMSA boundaries was only 1.4 times the 1900 population. In every decade from 1900 to 1970, the proportion of people living in metropolitan areas increased. Since the average family size for families in nonmetropolitan areas throughout this period was larger than in metropolitan areas, the increasing metropolitan structure of our population was in large part a consequence of the flow of migrants from America's nonmetropolitan areas, although during the first few decades metropolitan growth was also enhanced by substantial immigration from foreign countries.

Since our discussion of population distribution in the United States will focus on metropolitan and nonmetropolitan areas, it is important to note how these terms differ from the rural-urban classification. The Census Bureau defines a Standard Metropolitan Statistical Area (SMSA) as:

a group of contiguous counties which contain at least one city of 50,000 inhabitants or more, or "twin cities" with a combined population of at least 50,000. In addition to the county or counties containing such a city or cities, contiguous counties are included in an SMSA if, according to certain criteria, they are essentially metropolitan in character and are socially and economically integrated with the central city[2]

1. Calvin L. Beale, *The Revival of Population Growth in Nonmetropolitan America* (Washington, D.C.: Economic Development Division, Economic Research Service, U.S. Department of Agriculture, ERS-605, June 1975).

2. United States Bureau of the Census, *Current Population Reports*, Series P-20,

TABLE 1

POPULATION DISTRIBUTION OF THE UNITED STATES, 1900 TO 1970

| CENSUS YEAR | TOTAL UNITED STATES POPULATION | WITHIN SMSA's* | | | | OUTSIDE SMSA's | |
|---|---|---|---|---|---|---|---|
| | | TOTAL | % | WITHIN CENTRAL CITY | % | TOTAL | % |
| 1900 | 75,994 | 31,836 | 41.9 | 19,785 | 26.0 | 44,158 | 58.1 |
| 1910 | 91,973 | 42,028 | 45.7 | 27,122 | 29.5 | 49,944 | 54.3 |
| 1920 | 105,711 | 52,508 | 49.7 | 34,641 | 32.8 | 53,203 | 50.3 |
| 1930 | 122,775 | 66,712 | 54.3 | 43,070 | 35.1 | 56,063 | 45.7 |
| 1940 | 131,669 | 72,576 | 55.1 | 45,473 | 34.5 | 59,093 | 44.9 |
| 1950 | 150,216 | 88,964 | 59.2 | 52,138 | 34.7 | 61,252 | 40.8 |
| 1960 | 178,467 | 112,385 | 63.0 | 57,710 | 32.2 | 66,082 | 37.0 |
| 1970 | 202,143 | 130,257 | 64.4 | 61,452 | 30.4 | 71,886 | 35.6 |
| 1970† | 202,143 | 138,790 | 68.7 | 63,472 | 31.4 | 63,353 | 31.3 |

SOURCE: Irene B. Taeuber, "The Changing Distribution of the Population in the United States in the Twentieth Century," in the Commission on Population Growth and the American Future, *Population, Distribution, and Policy,* vol. 5, ed. Sara Mills Mazie (Washington, D.C.: United States Government Printing Office, 1972), p. 78, table 19.

* Standard Metropolitan Statistical Area (SMSA) boundaries as of 1960 have been used to eliminate effect of additions and deletions of areas from the SMSA classification.

† SMSA boundaries as of 1970.

The census definition of urban has changed several times since 1900, but in general people living in places with population greater than 2,500 are classified as urban residents. Thus, people living in isolated places between 2,500 and 50,000 population would be classified as urban but not metropolitan, and conversely people living in sparsely populated areas of metropolitan counties might be classified as rural. In 1900, 60.3 percent of the United States population was classified as rural and 58.1 percent as nonmetropolitan while by 1970, 26.3 percent was classified as rural and 31.3 percent as nonmetropolitan.[3] Even though nonmetropolitan and rural do not define equivalent categories, the population dynamics

using either definition result in much the same pattern for the large majority of the United States population now classified as both urban and metropolitan.

Table 1 also indicates that even though Americans increasingly live in metropolitan areas, the central cities of these areas are declining in population. This trend, which started in the 1930s and accelerated since 1950, indicates the well-known suburbanization phenomenon. The dynamics of urbanization in the United States has thus included limited decentralization within metropolitan areas.

The large-scale migration which accompanied metropolitan population growth often has been cited as evidence for nonmetropolitan population decline. However, the

No. 285, "Mobility of the Population of the United States: March, 1970 to March, 1975" (Washington, D.C.: United States Government Printing Office, 1975).

3. Irene B. Taeuber, "The Changing Distribution of the Population in the United States in the Twentieth Century," in the

Commission on Population Growth and the American Future, *Population, Distribution, and Policy,* vol. 5, ed. Sara Mills Mazie (Washington, D.C.: United States Government Printing Office, 1972), pp. 31–108.

data in table 1 indicate that while the rate of growth for the nonmetropolitan population was less than for the metropolitan part, the number of nonmetropolitan residents continued to increase slowly throughout this century. Many small towns and rural areas, of course, have actually declined in population, but in each decade since 1940 the percentage of growing small towns in nonmetropolitan areas has consistently been greater than the number of small towns declining in population;[4] and it has been the small towns with populations greater than 2,500 which have demonstrated the greater capacity for continued population growth during this period.

## EVIDENCE FOR A CHANGE IN THE 1900 TO 1970 TREND

Since the United States presently takes a complete census every 10 years, evidence of changes in population growth and migration patterns since 1970 must be based on less complete count data sources. Between the decennial censuses the Census Bureau makes estimates of population for counties, and although individual county estimates may sometimes be inaccurate, in grouped form these estimates provide a reasonably accurate picture of population changes. County population estimates can now be validated against independent record systems such as Social Security recipients and aggregated Internal Revenue Service returns. These sources generally confirm the picture which emerges from census estimates.

Using the Census Bureau's 1974 definitions of SMSA boundaries, Calvin Beale and Glenn Fuguitt have convincingly demonstrated that the long-term net outflow of people from metropolitan America was halted between 1970 and 1973.[5] In the 30 years from 1940 to 1970, about 9 million more people left nonmetropolitan areas than moved into them, but in the three-year period between 1970 and 1973, over 1 million more people moved into nonmetropolitan areas than left them.

An important question is to what extent this migration turnaround phenomenon is an aspect of continued suburbanization, a trend which dates back at least to the 1930s. To provide at least a partial answer to this question, nonmetropolitan counties were grouped as adjacent to SMSA's and not adjacent to these larger cities. These data, summarized in table 2, show that although counties adjacent to metropolitan areas are slightly more likely to have increased in population than are nonadjacent counties (68 percent versus 60 percent), nonmetropolitan population growth in the 1970s has not been confined to areas within commuting distance of metropolitan centers. When compared with net inmigration for the 1960–70 decade, the migration turnaround in table 2 actually has been more dramatic in the nonadjacent counties.

In addition to county population estimates, the Bureau of the Census conducts a monthly Current Population Survey. In March 1975 this survey of over 50,000 households asked people where they lived in

4. Glenn V. Fuguitt, "Population Trends of Nonmetropolitan Cities and Villages in the United States," in the Commission on Population Growth and the American Future, *Population, Distribution, and Policy*, vol. 5, p. 117.

5. Calvin L. Beale and Glenn V. Fuguitt, *The New Pattern of Nonmetropolitan Population Change* (Madison: Center for Demography and Ecology, University of Wisconsin, Working Paper 75-22, August 1975).

TABLE 2

Percent of Counties Gaining Population by Net Migration
1950–60, 1960–70, 1970–73

| County Designation | 1950–60 (%) | 1960–70 (%) | 1970–73 (%) | N |
|---|---|---|---|---|
| Metropolitan | 58 | 62 | 68 | (630) |
| Nonmetropolitan | 12 | 22 | 63 | (2470) |
|   adjacent to an SMSA* | 17 | 30 | 68 | (1009) |
|   not adjacent to an SMSA | 10 | 18 | 60 | (1461) |
| All counties | 21 | 31 | 64 | (3100) |

Source: Calvin L. Beale and Glenn V. Fuguitt, *The New Pattern of Nonmetropolitan Population Change* (Madison: Center for Demography and Ecology, University of Wisconsin, Working Paper No. 75-22, August 1975), p. 23, table 3.
* SMSA—Standard Metropolitan Statistical Area.

March 1970. Based on answers to this question, the Census Bureau estimates that, between 1970 and 1975, 6,721,000 people left metropolitan areas while 5,127,000 moved into metropolitan areas.[6] This represented a gain of 1,594,000 people through migration by America's nonmetropolitan areas. By comparison, for the five-year period between 1965 and 1970, 352,000 more people moved *to* metropolitan areas from nonmetropolitan areas. Including population change from natural increase as well as internal and international migration, the Current Population Survey estimates the 1970 to 1975 population increase was 3.6 percent for all metropolitan areas in the United States and 6.3 percent for all nonmetropolitan areas.[7] Current Population Survey and county population estimates, along with the collaboration of Social Security and Internal Revenue Service records, lead to the conclusion that the metropolitan-nonmetropolitan pattern of population redistribution is real, that the phenomenon is widespread, and that it is not confined to areas immediately surrounding metropolitan areas. Clearly an increasing number of Americans are choosing to move beyond the daily influence of metropolitan living toward those areas which have historically provided the population for our cities.

## Alternative Explanations of Nonmetropolitan Population Growth

The current state of the arts on regional population growth and economic development does not provide a well integrated, high level theory to explain the recent population trends in nonmetropolitan America. Rather there seems to be several general sets of tentative hypotheses that emerge from empirical analyses, such as the county population change research of Calvin Beale and Glenn Fuguitt.[8]

One of the major theories of spatial population growth patterns is suggested in the urbanization

6. United States Bureau of the Census, *Current Population Reports*, Series P-20, No. 285.

7. United States Bureau of the Census, *Current Population Reports*, Series P-20, No. 292, "Population Profile of the United States: 1975" (Washington, D.C.: United States Government Printing Office, 1976).

8. Beale and Fuguitt, *The New Pattern of Nonmetropolitan Population Change.*

literature of human ecology.[9] The fundamental social processes which underlie urbanization are industrialization and the accompanying increased specialization in the labor force and the spatial differentiation of population and land-use patterns. Population distribution patterns are primarily affected by the migration of people in response to industrial location and residential class and ethnic heterogeneity. Consistent with these basic processes is the hypothesis of metropolitan decentralization outward from metropolitan central cities to suburban rings and beyond into "exurban" nonmetropolitan areas. From this perspective, the population spillover is largely in areas of physical proximity and accessibility to a metropolitan center with transportation routes facilitating the commuting pattern of the spillover population to work places within the metropolitan region. Consistent with this theory, Calvin Beale and Glenn Fuguitt's analysis shows that nonmetropolitan counties adjacent to metropolitan counties did increase in population during the 1970–73 period. However, the rate of population increase in these nonmetropolitan counties was not as rapid as the rate for entirely rural counties which were not adjacent to a metropolitan area. Thus, it would appear that urbanization theory provides only a partial explanation for the recent nonmetropolitan population growth trend.

A second possible explanation for nonmetropolitan population growth emerges from a related fundamental tenet of human ecology that residents in a community seek to maintain an equilibrium between their numbers and the life chance or sustenance activities presented by the social organizations within a community.[10] Thus an increase in employment opportunities leads to an increase in the size of the population that can be supported in a community. These dynamics, in turn, frequently change the pattern of in- and out-migration. Consistent with this theory is the attempt to explain nonmetropolitan population growth as a function of industrial development in nonmetropolitan areas. Again, Calvin Beale and Glenn Fuguitt's evidence suggests that nonmetropolitan counties with an above average proportion of the labor force employed in manufacturing did increase in population and experienced net in-migration during the 1970–73 period. Overall, however, the increase in industrial activities, as indicated by employment in manufacturing, is a relatively weak explanation for the newly emerging nonmetropolitan population growth trend. Nationally, the rapid increase of service industries represents the significant new area of employment opportunities, and as of yet many of these opportunities are only beginning to locate in nonmetropolitan areas.

A somewhat stronger explanation for the recent nonmetropolitan population growth is the presence of a senior state college within the county. This explanation can be seen as a long-term latent consequence of earlier decisions concerning the

9. Amos H. Hawley, *Urban Society* (New York: Ronald Press, 1971).

10. Amos H. Hawley, "Human Ecology," in David L. Sills, ed., *International Encyclopedia of the Social Sciences* (New York: Crowell, Collier and MacMillan, 1969), pp. 328–32; and W. Parker Frisbie and Dudley L. Poston, Jr., "Components of Substenance Organization and Nonmetropolitan Population Change: A Human Ecological Investigation," *American Sociological Review*, vol. 40 (December 1975), pp. 773–84.

spatial location of state supported institutions of higher education. The relative importance of this explanation for the recent population trend is closely tied to the current effects of the post-World War II "baby boom" in the United States. However, the primary causal factor in the location of the state colleges, as well as the spatial location of military bases and other governmental expenditures, is public policy decision making. The latent, sometimes unanticipated impact of public policy on population distribution in the United States is different in kind but not in its effect from the more direct population dispersal policies of many European countries.[11]

A fourth and stronger potential explanation that emerges from Calvin Beale and Glenn Fuguitt's analysis focuses on noneconomic factors which seem to attract people to counties that can be characterized as retirement and recreational areas. Frequently located near mountains, lakes, or other areas of natural beauty, the high net in-migration to these counties is consistent with the general hypotheses that residential preferences for areas with non-economic amenities are playing a significant role in determining migration and population redistribution to nonmetropolitan areas. The available evidence for counties does not permit an adequate test of this general thesis of migratory motivational factors, but we have data from a longitudinal survey which will permit us to explore the impact of residential preferences on population dispersal migration behavior.

## RESIDENTIAL PREFERENCE AND MIGRATION BEHAVIOR

The emergence of personal preference in migratory behavior is emphasized by the geographer Wilbur Zelinsky in his analysis of internal migration patterns at different stages of national socioeconomic development.[12] He notes that in the most advanced and affluent societies, residential change and movement have become a way of life. Furthermore, the most distinctive feature about migration in advanced societies is the emergence of noneconomic motivations for migration. With specific reference to America, he hypothesized "that the increasingly free exercise of individual preferences as to values, pleasures, self-improvement, social and physical habitat, and general life-style in an individualistic, affluent national community may have begun to alter the spatial attributes of society and culture in the United States."[13] The pointed emphasis on a range of individual preference factors, particularly the possible impact of residential preference factors on population dispersal was considered significant enough to be included in the deliberations of the Commission on Population Growth and the American Future.

Theoretically, residential preference is a dimension of an individual decision-making model of migration

11. James L. Sundquist, *Dispersing Population: What America Can Learn from Europe* (Washington, D.C.: The Brookings Institute, 1975); and Gordon F. De Jong, "Population Redistribution Policies: Alternatives from the Netherlands, Great Britain, and Israel," *Social Science Quarterly*, vol. 56 (September 1975), pp. 262–73.

12. Wilbur Zelinsky, "The Mobility Transition," *The Geographical Review*, vol. 61 (April 1971), p. 247.

13. Wilbur Zelinsky, "Selfward Bound? Personal Preferences and the Changing Map of American Society," *Economic Geography*, vol. 50 (April 1974), p. 144.

designed to be applicable to specific migration streams (in this case, streams affecting nonmetropolitan area population change). Two general approaches to residential preferences research emerge from the literature. The first approach examines residential preferences as a factor in housing and/or intra-urban neighborhood choice, while the focus of the second is on the issue of size of place preference and population dispersal. The interest of the Commission on Population Growth and the American Future was on this latter approach, due in large part to the results of public opinion polls which have reported for some time now Americans' strong preference for living in smaller cities, towns, and rural areas rather than in large cities.[14]

Size of place preference has been studied by Glenn Fuguitt and James Zuiches with a national sample and by the author in a report on Pennsylvania population redistribution.[15] In respect to size of place preferences, the results of these two studies are much the same in that they markedly qualify the public opinion poll conclusions. It appears that while nearly three-fourths of the

respondents do not want to live in a large city, neither do they want to live very far away from one. When respondents expressed a preference for a location by the degree of proximity to a large city of over 50,000 people, there is a marked preference for smaller towns and rural areas within commuting distance (about 30 miles) of a large city. Population growth has, in fact, taken place in these exurban residential area commuting zones, but many more distant nonmetropolitan areas have also experienced population increase and net in-migration. What emerges from this type of preference data is that, although people seem to want a small town or rural environment, they also want it to be near a metropolitan center.

### SIZE OF PLACE PREFERENCES AND MIGRATION BEHAVIOR

Attempting to relate where surveys say people prefer to live with census data on population change does not provide a direct test of the hypothesis that size of place or urban proximity preference is a factor in population dispersal migration behavior. We were able to test this hypothesis by means of a longitudinal survey of 1,096 Pennsylvania households, starting in spring 1974, of whom 227 had changed residences by the time of a spring 1975 follow-up survey.[16]

A major finding is the striking incongruity between the size of place where people say they want to live and the actual size of place of destination of their move one year

14. James J. Zuiches and Glenn V. Fuguitt, "Residential Preferences: Implications for Population Redistribution in Nonmetropolitan Areas," in the Commission on Population Growth and the American Future, *Population, Distribution, and Policy*, vol. 5, pp. 621–30.

15. Glenn V. Fuguitt and James J. Zuiches, "Residential Preferences and Population Distribution," *Demography*, vol. 12 (August 1975), pp. 491–504; and Gordon F. De Jong, "Residential Preference Patterns and Population Redistribution," in Wilbur Zelinsky et al., *Population Change and Redistribution in Nonmetropolitan Pennsylvania, 1940–1970*, Report submitted to the Center for Population Research, National Institute of Health, Department of Health, Education and Welfare, Washington, D.C., 1974.

16. Gordon F. De Jong and Ralph R. Sell, *Residential Preferences and Migration Behavior*, Report submitted to the Center for Population Research, National Institute of Health, Department of Health, Education and Welfare, Washington, D.C., 1975.

later. A total of 58 percent actually located in the central city or suburb of a large or medium-size city while only 24 percent had expressed a preference for such a size of place. By comparison, 42 percent actually located in a smaller city, village, or the countryside while 76 percent stated a preference for these size of place locations. Most of those who were able to attain their preferred size of place were movers preferring the same size of place as they lived in one year earlier. Other than these people, only 11 percent of movers preferring a smaller size of place than their area of origin were able to attain that preference. Clearly, many people who expressed a preference for a smaller city, village, or countryside location actually moved to a larger sized place, while relatively few actually moved to a smaller sized preferred location. We repeated the analysis using preferences about proximity to a metropolitan center, but the basic findings remained the same. We thus conclude that residential preferences expressed in terms of small city, village, or the countryside, or proximity to a city location seem to have little relationship to actual population dispersal migration behavior. This conclusion does not minimize the favorable orientation to rural and small town life expressed by respondents. However, the findings do suggest that the links between size of place preference statements and area destination of movers one year later are not straightforward. One of the possible explanations is that size of place categories and proximity to a large city are relatively unimportant concepts to respondents when it comes to actual location decisions. These categories may be surrogates for specific home, community, or area

attributes or characteristics which members of the household desire. It is to a test of this possible explanation that we now turn.

## Residential Preference Attributes and Migration Behavior

As part of our longitudinal survey of Pennsylvania population redistribution, respondents were presented with an extensive list of 47 preference attributes about characteristics of residential locations. These included attributes of a new house, new neighborhood, the work situation in a new location, physical and cultural attributes of a new region, and convenience attributes of a new location. Respondents were asked to indicate whether each item was a very important, important, or not important characteristic to have if they could move to a new location. Our focus is on households which moved in a nonmetropolitan direction even though some of the new residential locations are within the outer suburban or exurban parts of a metropolitan area.

To test the hypothesis that residential preference attributes rather than size of place preferences are important in metropolitan to non-metropolitan migration, we present a comparative analysis among metropolitan households that between the spring 1974 survey and the follow-up survey one year later had moved out of a metropolitan center, moved elsewhere, or did not move. Our analysis is guided by Georges Sabagh and associates' approach of identifying factors on which non-migrants may differ from movers changing locations in various directional streams.[17] Using grid coordi-

17. Georges Sabagh, Maurice van Arsdol, Jr., and Edgar Butler, "Some Determinants

TABLE 3

MEAN RESIDENTIAL PREFERENCE ATTRIBUTE SCORES AND DIFFERENCES AMONG
METROPOLITAN NONMOVERS, NONMETROPOLITAN DIRECTION MOVERS,
AND OTHER METROPOLITAN AREA MOVERS

| | MOVE STATUS | | | | |
| | | | | NONMETROPOLITAN DIRECTION MOVERS | |
| | NONMOVERS | | | | |
| | | | | | MOVERS |
| PREFERENCE ITEM | SCORE | DIFFERENCE | SCORE | DIFFERENCE | SCORE |
|---|---|---|---|---|---|
| Weighted N | 1002 | | 33 | | 90 |
| Convenience to work | 1.8 | .2 | 2.0 | .4 | 1.6 |
| Convenience to shopping | 1.6 | .5 | 2.1 | .4 | 1.7 |
| Safeness of streets | 1.4 | .2 | 1.6 | .3 | 1.3 |
| Public transportation | 1.8 | .4 | 2.2 | .3 | 1.9 |
| Cost of housing | 1.4 | .1 | 1.5 | .2 | 1.3 |
| Availability of parks | 2.1 | .3 | 1.8 | .1 | 1.7 |
| Convenience to recreation | 2.2 | .1 | 2.1 | .1 | 2.0 |
| Spaciousness of yard | 2.0 | .3 | 1.7 | .1 | 1.8 |
| Quality of schools | 1.7 | .3 | 1.4 | .1 | 1.5 |
| Availability of entertainment | 2.5 | .3 | 2.2 | .1 | 2.3 |
| Contact with people | 2.4 | .3 | 2.1 | .1 | 2.2 |
| Opportunities for culture | 2.4 | .2 | 2.2 | .0 | 2.2 |
| Convenience to church | 1.8 | .2 | 2.0 | .0 | 2.0 |

SOURCE: Gordon F. De Jong and Ralph R. Sell, *Residential Preferences and Migration Behavior*, Report submitted to the Center for Population Research, National Institutes of Health, Department of Health, Education and Welfare, Washington, D.C., 1975, table 9.

NOTE: Scores represent means of the responses to questions pertaining to how important the characteristic would be in a new home, neighborhood, or area. Response categories were 1 = very important; 2 = important; 3 = not important. Differences of greater than .2 are conservatively significant at the .1 level.

nates of respondents' postal zones obtained from a cross listing of latitudes and longitudes of zip codes, a household was defined as in a metropolitan toward nonmetropolitan stream if: (1) at the time of the first survey in 1974 the household was located in the urbanized area of a large (over 500,000 population) or medium-sized city (50,000–500,000 population); (2) the area of destination was not another urbanized area; and (3) the distance from the new location to the nearest metropolitan center was further after the move than before the move. Other movers are primarily intra- and inter-metro-

of Intrametropolitan Residential Mobility: Conceptual Considerations," *Social Forces*, vol. 48 (September 1969), pp. 88–9.

politan movers in households which at the time of the first survey lived in a large city, suburb of a large city, or medium-sized city and relocated in an area not included in the above stream. Nonmovers are those urbanized area households which did not change residence between the first survey in spring 1974 and the follow-up survey in spring 1975. During this period, 3 percent of all metropolitan area households in our sample moved in a nonmetropolitan direction, 8 percent were classified as other metropolitan movers, primarily local movers, and 89 percent did not move.

Residential preference attributes which differentiate nonmetropolitan direction movers from other metropolitan area movers and nonmovers are shown in table 3. Nonmetropolitan direction movers listed quality of schools as a most important factor to look for in a new location. Other very important factors were the cost of housing and living in the new area, the safeness of streets, spaciousness of a yard, and the availability of parks. In general, these are items for which satisfaction should be facilitated by the nonmetropolitan move. Items for which the mean preference score indicates responses tending toward the less important end of the scale are more generally the metropolitan based qualities of public transportation, availability of entertainment, and opportunities for culture.

Turning to a comparison of the 13 items which showed substantial difference between at least two of the three groups, the three items that were more important to the people who did not move represent factors which are in fact easier to satisfy in more urban environments: public transportation, convenience to shopping facilities, and, to a lesser extent, convenience to church. Nonmetropolitan direction movers reported less importance for public transportation and shopping convenience, and hence their moves in a direction which indicates less ease in obtaining these services and amenities were probably facilitated by a lack of preference for these more metropolitan based services. On the "attraction" or "pull" side, the four items for which the nonmetropolitan direction movers show the greatest preference—spaciousness of yard, quality of schools, availability of entertainment, and opportunities for contact with people—were also important to other metropolitan area movers. In other words, all metropolitan area movers have a greater preference for these factors when compared with respondents who did not move.

The data suggest a similar interpretation for safeness of streets, cost of housing, and convenience to work, which were items most important to the other primarily local metropolitan area movers. These items are least important for nonmetropolitan direction movers, with nonmovers in between. This suggests that safeness of streets is important to the more local metropolitan area movers possibly because they will stay within the metropolitan environment where presumably the safeness of streets issue is more salient. Cost of housing may be less important for nonmetropolitan movers, because, as will be shown below, these movers have higher incomes and better jobs than other movers and nonmovers. Nonmetropolitan direction movers do not consider convenience to work as particularly important, and this perhaps represents a trade-off condition they are willing to accept to live in a nonmetropolitan area.

## SOCIAL AND DEMOGRAPHIC CHARACTERISTICS OF NONMETROPOLITAN MOVERS

Because family and socioeconomic status characteristics are such important factors in mobility behavior, we analyzed selected characteristics of metropolitan nonmovers, nonmetropolitan direction movers, and other metropolitan area movers. Several rather substantial differences among the groups are evident (table 4). When compared to nonmovers, nonmetropolitan direction movers are on the average 17 years younger, have almost two years more education, are in occupations with a higher socioeconomic status, and have incomes averaging about $1,500 higher. The income figure is particularly salient since nonmetropolitan direction movers are younger and presumably have less labor

TABLE 4

SOCIAL AND DEMOGRAPHIC CHARACTERISTICS OF METROPOLITAN
NONMOVERS, NONMETROPOLITAN DIRECTION MOVERS, AND
OTHER METROPOLITAN AREA MOVERS

| | MOVER STATUS | | |
| CHARACTERISTICS | NONMOVER | NONMETROPOLITAN DIRECTION MOVER | OTHER MOVERS |
| --- | --- | --- | --- |
| Weighted N | 1002 | 33 | 91 |
| Age of head of household | 50.2 | 33.3 | 34.7 |
| Education of head (yrs. completed) | 11.2 | 14.0 | 12.6 |
| Total family income: 1973 ($) | 9,200 | 10,700 | 8,400 |
| Socioeconomic status of head | 43.9 | 59.0 | 47.7 |
| Household type (% nuclear family) | 62.3 | 83.5 | 57.4 |
| Average household size | 3.3 | 3.1 | 3.4 |
| Marital status (% married, spouse present) | 68 | 87 | 64 |
| Sex of head (% male) | 74 | 92 | 74 |
| Race (% nonwhite) | 20 | 11 | 15 |

SOURCE: Gordon F. De Jong and Ralph R. Sell, *Residential Preferences and Migration Behavior*, Report submitted to the Center for Population Research, National Institutes of Health, Department of Health, Education and Welfare, Washington, D.C., 1975, table 10.

force experience than do non-movers. Family characteristics indicate that nonmetropolitan direction movers are more likely to be headed by a male and be a husband and wife family unit without other relatives than are metropolitan nonmovers. The average household size is slightly smaller, which is reflected in the nuclear family structure. The proportion of nonwhites among these movers is only about half (11 percent versus 20 percent) that of nonmovers.

When compared to other metropolitan area movers, nonmetropolitan direction movers average only about a year younger, rather than the 17 year differential when compared to nonmovers. Since the ages of these groups are quite similar, comparisons on the remaining factors have greater meaning since, in general, income, education, and household size are all strongly related to age. Nevertheless, nonmetropolitan direction movers have completed almost one and one-half years more schooling, are in occupations over 10 points higher in average socio-economic status, and have over $2,000 greater incomes. The fortuitous control for age between the two mover groups makes these findings particularly noteworthy.

CONCLUSIONS

While size of place residential preference was only minimally related to actual population dispersal migration behavior, we have identified some residential preference attributes which characterize nonmetropolitan direction movers. A high proportion of all metropolitan area movers expressed a preference for quality schools, spacious yards, availability of entertainment, and opportunities for contact with people. However, the crucial point seems to be, what are people willing to give up in order to attain these preferences, at least some of which are associated with a nonmetropolitan environment? It appears, given the low preference strength, that people moving in the nonmetropolitan direction are willing to give up the urban based items of convenience to shopping and work and public transportation. In the process, they are probably willing to pay more for housing. It thus appears that movement to satisfy preferences is contingent upon qualities that a household is willing to forgo or can realistically expect to circumvent in the movement to nonmetropolitan areas.

The social and demographic characteristics of nonmetropolitan direction movers help to explain the findings that, although there is widespread preference for smaller-sized places and amenities associated with these places, few people can act to satisfy their preference. Metropolitan people who actually moved toward nonmetropolitan areas are probably better able to satisfy their preferences due to their higher status positions and integrated family situation which often afford less dependence on a given spatial locality. The higher average income of nonmetropolitan migrants facilitates a reliance on a private car as opposed to public transportation, and this may make less convenient shopping of little consequence. The energy-related character of the interaction between residential preference attributes, social and economic characteristics of households, and population dispersal migration behavior becomes quite apparent. However, we must caution that, as with other relationships between attitudes and behavior, it is likely that extensive research will be necessary to identify the important dimensions and circumstances through which the numerous individual and household constraints, needs, resources, and preferences interact to precipitate a decision to migrate to a nonmetropolitan area.[18]

18. Howard Schuman and Michael P. Johnson, "Attitudes and Behavior," in Alex

## THE FUTURE OF POPULATION REDISTRIBUTION IN THE UNITED STATES

Although we have touched upon some current population estimation problems which must be confronted in determining the reality of the current metropolitan and nonmetropolitan growth trends, these technical issues do not provide a basis for assessing the long-term prospects for continued nonmetropolitan population growth in the United States. Population projection is at best an art and not a science, and to engage in such an enterprise with such sketchy evidence as is currently available is to risk total repudiation. The admonition notwithstanding, it is possible to identify some of the factors that would appear to underlie a continuation of the metropolitan to nonmetropolitan growth trend for the future. Some are facilitating factors, while others have their roots in more basic structural changes in the American society.

Heading the list of facilitating factors for nonmetropolitan population growth are communication and transportation advancements which permit business and personal interaction over wider areas of space. Telecommunications, interactive computing systems, as well as modernized highways are illustrative of the factors which permit the relocation of individuals, industry, and business to places increasingly remote from centers of industrial and commercial activity. The future would seem to bode a continuation of these communication-transportation developments and with it a continued facilitating factor for nonmetropolitan population growth.

Inkeles et al., eds., *Annual Review of Sociology*, vol. 2 (Annual Reviews Incorporated, 1976).

As a higher rate of urbanization is inexorably tied to a high rate of national population growth, so a lower rate of urban population growth is linked to the current United States trend toward a zero population growth society. Rural fertility is declining, further reducing urbanward migration response pressures. A low rate of total population growth also alters the long-term age distribution of the population toward an increased proportion of older citizens and a decreased proportion of young people who traditionally dominate metropolitan direction migration streams. As was noted earlier, many retirement areas are currently in the vanguard of nonmetropolitan population increase. A forecast of a continuation of the current below-replacement level rate of national population growth cannot be made with certainty; however, there is no evidence at present to indicate a return to the post-World War II fertility pattern of more than three children per family.

A third facilitating factor for nonmetropolitan population growth is the general level of affluence of the United States population. Increased commuting costs is but one example of the trade-offs which are often involved in the move to nonmetropolitan areas. While an increase in the general level of affluence of the United States population is by no means assured in the years ahead, an enhanced level of real income seems more probable than the reverse condition.

With these facilitating factors providing a favorable milieu for continued nonmetropolitan population growth, what are some of the basic structural factors which may determine the continuation or reversal of nonmetropolitan population growth? We suggest at least five basic factors.

*Demographic factors.* Future nonmetropolitan population growth is undoubtedly tied to the depletion of the excess reservoir of farm labor which has resulted from the modernization and mechanization of the rural farm enterprise in the United States. Facilitated by the reduction in rural fertility, the excess farm labor source of past rural to urban migrants has now been sharply curtailed. Correlated with this demographic factor is the increased ability of nonmetropolitan residents to find employment in the nonfarm sectors of nonmetropolitan area economics. Continuation of these trends would portend a reduction in the gross out-migration of nonmetropolitan workers.

*Economic factors.* The sometimes erratic trend in the national and international economic system is undoubtedly an important factor in the future of nonmetropolitan population growth. Periods of high national unemployment, particularly high industrial unemployment, have traditionally been associated with the reduction in the economically motivated "pull" of urbanward migration. High urban unemployment also contributes to return migration which for many migrants involves a nonmetropolitan destination. It is certainly significant that nonmetropolitan population growth has also occurred in many European countries and Japan during the early 1970s—a time of world economic recession.

*Social-cultural factors.* The past 10 years have been difficult times for urban government and urban institutions. To many of our citizens, the result has been a lowering of the quality of life, particularly in some of the older and larger metropolitan areas in the country. The host of social and environmental issues which compose the "urban problem" have undoubtedly tarnished the "bright lights" that attracted many migrants to the cities. Severe urban problems are not characteristic of all United States metropolitan areas, however, as most cities under 750,000 population, and especially cities in the South and West, have continued an above average rate of population growth. An important parameter of future nonmetropolitan population growth may be the reemergence of the image of large cities as desirable places to live and work.

*Population distribution related policy factors.* Although the United States may not develop population dispersal policies similar to those in many European countries, the latent impact of state and national policies on population redistribution trends cannot be ignored. Regional economic developments including tourism and retirement development programs, regional variation in federal spending, urban rehabilitation efforts, land use policies, taxation policies, and racially related policy decisions and practices are but an illustrative list of the often conflicting policy-based forces which affect the locational decisions of business and industry as well as individuals and families. If the situation in other industrial nations is any guide, continued uncontrolled urbanization and significant regional economic differentiation will become of increasing policy concern.

*Residential preferences.* As we have demonstrated in this paper, residential preferences for nonmetropolitan areas are correlates of metropolitan to nonmetropolitan migration. Although it is possible that there has been a recent increased preference for nonmetropolitan areas, the more reasonable

position suggests the preexistence of such a preference structure for many Americans. However, it may be only in recent times that constraints have been reduced enough so that these preferences can be attained by some people. If this line of reasoning is correct, we would expect residential preference factors to continue to exert an influence toward nonmetropolitan population growth.

In summary, we find some factors which argue for and others against continued nonmetropolitan population growth. At present, the numerical superiority of metropolitan-to-nonmetropolitan as opposed to nonmetropolitan-to-metropolitan migration is small and significant primarily in its departure from the past trend. It is possible that the future may see a fluctuating pattern of year-to-year variation in metropolitan-nonmetropolitan population balance. Barring the potentially crippling effect of an energy crisis on nonmetropolitan residents, the medium-range prospect for continued nonmetropolitan population growth appears to be highly plausible. Such a fundamental change in the basic population distribution trend may hold some desirable, as well as undesirable, consequences for the future of nonmetropolitan America. Can the nation and the states afford to foster such nonmetropolitan growth communities and assume higher capital costs of infrastructure and the higher operating costs of providing essential services over greater distances? Who should assume the higher costs? What are the consequences for metropolitan areas in population decline? And most important, how will population redistribution affect the happiness and quality of life of Americans?

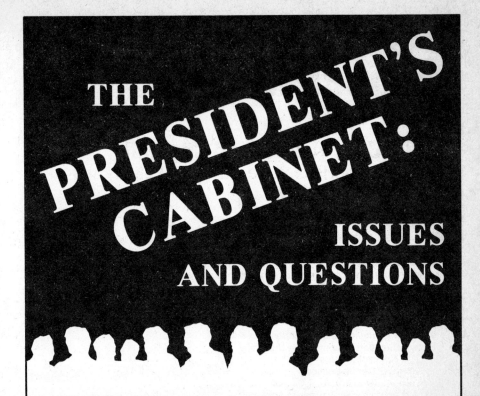

# Bright lights on the political scene.

### Morlan
## Capitol, Courthouse, and City Hall:
### Readings in American State and Local Politics and Government, Fifth Edition

Robert L. Morlan, University of Redlands
About 336 pages, paper. Now available.

Retaining the excellent balance between state and local government and politics that made the previous editions so popular, the new Morlan treats contemporary issues such as the New York City financial crisis, the growing power of municipal employee unions, and no-growth or limited growth politics in land use control.

### Jones/Ericson/Brown/Trotter
## Practicing Texas Politics, Third Edition

Eugene W. Jones, Angelo State University
Joe E. Ericson, Stephen F. Austin State University
Lyle C. Brown, Baylor University
Robert S. Trotter, El Centro College
500 pages, paper, with Instructor's Manual.
Now available. Study Guide available in April, 1977.

For the new Third Edition, Jones, Ericson, Brown, and Trotter retain the same effective balance of text and readings, but have updated the book throughout. They include new subjects such as the constitutional revision efforts of 1973-75, justice in Texas courts, money in Texas politics, and womanpower and Texas politics.

### Rouder
## American Politics: Playing the Game

Susan Rouder, City College of San Francisco
480 pages, paper, with Instructor's Manual.
Now available.

Rouder's text is designed expressly to teach students how to get the system to budge at all levels of government. An excellent preparation for effective citizenship, *American Politics* introduces the American political process in a *practical* way.

### Grieves
## A World in Conflict:
### An Introduction to International Relations

Forest L. Grieves, University of Montana
416 pages, with Instructor's Manual.
Now available.

Grieves covers the basic concepts and background necessary for an understanding of modern international relations. Students get a chance to examine the kinds of issues that concern professional political scientists. These include the nature of the nation-state, prominent theories, and the historical context of modern world politics.

144d

## The Humane Technologist

DUNCAN DAVIES, TOM BANFIELD, and RAY SHEAHAN. ☐ Because the increasing complexity of contemporary society demands that technologists consider their work in relation to present and future concerns about such topics as human behavior and organization, the environment, and the law, the authors propose a comprehensive approach for the exploration of alternative policies. (Science and Engineering Policy Series)

1976                190 pp.; 22 figs.                $10.50

## Science and the Media

PETER FARAGO. ☐ Analyzing the technical, social, and economic challenges which must be met in order to improve the flow of scientific information toward the general public, this study asks for a change in some of our social attitudes toward the ideas and embodiments of science, and for the acceptance of science as an outstanding part of our cultural heritage. (Science and Engineering Policy Series)

1976                104 pp.                $8.75

## March 1939: The British Guarantee to Poland
### A Study in the Continuity of British Foreign Policy

SIMON NEWMAN. ☐ Making full use of the new documents available, this work examines the origin and consequences of the British guarantee to Poland in March 1939. Although this study concentrates on an individual episode in the history of British foreign policy toward Hitler, the episode is used as a means of portraying a tenable, well-argued and well-documented interpretation of that policy in 1938 and 1939.

1976                264 pp.                $14.25

## English-Speaking South Africa Today
### Proceedings of the National Conference, July 1974

Edited by ANDRÉ DE VILLIERS. ☐ The eighteen papers collected here consider the contribution of the English-speaking South African to the development of the country and discuss such topics as public affairs, population and community, the economy, religion, education, language and literature, and the media. (Published for 1820 Settlers National Monument Foundation)

1976                396 pp.; 28 tables                $17.50

## The South African Economy
### Fourth Edition

D. HOBART HOUGHTON. An authoritative introduction to the South African economy for historians, political scientists, and sociologists as well as economists, this text has been extensively revised and updated to include the oil war, the collapse of the gold price, and the devaluation of South Africa's currency.

1976                328 pp.; 17 figs.; 25 tables; map                $12.25

*Prices are subject to change.*

 OXFORD UNIVERSITY PRESS
200 MADISON AVENUE
NEW YORK, N.Y. 10016

# Book Department

---

## INTERNATIONAL RELATIONS AND POLITICS

Herbert S. Dinerstein. *The Making of a Missile Crisis: October 1962.* Pp. xiv, 302. Baltimore, Md.: The Johns Hopkins University Press, 1976. $14.95.

This book is a useful addition to the already voluminous literature analyzing the Cuban Missile Crisis. It provides a detailed examination of the way in which the elites of Cuba and the Soviet Union viewed events leading to and during the crisis. Written by a distinguished student of Soviet foreign policy, the interpretation relies heavily on an exhaustive analysis of the Cuban and Soviet press of the period.

One thesis that the author develops is that the understanding that Cuban, Soviet, and United States elites derived from the overthrow of Arbenz in Guatemala in 1954 significantly contributed to how the three countries dealt with the development of the Cuban revolution. United States elites were impressed with how easily a regime could be toppled. Soviet elites saw the episode as evidence of American strength in the Caribbean, and both Soviet and Cuban elites were convinced that the United States had a strong propensity to intervene to block reform and revolution. With the memory of what had happened in Guatemala, the United States could unleash the Bay of Pigs invasion, not fearing that it would develop into the fiasco that it did. Both Cuba and the Soviet Union saw the invasion as confirmation of United States hostility toward leftist regimes, but both also saw the failure of the invasion as a sign of a shift in the balance of forces in the Caribbean and Latin America to the detriment of United States influence. Their fear of what the United States might attempt was heightened, but they also became somewhat contemptuous of the United States ability to order the course of events in the area. With these understandings, emplacing Soviet missiles in Cuba could seem to be a relatively low risk strategy for promoting the security of the Castro regime.

Emplacing Soviet missiles in Cuba could also serve other purposes of the U.S.S.R., and a second major thesis that Dinerstein advances is that there were different views within the Soviet Union about the proper course to be followed, particularly during the height of the crisis. This position is most persuasively argued by a careful, comparative analysis of the themes stressed in the Soviet Government Statement of 23 October

145

1962, and in the editorials in *Red Star*, *Pravda*, and *Izvestia* on 24 October 1962. Unexpectedly faced with Kennedy's resolve to remove the missiles, Khrushchev was prepared to back down, but there appeared to be some within the Soviet Union who wanted to challenge the United States determination, and those willing to compromise appeared to hold a spectrum of views.

Neither thesis is completely new; the contribution of the book is to provide detailed support for the arguments. The book also provides a fascinating chronology and analysis of the interaction among Castro, the *Partido Socialista Popular*—the Cuban communist party, and the Soviet Union. The Cuban revolution did not follow the Marxist-Lenist prescription for colonial countries, and eventually the Soviet Union was confronted with a self-proclaimed communist who after incorporating the PSP into his own Integrated Revolutionary Organization would purge several of the long-time leaders of the previously existing communist party. The situation could have posed a portentous dilemma for the Soviet Union, but Soviet policy appears to have promptly and pragmatically settled on support of Castro. This story has also been recounted previously, most recently in Alain Joxe's *Socialisme et Crise Nucléaire*, but never with such attention as Dinerstein has given to Soviet sources.

Because of the nature of the sources relied on in this book particularly for the analysis of Cuban and Soviet policy, much of the interpretation is inevitably speculative. Dinerstein acknowledges this, and he argues that his function is as much to raise questions as to provide answers. His attempts with respect to both purposes are wise, balanced and judicious. If one were to read only a single analysis of the famous crisis this book would not be appropriate, but it would be essential in a list of several analyses.

HAROLD K. JACOBSON
University of Michigan
Ann Arbor

MATTEI DOGAN, ed. *The Mandarins of Western Europe: The Political Role of Top Civil Servants*. Pp. 313. New York: Halsted Press, 1975. No price.

Eighteen European contributors have produced fourteen national analyses and cross-national comparative studies of eleven contemporary European political elites. Most of the difficulties and pitfalls of similar previous works (excessive abstraction, endless model building, unreasonable jargon, and prolonged description and definition) have been avoided in this well-integrated and obviously collaborative volume so ably organized and edited by M. Dogan of the *Centre National de la Rercherche Scientifique*.

In addition to a crisp and pointed introduction by the editor, there are two pieces each on the British and French high civil servants, three on Lowlander bureaucrats (two on Belgium and one on the Netherlands), one each on Italy, Switzerland, Norway, Denmark, Yugoslavia and Poland, and a highly competent comparative synthesis on attitudinal perspectives in Bonn, London, and Rome. If central public administration is the focal point, then the disturbing absence of the Brussels "mandarins" of the European Community is a minor defect of this otherwise invaluable production.

All of the essays provide the particulars on the augmented scope of modern state bureaucracy and the parallel decline of parliamentary power. The emphasis is on the economic role of government, mainly the budget process, nationalized industries and central planning, which are the basic ingredients for this massive transfer of power from legislative entities to the senior state officials. Many specific and unique factors have favored the growth of civil administrators, such as administrative centralization and ministerial instability in France, Italy's prefectoral system, the Dutch proclivity to select top bureaucrats as ministers, or the Belgian practice of institutionalizing ministerial cabinets of civil servants in quasi-political positions. Different relationships between power and politicization are evaluated, with Polish and Belgian politicized and relatively powerless administrators contrasted with the French and Swedish lack of partisanship and strong influence and power. Variants of public elites exist and are depicted, but similarities of the new technocrats appear frequently. The vast technostructure they populate appears more complex and difficult to comprehend than the mandarins themselves.

In the process of locating and dissecting top civil servants within pluralistic power structures, this book documents the decline of the traditional mandarins (the ambassadors and prefects) and the rapid ascent of the finance and business trained and oriented chiefs who control the summits of the administrative hierarchies. The essential and penetrating point about these *appointed* modern mandarins who have often displaced the *elected* politicians in many sectors of power is that they all derive their strength from the executive and importantly function as decision-makers in collectives such as agencies, commissions, boards, or committees. This survey sheds significant light on the advantages and limitations of this change in the power factor as it has moved from parliaments to executives and ministers to the top civil servants.

PIERRE-HENRI LAURENT
Tufts University
Medford
Massachusetts

CHARLES FRANKEL, ed. *Controversies and Decisions: The Social Sciences and Public Policy.* Pp. v, 299. New York: Russell Sage Foundation, 1976. $10.00.

From tentative beginnings around the turn of the century, involvement in policy making by the social sciences expanded slowly in the interwar period, becoming significant in national affairs after World War II. However, at the very time social science involvement peaked in the 1960s a series of misadventures, beginning with the aborted Project Camelot, began to call it into question. The crisis of confidence in government following upon disillusionment with the IndoChina War, the Watergate scandals and revelations of illegal activities by the C.I.A. and F.B.I. created an atmosphere of suspicion around liaisons between government and the social sciences. It is hardly surprising, in view of these developments, that a series of reviews of the promise and risks in the involvement of the social sciences in policy making have been undertaken recently. Of them *Controversies and Decisions* is without peer.

The essays comprising *Controversies and Decisions* fall into two general groups: one seeking to answer the charge from both the extreme left and extreme right, that no line can be drawn between "is" and "ought" and hence, ultimately, between science and politics; another which accepts the view that science (including social science) is an objective study of matters of fact which thrives when permitted autonomy and encouraged by an atmosphere of freedom, but which nevertheless faces grave risks of corruption when its findings are employed, as they inevitably will be, in the formation and execution of social policy.

Among the first group of essays: Charles Frankel defends the distinction between "is" and "ought" introduced by Hume and Kant and forming a tradition culminating in Max Weber; Stephen and Jonathan Cole present evidence for the role of universalistic (objective) criteria in the determination of the award system of science; Hugh Hawkins traces the uneven progress of the separation of objective social science from social reform; Robert Nesbit traces the sources of Weber's concepts of value-neutrality and academic freedom to the ideas and practices of Wilhelm von Humboldt.

Among the second group of essays: Lee Cronbach traces the career of the public controversy over mental testing; Yaron Ezrahi reviews the Jensen controversy, the recent form of the nature-nurture dispute; Paul Doty explores the ambiguities in scientific roles when they polarized on opposite sides of the Anti Ballistic Missile debate; Kenneth Boulding employs the imagery of ecology to locate the precise niche of science in the total framework of human affairs; H. Field Haviland traces the growth over time of social science involvement in public policy making; Adam Yarmolinsky formulates the contrasts in time schedules and suppositions as between social scientists and public policy makers; and Edward Shils explores problems in the simultaneous legitimation and public use of social science.

To all persons fascinated by the Faustian bargains so often struck when science makes itself the handmaiden of power, this book of essays will be of interest.

DON MARTINDALE
University of Minnesota
Minneapolis

DAVID B. ROBERTSON. *A Theory of Party Competition.* Pp. x, 210. New York: John Wiley & Sons, 1976. $15.95.

Since its founding in the early 1960s, the University of Essex has established a reputation for having a first rank political science program. In part this book is a by-product of the stimulating intellectual atmosphere associated with Essex political scientists such as Jean Blondel, Anthony King, Ian Budge, Anthony Barker, and Michael Taylor.

David Robertson's book reflects the empirical and mathematical bent which characterizes the political science curriculum at Essex. The book is a detailed re-examination, critique, and extension of the theory of party competition that Anthony Downs, an economist, formulated twenty years ago in *An Economic Theory of Democracy.* Moreover, this book reviews various subsequent refinements and interpretations of Downsian theory. Robertson contends that Downs overlooked elements essential to a theory of party competition—for example a failure to attend to the differing motives of party voters, party activists, and party leaders. The argument

is detailed, complex, and at some points, disjointed. Robertson posits several additional hypotheses to the basic Downsian theory and then proceeds to test them.

For data, Robertson uses the results of British general elections but mainly the party manifestoes (1924–1966), and the election addresses of individual candidates for the House of Commons. These are subjected to various quantitative research tools: content analysis (of themes—not individual words—in the manifestoes and speeches), factor analysis, regression analysis, path analysis, and various diagrammatic presentations. The manifestoes are the basis for examining the shifting appeals of the two major parties over a forty year period. Election addresses of candidates in 50 sample constituencies each from the 1924 and 1955 elections and the results in those constituencies are employed to examine the impact of party appeals at the level at which a voter makes his decision, that is, the constituency rather than the nation as a whole as is the case only for presidential systems. Basic to these enterprises are Robertson's dual assumptions that voters are essentially rational and that party identification is critically defective in explaining voter behavior. Overall the book is provocative and often persuasive.

Unfortunately, the book is marred by several copy errors and other inattention to scholarly detail. For example, decimal points are missing from several tables that report loadings for factor analysis; the notation or numbering system for chapter subjections is inconsistent and confusing; there are numerous spelling errors such as Herig for Henig (pp. 36 and 210), cannons for canons (p. 141), Eysack for Eysenck (p. 56), and Duvergar for Duverger; and the citation form—the author's name followed by publication date in parentheses—makes the reader a slave to *passim* if he wishes to pursue the citation. Finally, there is no index, which greatly limits the reference quality of the work.

Despite these flaws, specialists in voter behavior and democratic theory should peruse the book. Those who are uncomfortable with quantitative methods can easily absorb chapters 1, 2, 6 and the three appendices.

T. PHILLIP WOLF
Indiana University Southeast
New Albany

ARTHUR ROSETT and DONALD R. CRESSEY. *Justice By Consent*. Pp. xiii, 227. New York: J.B. Lippincott Company, 1976. $10.00.

This is an excellent primer on plea bargaining for pre-law and law enforcement students, recent law school graduates and those inexperienced persons concerned with the daily functioning of the American criminal justice system. Plea bargaining is one of the most important and controversial issues of the day. The authors, a professor of law and a professor of sociology—two of the nation's most prominent scholars, point out that ". . . of the one hundred adults arrested on felony charges and arriving at the front door of an American courthouse . . . only two or three will be escorted out the back door . . . to a state prison" (p. 34).

Each chapter deals with a different aspect of plea bargaining. For example, Chapter 4 discusses the role that judges perform. Chapters 5 and 6 describe the special problems of prosecutors and public defenders. Chapter 8 is of special importance for it systematically rejects the principal demands for reform of plea bargaining advanced by its critics. Finally, all eight chapters are cleverly linked by describing in each chapter the daily experience with plea bargaining of an imaginary person who had been arrested and charged with burglary in the first degree.

There is one significant disappointment that requires some discussion. The authors mistakingly equate plea bargaining, the administration of justice with rendering justice. They attempt to persuade the reader that negotiation and compromise, the etiquette necessary for successful plea bargaining, constitute justice. Justice is reduced to mere form or procedure. The substantive aspects of justice such as sameness of treatment,

impartiality and predictability are ignored.

Plea bargaining is never recognized for what it is, simple arbitrariness. And arbitrariness has always been the antithesis of sameness of treatment, impartiality and predictability. This arbitrariness forces an accused person to stand helpless before the authorities. His or her fate is determined by expediency, rather than more noble societal values. The rule of law is imperiled. In conclusion, if this work is to be really beneficial, the reader ought to have first read a first-rate philosophical treatise on the meaning of justice. John Rawl's *Theory of Justice* (1971) is an excellent example of such a work.

J. F. HENDERSON
Ohio University
Athens

JOHN D. STEINBRUNER. *The Cybernetic Theory of Decision: New Dimensions of Political Analysis*. Pp. xi, 366. Princeton, N.J.: Princeton University Press, 1974. $14.50.

John Steinbruner has attempted something laudable but difficult: to construct a general theory and then to show that it illuminates a complicated event. The theory is cybernetic decisionmaking; the event, the rise and demise within the NATO alliance of the multilateral nuclear force (the MLF). The book is divided evenly between a theoretical discussion of three paradigms of decisionmaking (the analytic, the cybernetic, and the cognitive) and a careful, rich reconstruction of the MLF debacle from 1956 through 1964. Others may disagree, but I do not find that the MLF case demonstrates the validity of the cybernetic paradigm for analyzing how large, fragmented, competitive, executive bureaucracies deal with intractable foreign policy problems. It is not that the theory has no utility whatsoever (although, as will be argued below, I find the theory to be counter to the political essence of statecraft); but rather that the MLF case substantiates the theory only weakly and, indeed, perhaps not at all.

In the theoretical section, Steinbruner

focuses on two central facets of foreign policymaking: first, how decisionmakers cope with the uncertainty of their craft; second, how they deal with the ofttimes inherent conflicts among the goals they pursue.

In dealing with uncertainty, Steinbruner follows the tradition of Simon, March, and Lindblom. He rejects what he calls the analytic paradigm (what Simon called "economic man" and what Lindblom called "synoptic rationality") because it requires that statesmen, in order to make decisions, have perfect or nearly perfect information about their circumstances. The analytic paradigm does not accurately describe the way decisionmakers operate because it stipulates conditions that cannot be met. It is the second requirement of the analytic, paradigm, however, with which Steinbruner is centrally concerned. The heart of his theory is this: a decisionmaker does not integrate values; instead, he separates them. The failure to construct tradeoffs occurs both because of the complexity of the issues to be analyzed and because of the strivings of the human mind toward consistency in its beliefs. Statesmen can handle complex issues only by breaking them down into their simpler component parts and then by giving each part to the organizational subunit most knowledgeable with its intricacies. These units will analyze the component part according to their standard operating procedures, which means that they will consider only a few, highly selective variables and will provide solutions that protect or enhance only their vested organizational interests. Partial solutions based on selective analysis and on vested interests are not likely to yield careful tradeoffs among conflicting goals. Modern governments, by nature fragmented, thus facilitate value separation.

What governmental institutions separate the human mind does not put back together. When told that there is an inherent conflict among his goals, either a stateman will deny that such a conflict exists by arguing that the goals are unrelated to one another; or, he will assert that the goals are supportive by arguing that the attainment of one will facilitate the attainment of the other(s). Outright denial is more common than rationalized support; both occur because the mind strives toward consistency (harmony) among its beliefs. Thus, the cybernetic part of Steinbruner's theory tells us that top level decisionmakers by necessity must parcel out complex problems to subunits that consider only a few variables when choosing from among options. The cognitive part tells us three additional things: first, these top level statesmen initially make categorical judgments about what is desirable and attainable; second, subsequent evidence to the contrary is not likely to alter those judgments; and, third, therefore, when faced with conflicts among the partial solutions offered to them, decisionmakers will not construct the careful tradeoffs necessary for an optimal solution.

Does the MLF bear out the postulate of value separation? Consider the two value problems that NATO presented to American presidents from 1956 through 1964. First, Eisenhower, Kennedy, and Johnson wanted to maintain (or acquire, depending on your perspective) centralized (American) control over any nuclear war that NATO might fight; second, they wanted to respond in part to the Europeans' desire to regain autonomy over their own fates and in particular to assuage their doubts over America's nuclear guarantee to them, doubts that were generated by Russia's presumed lead in nuclear forces and then by America's flexible response doctrine. (The emphasis on conventional defense in flexible response seemed to Europeans to cast doubt on the reality of the American nuclear umbrella.) Centralized, presidential control over the use of nuclear weapons was designed to minimize the chances of nuclear war occurring and to keep damage to a minimum if it did occur. The attempt to redress Europe's loss of independence was designed to preserve the cohesion of the NATO alliance and to halt or reverse the proliferation of nuclear weapons among its member states. The first goal, however, conflicted with the second. The only way the Europeans could truly regain their sense of independence from the United States would be to acquire or augment their own nuclear forces. America's continued control over Europe's fate was at loggerheads with America's attempt to aid Europe in regaining control over its own fate. It was impossible to proliferate and not to proliferate nuclear weapons with the same policy.

The MLF attempted the impossible. America would assist the Europeans in developing a European nuclear force, but she would retain a veto over its use. The original proposal made by the Kennedy Administration required that any MLF which materialized be integrated fully with America's strategic nuclear forces (the retention of the American veto); but it also promised that the United States would be flexible on the issue of control over firing (the relaxation of the American veto). There was a rationale to this apparent madness: once the Europeans became deeply involved in planning the details of a joint nuclear force, they could be educated by the Americans into the horrors of nuclear war, into the need to maintain rigorous, deliberate control over it should it occur, and, consequently, into the need for centralized (presidential) conduct of it. The MLF offered many different things to many different people; but to Kennedy it offered a chance to resolve his NATO dilemma even though he always remained dubious of the MLF's chances of success.

Were there any alternatives to the MLF? This is not an idle question. Before one can dismiss the MLF as a poorly constructed policy, one must present a viable alternative. Steinbruner presents only one, but then promptly offers compelling evidence for rejecting it. Rather than sharing nuclear weapons the Administration could have shared nuclear information, such as its targeting plans and intelligence data. Presumably, this was done beginning in 1965, after the demise of the MLF. Why not before? Steinbruner states that such candor was rejected out of fear that it would heighten, not diminish, the Europeans' desire for their own nuclear forces.

Sharing information risked ". . . opening up for stark review the vulnerability of Europe to Soviet IRBMs" (page 212). By 1965 or 1966, the United States would have enough ICBMs to target those IRBMs; but in 1961 and 1962, it did not.

When viewed together with America's massive ICBM buildup, the MLF does make some sense. It was a device that might have bought time until America could confront the Europeans with her massive superiority. By itself, it might even have moved the Europeans to acquiesce more completely in their dependence on the United States. The MLF and the massive American buildup of ICBMs in the early 1960s were two integrated responses to a difficult problem: how could the United States completely persuade the Europeans that it would come to their defense even in the process it would subject itself to devastation. That the MLF did not work perhaps suggests, not that its assumptions were faulty, but that the problem was irresolvable. To assert, then, that the proponents of the MLF did not squarely resolve the inherent conflict between stemming nuclear proliferation within NATO and enhancing Europe's sense of autonomy misses the central point. The MLF was an attempt to straddle a conflict for which no solution was then available. It was a policy that deliberately tried *not* to make an explicit tradeoff, but to slide, fudge, and waiver as much as the political conditions would allow. Steinbruner has missed the *political* point of the MLF in his attempt to make the facts fit his psychological theory.

Finally, if the cybernetic-cognitive paradigm does not work for the MLF case, will it work for others? Obviously, no definitive answer can be given; but I offer two general reflections. First, the cybernetic aspect of the theory reduces to the question of whether American Presidents are institutionally prevented from making coherent policy amidst executive fragmentation. If Presidents cannot control their bureaucratic underlings, then they cannot begin to make tradeoffs. I have written elsewhere on this subject and have not found the evidence to be persuasive that a President cannot have his way with his *executive* subordinates on those issues that he deems crucial to his presidency. Second, the cognitive aspect, although intriguing, strikes me as counter to the spirit of politics. After all, politics is the art of the possible. Whether domestic or international, politics means making compromises. And that, by definition, consists in consciously confronting value conflicts and in carefully constructing the optimal tradeoffs. And even when we find no evidence that this has been done, there is always the additional reflection: the true political animal will be vague and ambiguous when he senses that decisiveness and clarity can be dangerous to him.

ROBERT J. ART

Brandeis University
Waltham
Massachusetts

BARBARA WARD. *The Home of Man.* Pp. xii, 297. New York: W.W. Norton, 1976. $8.95.

In 1972, Lady Barbara Ward Jackson and Dr. Rene Dubos prepared the definitive report on the state of the human environment for the Stockholm Conference Secretariat. The ensuing volume, *Only One Earth: The Care and Maintenance of a Small Planet*, established the conceptual framework for the U.N. Conference on the Human Environment. *The Home of Man* provides an overview of the issues with which Habitat, the U.N. Conference on Human Settlements, dealt at Vancouver in June 1976.

Lady Ward points out that it is extremely difficult to get a "coherent" grip on the issue of the human habitat because (1) the habitat includes everything; and (2) never before has the man-made environment been in such a state of "convulsed and complete crisis." The greatest wandering of the people is taking place at a time when mankind has a clearer vision of equality and human dignity for all people, when they are much more aware of the limits of the environment. She estimates that 1,-500,000,000 people will pour into the world's cities between now and the year

2,000 A.D. How will they be provided with housing, food, jobs, and essential services? How will the destitute villages be given new purpose, vitality and expanded vitality? Essentially, the book is divided into six parts beginning with the advent of the city, and then moving swiftly into the city as we know it today. She then treats of the technological order, the poor world's settlements, the problems of management, and the universal city.

As Mr. Penalosa writes in his introduction, "*The Home of Man* is a synthesis of Barbara Ward's writing, teaching and lecturing, in which she has so eloquently pleaded for a new understanding of the interdependence of peoples, for planetary management of both the human and the natural environment, and for the moral as well as economic justification and need for a new world order." She observes that if we accept the goal of a world order designed to secure a fairer distribution of the planet's resources and to put an end to concentration of wealth, within and between nations, which are incompatible with human justice, dignity and self-respect, we must then determine the instruments, scale and priorities. Until the necessary institutions are in place and functioning, "life for man on earth, life in his settlements, rich and poor, North and South, in village or megapolis, must remain a haunted danger-shadowed uncertain risk." Nevertheless, however muddled the outlines may appear, a new international economic order, "aiming at justice and cooperation, is, quite literally, a matter of life and death."

Lady Ward writes from a broadly philosophical, but undogmatic and practical point of view. She buttresses her position with a solid command of the pertinent data at hand. This is a challenging book which should be read and pondered not only by students of sociology, economics and politics, but by statesmen who presume to lead us in consideration of the basic problems of the contemporary world, and by the general public. That alone, of course, will not lead to solutions of problems — but it could point to ways and means.

Where there is no vision, the people perish. There is much vision in this volume.

HARRY N. HOWARD
Bethesda
Maryland

DAVID WILKINSON. *Revolutionary Civil War: The Elements of Victory and Defeat.* Pp. vi, 229. Palo Alto, Calif.: Page-Ficklin Publications, 1975. $6.95. Paperbound.

Civil wars are usually long, intense, and violent combats among large, organized forces struggling to control a state. Although the best cases of this type of "internal warfare" belong to the 20th century (especially in Mexico, China, Spain and Russia), this phenomenon is not a new one; it appears and reappears across centuries as well as across cultures.

Because revolutionary civil wars are long, large, organized and polarizing conflicts they portend a drastic change of regimes and of foreign policies; they influence foreign states and attract foreign interventions. The United States, interestingly enough, has involved itself in several such conflicts, and as Wilkinson points out, "without success or distinction" and frequently "without understanding their characteristic features."

The study of the outcomes of such wars is less advanced than the study of their origins, although it raises such engaging questions as: Why do wars end as they do? Why do the winners win and the losers lose? Wilkinson directs himself to the question of the causes of victory and defeat in revolutionary civil wars, and abstracts and synthesizes historians' and observers' explanations for victories in eight revolutionary civil wars fought in several countries, in several areas, by factions with widely diverging political complexions. The eight cases are: Rome (83–82 B.C.); England (1642–46); Mexico (1914–15); Russia (1918–20); China (1926–28 and 1930–34); Spain (1936–39); and China (1946–49).

After presenting these eight cases, Wilkinson then covers Political Factors (Resources, Time, Leadership, Strategy, Program, Organization, Political Work, Political Control, Mobilization and Political Base); Military Factors (Position, Leadership, Strategy, Organization, Security of the Rear, Troops, and Supply); and Analysis (The Model Loser, the Ideal Victory, the Dilemma of the Moderates, and the Question of Strategy).

While the text covers 129 pages, 80 pages are devoted to Appendices, Notes, and Bibliography. This indicates the richness of the sources Wilkinson has consulted (especially Sorokin, Edwards, and Brinton—in addition to others). Fortunately, we cannot even summarize many of his hypotheses and conclusions. Some of them could be easily questioned; but, at any rate, they are very interesting.

JOSEPH S. ROUCEK
City University of New York

*AFRICA AND ASIA*

SUFIA AHMED. *Muslim Community in Bengal, 1884–1912.* Pp. 425. Bangladesh: Oxford University Press, 1976. Tk. 85.00.

The author teaches in the Department of Islamic History and Culture at Dacca University. Her book is an expanded version of a London thesis accepted in 1960. Despite the many hardships which her community has recently undergone, the author has made good use of her years since London, and we can recommend her book to libraries which have a special interest in Islam, South Asia and the sociology of religion. Her material, drawn in the main from London archives, is divided into five big chapters: (1) educational developments, (2) economic conditions, (3) social and political activities, (4) partition of Bengal and (5) Muslim writings in Bengali. The author's principal contribution appears at the very end of her long book—that the Muslims of Bengal, if they felt themselves to be distinct from the Hindus, also felt themselves to be distinct from other Muslims in India (p. 374). The author's path to this conclusion, so fateful for Pakistan's prospects, forces the reader to go through a sudden change of direction which centers around the Arabic concept of *adab* (belles-lettres, good manners, and the like). The author never mentions *adab*, nor does she underscore the relevance to her community and its history of the Muslim class system, but she deals with these matters as her documents would have them dealt with, namely, by way of the importance of Urdu in Bengali Muslim education. The Muslims, thus, are first seen as standing fast in their loyalty to Urdu ("... whatever the poorer classes might speak, they wished Urdu to be the medium of instruction in their schools," p. 28), but in her important chapter on literature the author records the names of numerous Muslim authors who wrote in standard Bengali and who made it an acceptable medium even for the orthodox. The author performs an important service by describing this change in the appeal of literary Bengali, but she does not try to explain it. Perhaps there can be no satisfactory explanation until the map of Muslim humanism in South Asia has been better drawn, but there have been attempts worth consulting, such as Mahmud Shah Qureshi, *Etude sur L'Evolution Intellectuelle chez les Muslmans du Bengale, 1857–1947* (Paris, 1971).

Numerous printing errors will have to be corrected in the book's second edition, but these do not mar the author's basic achievement at the present time.

MORRIS DEMBO

University of Pennsylvania
Philadelphia

ADDA B. BOZEMAN. *Conflict in Africa: Concepts and Realities*. Pp. xiv, 429. Princeton, N.J.: Princeton University Press, 1976. $27.50. Paperbound, $12.50.

RICHARD HARRIS, ed. *The Political Economy of Africa*. Pp. ix, 270. New York: Halsted Press, 1975. $15.95. Paperbound, $6.95.

At first glance these two books appear so different that one wonders how they could be handled in the same review. What they have in common—at second glance—is that each questions conventional "Western" ways of analyzing and evaluating our political and economic relationships with Africa. Bozeman argues that African folkways have not been adequately understood by the West, a failure which has had profound implications in both the colonial and postcolonial eras. Harris and his authors, on the other hand, would argue that the West has understood Africa too well, and that we have taken undue economic and political advantage through our superior knowledge.

The Bozeman book does not have a political axe to grind; it is scholarly, explanatory and analytical of ways in which conflict is handled differently in Africa from the West. The Harris book, on the other hand, is avowedly political; it is grounded on left-wing doctrines.

Bozeman cites three principal distinctions between African and Western modes of conflict resolution. The first relates to literacy. Not only have African societies not long been literate, but merely creating a way of writing does not materially alter thought processes that have been moulded by non-literacy. Abstract intellectual activity cannot evolve in non-literate societies, and precise records of past events are not possible. Non-literacy leads a society away from positivism. The second distinction relates to time, which Bozeman declares is circular rather than linear in African societies. The past, present, and future; the dead, the living, and the unborn, become inextricably mixed, as if all existed simultaneously. The third relates to tribalism and kinship patterns. Non-literate societies must be small and self-sufficient if they are to endure.

From these three principles, Bozeman develops a set of propositions which she believes are common to African societies and which differ from Western concepts. In the West, the predominant view is that all wars are avoidable and all conflicts can be solved. In African societies, she argues, war is a norm, and disputes need not be resolved. The British made the mistake of believing that African tribes

were the analog of European States, and
that treaties would bind. They discovered tribes to be fluid, dividing and
re-forming in different patterns, often
migratory. Treaties did not bind, and it
was difficult to pin down authority and
responsibility.

Order and disorder are seen in Africa
as functions of magic, power, and death.
Since all human beings come from a
superior magical order, all are suspect as
potential carriers of evil forces. This
characteristic would obviously affect the
manner in which commerce and industry
are carried on, and raise the question of
the minimum amount of trust necessary
for fruitful relationships.

Although Bozeman is less categorical,
and more qualifying, than may appear in
the short space allotted for this review,
even so her opinions are bound to be
challenged in the liberal West. Now that
we have presumably passed the Spencer-
ian age of believing in "superior" and
"inferior" cultures—only different
ones—it will come as a shock that a
Professor of International Relations in a
prominent American college points to
African cultural characteristics which—
though the author does not say so
outright—could readily explain under-
development, instead of by lack of
capital or modern skills.

It is, furthermore, not a large step to
conclude that modern economic
analysts, in applying macro models, are
repeating the errors of the British in
attributing certain behavior patterns to
the Africans. Yet the Bozeman book is
well documented, and it is worthy of
serious, if disquieting, consideration by
Western scholars.

Of an opposite bent is the book by
Harris. In addition to an introduction by
the editor, it contains articles on Ghana,
Nigeria, Zambia, and South Africa, and a
comparative analysis of Kenya and Tanzania. Harris's opening salvo attacks the
prevailing Western notion that "modernization of the underdeveloped countries . . . . has been impeded by a variety
of obstacles and conditions within each
of the underdeveloped countries." He
draws his model from the left-wing
economist, Andre Gundar Frank, with

virtually no modifications or further
development, only repetition of left-
wing arguments that have already been
heard ad infinitum. Harris writes of how
British colonialism disrupted African
society by the slave trade (p. 5), in
contrast to Bozeman who points out that
the slave trade was a way of life in Africa
from the seventh century (p. 125).

Fortunately, some of the authors that
Harris picked (not all of them) partially
redeem the book for him. The essay on
Ghana (by Emily Card) is informative
and objective in its criticisms, which are
aimed at capitalist and socialist
economic theory alike. The author is so
balanced in her writing that it is difficult,
finally, to see how she arrives at her
"socialist type" conclusions. The essay
on Nigeria (by Barbara Callaway) is also
objectively written. Although "political
economy" is written into the title, it is all
politics and no economics. It contains an
informative description of the events
leading to the Biafran secession. The
essay on Kenya/Tanzania (by Lionel
Cliffe) is too rambling; it should have
been further edited. It contains no
economic analysis but depends on the
author's faith that socialism is superior to
capitalism. No studies are cited that
demonstrate effectively that Tanzania
has had a more worthwhile experience
than Kenya, although the author asserts
that this is the case. The article on
Zambia (by Dennis Dresang) contains
some useful facts in the history of
Zambia's independence, but it is superficial. Once again, there is no economic
analysis, and the case for "dependence"
is far from made. The article on South
Africa (by Martin Legassik) is highly
informative on political events. One does
not have to be a socialist, however, to be
convinced that South Africa is a country
of oppression, and the author has a field
day listing the evil things that the
government has done to the Blacks. The
non-socialist reader, however, would
remain unconvinced that South Africa
constitutes a "typical" case of capitalistic
oppression; therefore, it may have been a
bad choice for the volume.

Furthermore, the author uses language
of insinuation (such as the "alliance of

gold and maize"). He makes sinister those productive activities (for example, mining and farming) that other would find laudable. Is it not the manner in which they are conducted, rather than the activities themselves, that is sinister? The author should be more careful in sorting out one from the other.

In sum, the Bozeman book is a scholarly, but unsettling, effort to analyze the conflict mechanism in Africa, which has implications far more widespread than are carried by the author. The Harris volume reiterates much of left-wing rhetoric concerning the economic imperialism of the West. Its principal virtue is the amount of factual information and political (not economic) analysis that it contains.

JOHN P. POWELSON
University of Colorado
Boulder

JOHN F. CADY. *The United States and Burma.* Pp. vi, 303. Cambridge, Mass.: Harvard University Press, 1976. $17.50.

At the end of World War II, the Harvard University Press inaugurated a new series of original studies of foreign countries, under the editorship of Sumner Welles. Its goal was to produce a clearly written, unbiased authoritative work on a specific country "to give Americans a reliable and objective basis on which to do their own thinking about foreign policy. . . ." The authors, for the most part, were already established authorities on their particular country. The texts were presented without footnotes or specific references and the greater portion was given to examining the history, culture, institutions and economy of the country; only a small section, usually at the end of the volume, was devoted to a review of the relations of the particular country and the U.S. Within that frame of reference, the latest addition, John F. Cady, *The United States and Burma*, meets all the established criteria. It is essentially a history of Burma with only meager references to its relations with the United States. For the most part, it repeats in somewhat condensed form what Cady wrote nearly two decades ago in his well-documented and well-received *History of Modern Burma* (Cornell University Press) with the addition of two new chapters devoted to the events of the last decade and a half.

As so many in this series before it, this volume fails in its discussion of the particular country's relations with the U.S., past and potential. The present editor of the series, Edwin O. Reischauer, acknowledged in his preface that "Burma has never loomed large in American eyes, nor is it likely to do so soon." However, this can only become meaningful if Burma is placed in its Southeast Asian context and as the near-neighbor of China and India, Laos and Thailand. Given its location and its determination not to be drawn into the "cold war" of the United States and the Soviet Union or to become a pawn of its larger neighbors, it is vital for anyone seeking explanations to know why Burma's neutralism apparently succeeded, while that of Laos and Cambodia failed. For the reader more interested in internal politics than in foreign relations, the problem of how Burma struggled with the issue of uniting several ethnic minorities into a nation or how Burma managed to live for nearly thirty years with Communist and multi-ethnic insurgency, there is little in this study to answer the questions.

For anyone unfamiliar with Burmese history before independence, this is a good introduction. It is unfortunate that Cady's editor did not encourage him to depart from the series' format and develop a fresh approach which would have allowed him to use his rich knowledge of early post-war U.S.-Burma relations, or to draw more fully on his personal experiences as a teacher and researcher in Burma. For this reviewer, it is this that should have been at the center of this study and not what we have been given.

JOSEF SILVERSTEIN
Rutgers University
New Brunswick, N.J.

CHARLES GRINNELL CLEAVER. *Japanese and Americans: Cultural Parallels and Paradoxes.* Pp. ix, 290. Minneapolis: University of Minnesota Press, 1976. $12.75.

Comparative study as a method is employed in many fields although one will find few serious efforts in which several disparate dimensions of two cultures are carefully juxtaposed and analyzed for similarity and dissimilarity. More frequently such a study will focus on only those elements of concern to a particular discipline or will be preoccupied with some fundamental comparative model.

Professor Cleaver's effort may indeed have its limitations in terms of orthodox methodology and he admits a personal limitation in terms of language capability. Nonetheless, Americans and Japanese alike will benefit from this fascinating study of their two cultures. Cleaver looks at the folkways, mores, arts, social attitudes, symbols, work habits and living accommodations as media for discovering mutual likenesses and differences.

The author's approach is to examine within a general topic the symbols and attitudes of the respective peoples. He relies on both his own observations and those of others as manifest in literature, academic writings and related resources. He then seeks to crystallize as finitely as possible the relative characteristics of the two peoples and cultures. For example, in his chapter on "The Old Environment: Nature" he metaphorically concludes as follows, "The Japanese marriage to their homeland has lasted for a long time, and their infidelities, their flirtation with gaudier mistresses have been of relatively short duration. Yet their wife is frailer than the Americans'. The Americans' land is robust, but their attentions have been rapine, and their affection has never been unambiguous. And they seem less eager to swear off dalliance with shiny profits. Both peoples must necessarily change their ways, or their old wives will curl up and die."

As can also be deduced from the above quotation, Professor Cleaver regularly inserts a note of doom unless the two peoples repent their "wicked" ways. Perhaps this tendency causes some disservice to his effort in that some of the elements of beauty and value in the two cultures are thereby subdued or reduced in their appreciation.

Still and all, this study is valuable and insightful and provides both scholar and layman a resource for reflection and introspection. In the reviewer's judgment the greatest weakness is the author's lack of knowledge of the Japanese language, for with that added element he could have refined his appreciation of the nuances of the different perspectives. Yet, to criticize for this reason does not do justice to what is nonetheless a worthwhile study.

ARVIN PALMER
Northland Pioneer College
Taylor
Arizona

MICHAEL LIPTON and JOHN FIRN. *The Erosion of a Relationship: India and Britain since 1960.* Pp. xv, 427. New York: Oxford University Press, 1976. $32.50.

The main argument of this richly detailed and spirited book is that throughout the 1960s there was an accelerating, many-sided and to some extent avoidable erosion of good relations between Britain and India. The authors (both academic economists at British universities) contend that since 1960 most of the main linkages—trade, capital flows, population movements, publishing connections—have been severed, or at least severely weakened. And they strongly, and repeatedly, deny that this erosion is either the inevitable consequence of decolonization or still less it is inexorably the result of deliberate skillful redesigning and diversifying of their policies by the two countries. Indeed, one of the authors' main contentions is that Indo-British disengagements have stemmed in large measure from mutual disenchantments, misperceptions and drift, through "inattention rather than intention," and have been carried far beyond what might have resulted from a sustained and genuinely practical calculus of mutual interests, even from a calculus which accorded due weight to Britain's growing links with western Europe and India's desire for real diversification and increased self-reliance.

It is, of course, arguable that 1960 represents no important watershed in Indo-British relations comparable in any way with 1947, or even 1956 or 1973. The authors are most concerned, however, to measure as clearly and fully as possible, displaying their methods and evidence fully in the process, the elements of entwined interest which in the 1960s bound, and which could and in their view should continue to bind, the two countries together. While Lipton and Firn are aware of the ambiguities of "interest" and know that it is ingenuous to believe that peoples and politics always maximize their interests—for they often fail to conceive and calculate them with clarity and accuracy—there is, none the less, at times a neo-utilitarian touch of overweening rationalism about their analysis. The powerful negative side of the authors' argument is to stress—and lament—the triumph of in-advertence and drift. Their more important and valuable positive contribution is, however, to document and measure, wherever possible, the changing condition of Indo-British relations throughout the 1960s; and this they do in greater depth and detail than has ever been done in any publication hitherto.

Their last, thirty-page, chapter, entitled "Indo-British Relations in a Divided World, 1960–80," attempts prognosis and prescription as well as description, and somewhat anxiously and queru-lously adopts a moderately optimistic note.

This book was written mostly between mid-1974 and mid-1975 and asserts on its last page of text (p. 236) that there is "at present [a] fairly favourable Indo-British *political* climate." This was before the declaration of the Emergency and Mrs. Gandhi's incumbency coup. There is much material provided in this book with which to contest the authors' conclusions as well as to substantiate them.

PETER LYON
Institute of Commonwealth Studies
University of London
England

RAUL S. MANGLAPUS. *Philippines: The Silenced Democracy.* Pp. ix, 205. Maryknoll, N.Y.: Orbis Books, 1976. $7.95.

This is a disturbingly disappointing book and not well written to boot. At a time when considerable attention is focussed on the Philippines with the renegotiation of our bases agreement with the Marcos regime, the fate of democracy and human rights in the Philippines deserves better treatment than has been given by the President of the American-based "Movement for a Free Philippines." Unfortunately, Manglapus is somewhat typical of those in opposition to Marcos. He blames the United States—not the Filipino—for Marcos' rise to power and the continua-tion of martial law in the Philippines. He criticizes Marcos for the abuse of human rights—as well he should—and for an unfinished land reform program. But Manglapus, like others in opposition, has yet to put forth serious suggestions for programs which might help solve the monumental problems which must be tackled if the Philippines is to survive—population, economic growth and the redistribution of wealth. What he seems to be saying is that Marcos has been in power long enough, let us in opposition have a crack at the power and wealth that go with traditional rotation of political rule in the Philippines.

Manglapus devotes considerably more space to criticism of the U.S., its values and leadership than to a hard look at Philippine problems. He, as with so many other Philippine leaders, finds it much easier to blame the United States for all of the ills of the Philippines rather than face the unhappy truth that Filipinos are captains of their own fate.

It is perhaps significant that two thirds

of this book is a reprint of a musical play "Manifest Destiny" which Manglapus wrote while at Cornell. The play itself reflects some superficial research into the 1898–99 period when the United States began its colonial rule in the Philippines. In this metier, Mr. Manglapus shows that he is better at writing off-color limericks than handling banners at the barricades. His lively interest in his female characters makes one wonder whether Imelda Marcos some day might not be able to charm Manglapus into giving up his comfortable "refugee status" in the United States and to return to the Philippines where at one time he did indeed give noble service to his country and the cause of freedom.

In the meantime, Mr. Manglapus may be expected to continue his efforts to convince us that we can start solving the problems we created in the Philippines by cutting off all aid to the Marcos regime.

Unfortunately neither Manglapus, other political opposition leaders nor the church show convincing signs that they or the Philippine people are sufficiently riled up over the loss of human rights, the absence of democracy, corruption or any of the other abuses attributed to Marcos, to really do much about it except philosophize and blame someone else for their woes. At this time the Philippines does not appear to be ready to pay a very high price to return the voice to democracy.

Harrison Salisbury's foreword is a good shorthand rendition of our relations with the Philippines although he too attributes to the U.S. Government greater support for, and satisfaction with, the Marcos regime than the record warrants.

LEWIS M. PURNELL

Rehoboth Beach
Delaware

ROBERT M. MARSH and HIROSHI MANNARI. *Modernization and the Japanese Factory.* Pp. vii, 437. Princeton, N.J.: Princeton University Press, 1976. $27.50. Paperbound, $11.50.

WILLIAM BRUGGER. *Democracy and Organization in the Chinese Industrial Enterprise, 1948–1953.* Pp. v, 374. New York: Cambridge University Press, 1976. $27.50.

This sociological study of Japanese modernization questions the extent and success of the "paternalism-lifetime commitment Japanese factory model," claims that "the most successful firms have in fact moved in the direction of a more modern organizational structure and will continue to move in this direction... [and] those firms that have not... will suffer significant organizational strains," and gives greater weight to the impact of "universal" organizational elements than to "Japanese" characteristics in the effective functioning of enterprises. The Japanese "miracle" of swift, robust economic growth after World War II and into the seventies is seen as the consequence of technological convergence of Japanese industry toward a modernized social organization rather than to any set of cultural and institutional facts.

These conclusions are inferred from nine months' field work divided among three large main Japanese firms (electric, shipbuilding, and sake companies) in which observation, consultation, analysis of firm records, personnel interviews, questionnaire response from production, staff and managerial employees provided quantitative data (subject to multivariate statistical analysis) as well as the ethnographic context. The authors were concerned with several theoretical questions on the modernization process: How much convergence of technology without convergence of social structure in organizations can there be? Which organizational type maximizes effectiveness? To what degree do culture and social history, on the one hand, and organizations' technological and structural characteristics, on the other, explain attitudes and behaviors of factory personnel?

Professors Marsh and Mannari, in seeking understanding from their data, attempt to relate technological modernization, the modernization of social organization, and organization results of industrial manufacturing firms and their operating units. Toward that end their research deals elaborately with salient dimensions of the factory: formal structure, systematic procedures (rules), division of labor, status structure, economic and social rewards, social integration (employee cohesiveness, paternalism, recreational participation, company identification, conflict, interfirm mobility, and lifetime commitment norms and values), job satisfaction, work values, technology, and performance. For each firm, detailed questionnaire answers were secured covering each of these structured elements. The book's chapters follow the above structured elements in exposition. Four appendixes set forth: the research methods, construction of indexes of the above elements of social organization, correlation matrices, and multiple regression analyses.

Since the authors do not claim either that their three firms were selected at random or that they are representative of large firms in general, in their industry or not, their study primarily describes and explains in great detail patterns of social organization, attitudes, and behaviors in the firms studied. In this context the study provides a wealth of material and insight on these three Japanese factories. Unquestionably much of what is described and explained has relevance for large Japanese plants in general, just as much may be valid only for the three firms. Understanding the process of modernization in Japanese industry cannot help but be advanced by this thorough work, if used carefully, not only from the wealth of information, but also for the unanswered questions that must be pursued by other researchers who deal with the modernization process in Japan and elsewhere. This reviewer wonders, however, how, on the basis of the three firms' patterns, the convergence theory can be so strongly upheld and the paternalism-lifetime commitment model equally strongly rejected. After all, sustained Japanese economic growth rates, significantly higher than in numerous other advanced industrial societies, cannot be explained

primarily by convergence toward the social organization of economies such as the United States with markedly poorer industrial performance. Similarly, significantly lower Japanese unemployment rates than those in the United States most probably can be related to important institutional differences in the two cultures.

*Democracy and Organization in the Chinese Industrial Enterprise, 1948–1953* goes considerably beyond its title, and its author provides perceptive descriptive analysis of salient strategies and tactics of the Chinese Revolution reflected in industrial organization and control from 1948 to 1953. Focusing on the Chinese Communist Party's (CCP) attempts to implement a new factory system embodying revolutionary objectives and based on a Soviet model, the author throws light not only on groping efforts to fashion a proletarian industrial society, but also on the process and thinking that led ultimately to a rejection of the USSR's example.

Dr. Brugger's approach is broadly sociological and political but he also considers important economic issues and deftly puts the CCP's socialist modernization attempts in the comparative context of Russian, Japanese, and pre-revolutionary Chinese industrial experience. Then he analyzes insightfully the political environment in which CCP industrial organization policy and practice unfolded from 1948 to 1953. The control scheme for rational socialist industrial organization in its planning, accounting, and incentive aspects is then critically described followed by an appraisal of the curbs developed on managerial bureaucratism and authoritarianism.

The author's major theme—that the CCP's attempted implementation of a Soviet organizational and motivational model conflicted with pre-1949 Chinese patterns—poses significant questions answers to which clarify our understanding of the Chinese development strategy process. There was a contradiction between CCP policy for democratization and organization of factories and the limited human resources available; the Soviet model being copied was unclear; there were further contradictions between different leadership types and the handling of internal conflicts; the Soviet and Chinese approaches to planning, motivation, and organization were quite different. Dr. Brugger infers that "there existed within the [Chinese] Communist Party a tradition of 'centralised leadership and divided operation,' a genuine commitment to participatory democracy and an attitude towards conflict that was not merely 'suppressive.' . . . this tradition conflicted with the [Soviet] model of organization. . ." (p. 258).

The alien Soviet model was never really put in operation and the CCP attempt failed. The result was that the Chinese were forced to shape their own organizational process and in the Great Leap Forward and Cultural Revolution (CR) the pre-1949 tradition was a principal source for mechanisms and tactics experimented with in factories and mines in the rejection of the "one-man management" model. The author sees some hope for the Chinese realizing democratic industrial organization based on worker participation during the CR and expanded since and the extension of CR-developed "creative" approaches to education that undermine the mystique of the expert.

CHARLES HOFFMANN
State University of New York
Stony Brook

ALFRED C. OPPLER. *Legal Reform in Occupied Japan*. Pp. xx, 345. Princeton, N.J.: Princeton University Press, 1976. $20.00.

As an autobiography, this book provides appropriate and interesting reading. However, as a source of much new information for the legal scholar, it hardly fulfills one's expectations. It deals largely with the well-known bureaucratic method of reaching conclusions about disputed legal points, sets forth the author's estimate of his colleagues and expresses his own opinions on numerous political and non-legal topics. No more

than about one third of the material relates directly to "Legal Reform in Occupied Japan" but that part is worthwhile, is clearly and intelligently presented and is implemented by reference to some actual cases in Japanese courts.

The author states that the present Japanese Constitution, which was fathered by the American Occupation Authorities, adopted by the Japanese Diet and provided for legal reform, "merely pushed forward existing reforming and liberalizing trends that would have effectuated similar results although at a slower tempo," but he fails even to intimate how slow that tempo might have been. He emphasizes that the retention of the institution of the Emperor eased the acceptance of new democratic ideas by the Japanese people. This reviewer when Chief of the Japanese Staff, Property and Institutions Section of Foreign Economic Administration had also advocated this course. The current independence of the Judiciary is noted as well as the facts that largely because of the Japanese traditional respect for judges, the jury system was not imposed and the Revised Codes display inquisitorial as well as adversary traits. The author's evident understanding of and empathy with the Japanese people most likely did help to avoid excessive Americanization of the Japanese legal system. As he rightly claims, the success of the American Occupation legal staff can be judged by the fact that the implementing legal and judicial reforms have remained virtually unchanged although they could have been abolished or revised by a simple majority of the Japanese legislature.

ALBERT E. KANE
Washington, D.C.

ROBERT M. PRICE. *Society and Bureaucracy in Contemporary Ghana*. Pp. 275. Berkeley: University of California Press, 1975. $12.50.

In his book, Price sets out to prove through a series of surveys something which is obvious to the observer of Ghana—or almost any transitional society—that individuals in governmental roles are torn between loyalty to the system of government and to the family background from which they came. He describes the alternatives as "universalistic" and "particularistic." The universalist will adhere to standards of ethical behavior which do not differentiate between the applicants for the services he can provide. The particularist will be motivated to act in accordance with traditional patterns which will mean in practice aiding those to whom he has ties of family, clan or tribe.

In determining the behavior of Ghanaian civil servants, Price surveyed three groups. First he interviewed civil servants themselves. He then talked with university students, many of whom would be candidates for government positions and who then were among the "consumers" of the services of government employees. His third group was a segment of the general population in order to ascertain impressions of civil servant behavior. In general, the questions, notably those to the civil servants, were (1) what would you do in a particular situation, and (2) what would you expect others to do in the same situation. He found, not unexpectedly, that even among the most highly educated civil servants there was a lingering of particularistic behavior and a higher degree of expectation of particularistic behavior on the part of others. Among university students there appeared to be a level of idealism with respect to their own future behavior, but a more realistic attitude toward the behavior of others already in office. The third group tended to think in terms of traditional patterns when they required services from government officials. None of this strikes the reader as exceptionally original.

The development of the theme is labored and the writing turgid and prolix. In good dissertation form, many pages are devoted to a review of the literature with ritualistic citations of sources from Max Weber to the present. The samples are small and are not scattered throughout Ghana. This is defended, with justification, by mention of limitations on time and funds. It could perhaps be further justified by noting that Accra is, after all, the center of much governmental activity and holds a cross section of Ghana's population. However, it seems almost certain that a study of the local government level would show higher particularistic behavior and expectations.

There must be some doubt as to the knowledge of Ghana itself on the part of Price. For example, he concentrates on family relationships but appears (pp. 98–99) to miss the matrilineal character of most Ghanaian tribes when he seems uncertain about an explanation of a person in the mother's side of the family receiving greater preference than a "closer" relative on the father's side. He does bury an explanation in a footnote, but one would think this would be a primary consideration which was worthy of closer examination. In his limitation to family ties, he does not look at wider tribal affiliations which are also important, that is, in dealing with a consumer of his own tribe as opposed to one of a different tribe would the civil servant tend to give preference to his tribal colleague. The record seems to indicate that he does, but this is not considered by Price. Also he has come rather late to the realization that wives of government officials often have their own sources of income (p. 157).

The book is useful so far as it goes. There is too much attention to the jargon of the subject and the topic warrants exploration of broader aspects than it has been given.

CRAIG BAXTER

Accra
Ghana


## EUROPE

MICHAEL HECHTER. *Internal Colonialism: The Celtic Fringe in British National Development, 1536–1966.* Pp. xviii, 361. Berkeley: University of California Press, 1975. $15.75.

In the period from the annexation of Wales (1536) to the 1966 British census, Hechter concerns himself with the relative merits of diffusion and internal colonial models of national development as exemplified in the British Isles. He starts by maintaining that the "current flourish of national consciousness among cultural minorities in advanced industrial societies poses something of a sociological dilemma." It is only a dilemma to those who have assumed it "to be endemic to the early stages of national development" (p. 15). Thus he devotes himself arduously to the support of internal colonialism at the expense of diffusionism even though both are demonstrably operative, and he fails to take into full account the extent to which ethnicity and religious organization can grow out of or substitute for class-based struggles.

This work highlights contrasts between certain types of historical studies and of sociological studies based upon historical data. Hechter appears impatient with the uniqueness of events, with historical ambiguities, and with changing banners and rationales for intergroup and especially interclass competition, domination, and conflict. He sets up and tests quite specific and simplified models and hypotheses. His book is thus cluttered with repetitious theorizing to maintain favored conceptions that will presumably withstand social change and to compare alternative hypotheses that can be contrasted only after oversimplified definition of their terms.

He finds "problematic in complex society ... the social conditions under which individuals band together as members of an ethnic group" (p. 37). This becomes especially problematic because of the limited definition he gives to "culture" as "a set of observable behaviors which occur independent of a group's relationship to the means of production and exchange" (p. 312)! Few cultural anthropologists would accept that limited viewpoint, but it enables him to place "ethnicity" in a setting of such a notion of "culture" rather than as one of the guises of intergroup and interclass domination and conflict in society.

Perhaps if Hechter had devoted more attention to the machinations of the elites controlling the evolving core of the United Kingdom, he would not have concluded that "very little is known ... about the prevalence of ethnocentric attitudes towards inhabitants of the peripheral regions on the part of key decision-makers. This kind of information may be worth pursuing" (p. 347). It might, indeed.

ALFRED MCCLUNG LEE
Brooklyn College of the City
University of New York

JOHN ROBERTS. *Revolution and Improvement: The Western World, 1775– 1847.* Pp. xii, 290. Berkeley: University of California Press, 1976. $20.00.

Tolstoy, in the second part of the epilogue to *War and Peace*, was ironically amused by modern history's belief that the aim of the whole historical process was "the welfare of the French, the German, or the English people, or its highest pitch of generalization, the civilization of all humanity, by which is usually meant the peoples inhabiting a small northwestern corner of the great mother-earth." John Roberts, Fellow and Tutor in Modern History at Merton College, Oxford, continues in the tradition held suspect by Tolstoy and affirms that what happened in Western Europe between 1775 and 1847 determined the subsequent destiny of the globe. The world is seen as following in the wake of Western Europe's history much as the small fishing boats of Ireland, packed with impoverished emigrants, captained by skippers who knew no navigation, waited, in the latter half of the nineteenth century, in the sea lanes of the North Atlantic to follow the great steamers to the New World, and into an unknown port after the great ships had dropped anchor. Roberts is not, however, concerned to establish in any detail how the West altered the world, but rather to reflectively analyze the cumulative and irreversible changes taking place in Europe and America in the seventy-two years ending in 1847.

Roberts is sensitively aware that the developments he charts occurred at different rates and times throughout

Europe. What matters to him is the reshaping of Europe that began on the eve of the American and French revolutions and was fixed by the eve of the revolutions of 1848. It is the great merit of his work to deftly, and in very brief compass, identify the cluster of changes that transformed the European state systems, politics, ideology, economy, rural and urban existence, collective mentality. His principle of organization is that of a series of thresholds passed sequentially within specific time zones by the states of Europe. The crisis of the old order, the *ancien régime*, provided one such common experience, the French Revolution another, and the urbanizing, industrializing commencements following 1815 offered the final gate into modernity.

A work of synthesis is rarely original in each of its parts and Roberts' book is no exception. His originality lies in his skill at juxtaposing the common and uncommon experiences of the European states and in holding together and linking events and trends seldom captured in a single frame. His dexterity astonishes and delights the reader upon whom no great demands are made. However, the reader may at times be less artful than the author when, for example, he is required to dodge, in the space of a paragraph, from contemplating the bright prospects of American expansion in California to considering the mournful plight of Poland at the half-way mark of the nineteenth century. It is not possible to object to Roberts' conclusion that by 1847 the Middle Ages was over for great parts of Europe. His wit and balance evoke admiration and it is churlish to observe the absence of profundity or of theoretical surprises. This history enlarges the reflective opportunities of its readers and admirably fulfills the intention of its author.

EDWARD T. GARGAN
University of Wisconsin
Madison

LAWRENCE SCHOFER. *The Formation of a Modern Labor Force: Upper Silesia, 1865–1914.* Pp. xvi, 207. Berkeley: University of California Press, 1975. $12.00.

HENRY WEISSER. *British Working-Class Movements and Europe, 1815–48.* Pp. viii, 226. Totowa, N.J.: Rowman and Littlefield, 1976. $17.50.

The Great Transition from rural, agricultural societies to urban, industrial types has been the subject of innumerable studies by economists, historians and sociologists over the past hundred years. Professor Schofer's study of the formation of an industrial labor force makes a contribution to some neglected considerations of this complex social process. The focus of this analysis is Upper Silesia, a region of southeastern Prussia defined on two sides by Russia to the east and by Austria-Hungary to the east and south. The area is important because it represents one of Germany's principal mining and smelting centers pre-1945.

The author begins with a *detailed* description of the economic setting covering its geography, geology, demography, labor force profile, and general entrepreneurial orientation. Moving quickly through an account of ethnic and geographic origins of the labor force, the main topic—the dynamics of the shift from the land to industry—is introduced. Here Schofer, concentrating on the mining and smelting industries, provides some insightful accounts of the multiple forces operating on the industrial labor market: The relationship between the landless and the landholding peasant to industrial employment; the recruitment process; the paternalism of the entrepreneurs; the problems of labor turnover and absenteeism; strikes; and finally, the evolution of a "modern labor force," which is implicitly defined as one which has reconciled itself to labor discipline and orderly behavior.

Emerging out of this wealth of detail is one main thesis. The author is at pains to argue that if one is to understand a modern labor force, it is imperative to adopt a multicausal historical framework, but does not place any particular emphasis on the conventional wisdom which sees early Labor exploited at the hands of avaricious Capital. Schofer argues that ". . . one can probably better comprehend the evolution of a modern labor force by regarding labor-management relations not merely as an adversary process but as a mutual learning experience for both groups in a total industrial context" (p. 138).

Professor Schofer's position is, to say the least, not shared by most students of early Labor-Capital relations — particularly those of Marxian persuasion. We can agree with his perception that new forms of analysis are needed to move social historians beyond "The working-class - labor - unions - conditions - of - the - workers structure" (p. 2). However, if we are to be convinced of this unusual thesis, it is going to take a broader data base than one anomalous case-study of one nonrepresentative industry. Case studies are of limited generalizability to begin with, and Upper Silesia is more problematic than most in this respect. Constraints on a free flow of labor from the surrounding areas is one major typical feature; the ethnic relations between the German and Polish workers of that period is another—as we will see when we examine Professor Weisser's study of the working classes in Europe at that time. In summary, it would seem reasonable to say that while Schofer offers some interesting hypotheses for further empirical investigation, the case for a generalization about the formation of a modern labor force remains to be made.

Comparing the two books, Professor Weisser's work is by far the more intellectually stimulating of the two. The setting is London during the tumultuous years, 1815–48, when the working-classes experienced an explosion of consciousness in both Britain and Europe. Here is a classic example of the dialectical process of class development as the various groups and individuals interact in moving the working classes of Britain and Europe toward the possibility of breaking out of their traditional "false consciousness" and into a "class for itself."

The role of the "ultra radical press" is treated in great detail. During the period under study, some sixty radical news-papers were in circulation for various periods of time. As outlets for radical organizers, these newspapers had tremendous influence in building and sustaining an internationalist perspective among the hitherto provincial British workers. The structure of political events on the Continent in the 1830s is shown to have been a major cause of the emerging international worker's movement. The July revolution in France (1830) is chosen as the beginning of a mature class consciousness. Weisser traces the contagious excitement generated by this uprising of the French workers for the political awareness of Britain and the rest of Europe. Belgian and Polish revolutions follow in rapid succession in the same year. Soon ". . . the Polish cause became a magnificent source of entertainment and interest for the British workers, and eventually served as a catalyst to bring together proletarian internationalists, exiles of various nations, and foreign intellectuals" (p. 48).

Among this great collage of social activists were the distinguished personalities of Karl Marx and Friederich Engels, both Germans who were to become the key figures among the architects of the internationalist platform. This platform soon became organized in the Chartist movement, a monumental social movement which originated in 1836 with the London Working Men's Association—a rather provincial organization of craftsmen dedicated to intelligent and balanced reform. Given the impetus provided by events on the Continent, the LWMA soon blossomed to the Chartist International with all of the ambitions implied by the grandiose name: ". . . emancipation of the producing classes, not only in Britain, but throughout the universe" (p. 72).

Professor Weisser skillfully communicates a sense of the electric ferment which surrounded the growth and development of the Chartists and its progeny, the Fraternal Democrats. The open rallies with banners "rippling in the breeze," vitriolic manifestos of the working-class, goals of emancipation— they all unfurl as a fascinating serial. Out of this gigantic internationalist undertaking came the Communist League, the famous (infamous) Communist Manifesto and socialist ideology which would eventually command a third of the world's allegiance. Sadly, the pacifism and brotherly sentiments which were central to the original movement floundered in the face of the nationalism typifying today's political arenas.

This essay can be credited with making a significant contribution to the literature of class consciousness. A particular strength can be attributed to the causal connections Weisser was able to demonstrate between the structure of the British and European political conflicts and the social-psychological consequences of their aftermath. Though clearly written for specialists in 19th century British history, this work is a fine addition to the libraries of economic historians and sociologists interested in early working-class dynamics.

THOMAS J. RICE
Denison University
Granville
Ohio

TONY SHARP. *The Wartime Alliance and the Zonal Division of Germany.* Pp. 220. New York: Oxford University Press, 1975. $19.25.

Tony Sharp of Dundee has converted his long doctoral thesis into a scholarly account of a significant topic which has been so far not fully understood. What was understood was the political aspect of the various wartime diplomatic conferences. What has been lacking was a study of the military context of the wartime diplomacy on Germany. The author has made a very exhaustive recitation of the military aspects of wartime diplomatic negotiations over occupied and divided Germany. He has combed through not only all the principal published materials in documents and secondary works but he has gone through the recently opened Foreign Office and Cabinet papers. In addition to this he has interviewed and/or corresponded with many of the main personalities in the decision making processes who are alive. Among them are U.S. Generals R.W. Barker and John H. Hildring; U.S. diplomats John J. McCloy and Robert Murphy; and British diplomat Lord Strang. Several of their assistants were also contacted.

The narrative presented is a long involved story which tells the interactions between military strategy and diplomatic negotiating. It is a maze of detail, difficult at times to follow but there for the curious reader to ferret it out. One of the misconceptions of some writers who followed the WWII diplomatic jockeying about the occupation of Germany was that the division of Germany was fairly well sealed by the European Advisory Commission setup in London in October, 1943. This was certainly far from the truth. Before then and ending with the final zone protocol of July 26, 1945, much transpired. One gets the picture of Roosevelt, Churchill, Stalin and de Gaulle all jockeying for positions involving political aims. Juxtaposed alongside these was Eisenhower stressing the military and nonpolitical objectives to have a complete and speedy victory. The fact was that in all the discussions about zones of occupation in Germany, enclaves in the northwest part of Germany and the sectors of Berlin, there was the transcending factor of military operations whose exact outcome neither Stalin nor the western generals knew precisely. Perhaps one of the most uncertain of the WWII allied leaders about the timetable of victory was Stalin himself. He did not know how fast his armies could push back the Nazis. This variable was also dependent on how fast the British and U.S. armies could move into Germany and how far they could penetrate in a specific time period. Tony Sharp shows how Stalin was concerned about legitimizing Soviet occupation of Berlin early in the game lest the western allies would get there first. The author takes the reader through a huge mass of detail concerning all the strategic planning and main military operations in the western front. He tells how the U.S. got the Bremen enclave and how Roosevelt thought about circumventing the support of U.S. forces in Germany through another route than through

France. He shows how indefinite were the zones that were to be given to the western allies, as to which was to get the northern part and which the southern part of Germany. He gives fascinating details on how the French secured their zone of occupation out of the American zone. He tells the history of how the sectors in Berlin were agreed upon as well as how many other thorny problems of occupation planning were decided.

This book is not easy reading, but it is a commendable study, impartial and objective and serves as a definitive reference book on what happened.

By giving summaries and conclusions at the end of the chapters, the author would have facilitated the task of the reader. Perhaps a popular edition of this encyclopedic work would rectify these minor shortcomings of this most welcome study.

WILLIAM B. BALLIS
University of Michigan
Ann Arbor

DENIS MACK SMITH. *Mussolini's Roman Empire*. Pp. xii, 322. New York: The Viking Press, 1976. $12.95.

Denis Mack Smith, Fellow of All Souls College, Oxford, has presented us with another of his lively, provocative studies of Italian history. This most recent contribution is an "essay" on the major facets of Mussolini's foreign, colonial, and military policy from 1922 to 1943, with particular attention devoted to the last half of that period. The author's theme is "how Mussolini deliberately and even carefully steered his Fascist movement into imperialism and into a succession of wars which eventually left Italy prostrate" (p. v). Mack Smith's prior assumption is that the nature of Mussolini's political career is better revealed by what Fascism became than by how it began. Thus the book is a study of political and military defeat and the reasons for that defeat; at the same time, it is a study of the effectiveness and dangers of propaganda. When the Duce in the final months of his life mused on his own triumph and defeat, he would

not concede that he had any major responsibility for what had gone wrong. Mack Smith, on the other hand, quite correctly places most of the blame for these disasters on the dictator himself.

*Mussolini's Roman Empire* is an excellent piece of scholarship at the expense of the Duce's ludicrous side. It is the result of careful study of a great number of memoirs, diaries, Fascist publications of the time, secondary works, and the photostat files of the *Segreteria particolare del Duce* which were seized by the Allies at the end of the war and are preserved at St. Antony's College, Oxford. The book will interest a broad range of readers and provide history teachers with innumerable examples of the Duce's bombast and inconsistencies to enliven their lectures. Its abundant footnotes, which unfortunately have been relegated to the back of the book, will be of much assistance to other scholars.

The author quickly skims over the 1920s, since those years have been thoroughly researched by Alan Cassels and others. For the later years, however, much more research needs to be done, and Mack Smith has made a noteworthy contribution to this period. His book significantly supplements such major studies in English as those by George W. Baer on the Ethiopian war, Elizabeth Wiskemann, Mario Toscano and others on the shaping of the Axis and the Pact of Steel, and F.W. Deakin on the years 1942–45. Difficulties remain. It is not yet easy to consult the records of Italian government departments for the 1930s. Historians are also handicapped by the fact that in Italy no official investigations of the conduct of World War II were undertaken comparable to those that took place during and after the first world conflict. Moreover, Fascism (or its memory) continues to be a burning political issue in Italy, making dispassionate historical investigation difficult at best. This fact has recently been underscored by the vigorous polemics (in which Mack Smith has participated) that greeted publication of the fourth volume of Renzo De Felice's massive "biography" of *Mussolini il duce: Gli anni del consenso, 1929–1936* (Turin: Giulio

Einaudi, 1974), a study which takes Mussolini and his regime in these years considerably more at face value than does Mack Smith's book.

*Mussolini's Roman Empire* brims with fascinating revelations. Among the most interesting are those pertaining to the brutal and often racist nature of Fascist colonial policy in Libya and East Africa. The policies pursued in Libya are discussed at greater length, however, in the important study by Claudio Segrè, *The Fourth Shore: The Italian Colonization of Libya* (Chicago: University of Chicago Press, 1976), which came out while Mack Smith's book was already in press. While Mack Smith does not claim to have presented an exhaustive treatment of Fascist foreign policy, it is nevertheless somewhat surprising to find almost no mention of relations with the Holy See. Several volumes of Vatican documents pertaining to World War II have now been published, and the reviewer's "Pius XII, Italy, and the Outbreak of War," *Journal of Contemporary History*, II, No. 4 (October, 1967), has some relevance to Mack Smith's discussion of events leading to Italy's entry into the conflict.

CHARLES F. DELZELL
Vanderbilt University
Nashville
Tennessee

JOHN M. STARRELS and ANITA M. MALLINCKRODT. *Politics in the German Democratic Republic*. Pp. vii, 399. New York: Praeger Publishers, 1975. $22.50.

It is still a real challenge to apply structural-functionalism à la Gabriel A. Almond to one of the countries behind the Iron Curtain. John Starrels and Anita Mallinckrodt have done so with regard to the economically most modern of the people's republics, East Germany, and produced a remarkable contribution to the Praeger Special Studies in International Politics and Government. Relying heavily on East German publications and writers of the official state party, the SED (Socialist Unity Party), the authors have succeeded in constraining the Communist waterfall of words and the myriad of impressions of this extraordinary system in strictly functional categories. The resulting analysis constitutes a challenge not only to the materials but also to the structural-functional framework which tends to give systems more logic and rationality than they may really possess. The book is full of the newest information and revealing glimpses, such as on the representation of women in public office (pp. 101–102), or of the interface between private and public life which is crucial to the understanding of any Communist system. The description of elections in the German Democratic Republic (pp. 154–156) and other aggregation and persuasion processes is pithy and eschews the kind of critical comment that has often taken precedence over factual knowledge in other Western accounts. The only criticism that comes to mind is the failure of this structural-functional model to account for the international environment (except for a few pages of straight narrative at the end) of the East German Republic to explain the extent to which this system can be considered "a penetrated system" or an example of the dependency model. This omission is all the more surprising since at least one of the authors has elsewhere written most knowledgeably about the foreign policy of the DDR. Apart from this omission, however, this book is a major systematic contribution that fills a gap of long standing in our knowledge of this rising industrial power. One can only hope that it will be made available in paperback for classroom use soon.

PETER H. MERKL
University of California
Santa Barbara

JOHN M. STEINER. *Power Politics and Social Change in National Socialist Germany: A Process of Escalation into Mass Destruction*. Pp. viii, 466. Atlantic Highlands, N.J.: Humanities Press, 1976. $22.50.

This book is a historical maverick, unclassifiable, methodologically eclectic, eccentrically organized, irritatingly repetitious, and fitfully brilliant. The author, former Auschwitz inmate and witness to some of our century's more ghastly events, has a definite point of view and many strong things to say. Striving to understand the psychological and social reality of National Socialism, he roams far and wide, on and off the beaten path, foraging and trespassing for deeper insights. In the end I think he brings some interesting quarry at bay.

The source material for this book includes extensive readings in the social sciences by authors such as Adorno, Arendt, Durkheim, Erikson, Fromm, Goffman, R.D. Laing, C. Wright Mills, Ortega y Gasset, Rathenau, and Weber; most of the basic Nazi literature; memoirs and diaries of Nazis, anti-Nazis, and survivors; and unpublished interviews, biograms, and 450 questionnaire protocols submitted to former members of the SS and German Armed Forces. All this material is presented in a somewhat discursive, unsystematic manner. Theories protrude throughout the empirical data. How, where, and when the author acquired the suggestive SS and Wehrmacht interviews is never clearly revealed. And yet it is evident the author is a sound scholar, careful with his evidence and attentive to ambiguities.

The first part of the book deals with a social psychological theory of power, ideology, political crime, and bureaucracy. Then comes the most significant section of the study. Taking the SS as an example of a totalitarian bureaucracy, Steiner delves deeply into the institutions, ethos, and "life styles" of these members of the black-shirted Nazi elite. It's a gruesome story of organized fanaticism and calculated terror. What Steiner brings to the often-told record is a conceptual framework that enables him to explain—quite effectively—the function of morality and honor in the SS, the unconscious meanings of racial discriminations, and the role of the "new religion" in the Nazi *Weltanschauung*. How these syndromes of ideological morality were projected outward into other Nazi institutions and the German bureaucracy, how they escalated into rationales for the "Final Solution" of the Jewish problem: these parts of the horrible story are vividly portrayed in terms of the sociology of deviance and accountability.

It is no easy task to come to terms with the ideas in this book. There are searing, agonized discernments scattered on nearly every page. Curiously the author fails to use H.V. Dicks' recent book on *Licensed Mass Murder: A Socio-Psychological Study of Some SS Killers* and Florence Miale and Michael Selzer, *The Nuremberg Mind*. He also neglects Gitta Sereny's *Into That Darkness*, a fascinating depth-psychological portrait of Franz Stangl, former Commandant of Treblinka. But Steiner's work gives historians new and valuable perspectives on old and dastardly deeds.

RICHARD M. HUNT
Harvard University
Cambridge
Massachusetts

DAVID VITAL. *The Origins of Zionism*. Pp. i, 396. New York: Oxford University Press, 1975. $22.00.

Zionism was described in 1906 by Solomon Schechter, Dean of the Jewish Theological Seminary of America, as "the declaration of Jewish independence from all kinds of slavery, whether material or spiritual. . . ." Evolving in the late 19th century, it gripped the imaginations of small groups of intellectual pioneers concerned with the "Jewish Question," and grew rapidly, largely under the impact of successive anti-Semitic developments in the world at large. It achieved its climactic success in 1948 with the establishment of the State of Israel, although "for a full third of all Jews the State of Israel came too late."

This work concentrates on the "origins" of Zionism in the period 1881–97, from the onset of Russian pogroms to the convening of the first Zionist Congress. Mr. Vital emphasizes that "the genesis of the Zionist movement occurred in the period immediately subsequent to, and to a large extent as a consequence of, the events of the years 1881–84 in Russia . . ." (p. 65). The pogroms as Russian governmental policy convinced both the ghettoized and the assimilationist elements of East European Jewry that the solutions to their problems would have to be sought outside Russia. Flight to the West (notably America) was the major option, but other alternatives were fostered as well, among them—the Zionist idea and movement.

Vital traces the development of the nascent Zionist movement—the *Hovevei Zion* (Lovers of Zion)— following the publication of Dr. Leo Pinsker's powerful manifesto, *Autoemancipation!* At its founding meeting in Kattowitz in 1884, it resolved to support the trickle of settlers and settlements in Palestine, to deal with the various governmental bodies, and to coordinate the activities of its constituent societies. After its initial enthusiasms, however, it began to fade and languish, as did the colonies in Palestine.

Occasional pockets of Zionist sentiment appeared in Western Europe at the same time, but these were largely composed of expatriates from the East, and as such made little impact on the indigenous population. Vital describes the roots of Western Zionism essentially as a "malaise," a disillusionment with the inadequate place of Jewish identity in the modernized social setting.

Zionism was thus going nowhere—in east or west—when Theodor Herzl burst onto the scene, in 1896, with the publication of his *"The Jewish State."* Assuming personal leadership of both arms of the movement, he welded it rapidly and forcefully into a significant new force in the Jewish world, and ultimately in the international community as well. Learning quickly that the western philanthropists were not receptive to his "political" Zionism, and that the Eastern Zionists were suspicious of his assimilated background, Herzl determined to call an international Zionist organization into being by convening a Zionist Congress of delegates in Basel in 1897. The rest is history.

Vital provides an in-depth social and intellectual history of this brief 16 year span and documents thoroughly his contention that this period was a decisive watershed in shaping the parameters of the subsequent stages of the Zionist movement. Such later issues as political initiatives versus philanthropic benevolence, socialism versus private enterprise, a state versus a protectorate, massive immigration versus cultural upgrading, immigration to America versus immigration to Palestine, secularism versus religiosity, open debate versus circumspect caution, ideology versus eclecticism; all of these were active considerations during this period and are dealt with in thoroughgoing fashion in this work.

In this type of scholarly analysis, one can easily create the impression that the pioneer *Hovevei Zion* were too cautious, limited and fearful (p. 160), that the western Zionists were too mercurial and out of touch with their respective realities (p. 228), and that Herzl was simply not sufficiently equipped to handle the great mandate (p. 260, 318). Vital, however, allows his material to speak for itself in its dramatic implications and achievements, and offers his personal, concluding judgment that

. . . it seems beyond question that this movement for revival and radical change in Jewry did attain results which may fairly be called revolutionary and, further, that its definitive form dates from 1897. For that reason alone the First Zionist Congress must now be judged one of the pivotal events in the modern history of the Jews.

HERBERT ROSENBLUM
Hebrew College
Brookline
Massachusetts

## UNITED STATES HISTORY AND POLITICS

THOMAS J. ARCHDEACON. *New York City, 1664–1710: Conquest and Change.* Pp. 197. Ithaca, N.Y.: Cornell University Press, 1976. $9.75.

In this book Professor Archdeacon has tried to apply methods currently associated with the study of pre-Revolutionary American communities and analysis of nineteenth century ethnic politics to research on late seventeenth century New York. His thesis is that the English conquest of New Amsterdam produced major economic and social changes which were reflected in ethnic political rivalry between Dutch and English culminating in Leisler's Rebellion of 1689. For Archdeacon, Leisler's Rebellion was a Dutch protest movement supported by those longing for older, better days before the English conquest. This thesis seems unsound and is not sustained by the author's own evidence. Archdeacon's analysis of earlier community studies in which he attempts to root his own work is partial and tendentious. More alarming, however, is his assumption that nineteenth century ideas of nationalism and national identity are applicable two hundred years earlier. His work shows little understanding of seventeenth century Dutch society and he ignores recent authors who have questioned whether a distinctly Dutch society existed in New Netherlands in 1664. Indeed the three most recent monographs on New Netherlands find no place in Archdeacon's bibliography.

The most valuable part of this study is the attempt to reconstruct the social and occupational structure of late seventeenth century New York. Tax and census rolls, church records, marriage licenses, indentures, wills, inventories and legislative records have been used to build up a picture of the occupations, wealth and places of residence of New Yorkers between 1664 and 1710. By the latter date sixty percent of the city's population was still Dutch in name, language and religious traditions, while English, Huguenots, Jews and Blacks made up the majority of a polyglot remainder. In a mercantile economy the wealthiest men were Dutch, but they shared power and prestige with a large group of English and Huguenot newcomers with whom they intermarried. The majority of the Dutch were to be found neither in the elite nor among the poorer sections of society. They were men of middling rank—small merchants, retailers and skilled artisans— living more separately from the newcomers than the Dutch elite. It is this large group of middling Dutch citizens whom Professor Archdeacon sees as downwardly mobile, but he provides no adequate discussion of their fathers' occupation nor of the relative size and complexity of the city's economy in 1664 and 1710. Although Archdeacon argues otherwise, this reviewer was more impressed by the evidence, which shows that men of various backgrounds supported the different political factions of the period. Archdeacon produces very limited material to support his claim of intense status frustration among the majority of Dutch. Throughout the book, too much is assumed as when the author extends his doubtful thesis from New York City to the whole colony (p. 147). In his preoccupation with a 'status revolution' Professor Archdeacon has marred what could have been an important social analysis of early New York.

LOUIS BILLINGTON
University of Hull
England

EARL BLACK. *Southern Governors and Civil Rights*. Pp. xi, 408. Cambridge, Mass.: Harvard University Press, 1976. No price.

Earl Black does a superlative job of gathering, correlating, analyzing and reporting comprehensive data on *what* happened to racial segregation issues in gubernatorial campaigns and elections in southern states from the period immediately preceding the Supreme Court's *Brown* decision in 1954 through the elections of 1972. Careful, systematic research and documentation pervade the 11 chapters, 54 tables, 29 figures, 2 appendixes (with 4 additional tables), 45 pages of notes and a serviceable index that comprise this vital new sourcebook of information and hypotheses. The author's conclusions, however, about *why* attitudes and rhetoric changed concerning segregation—which he sums up with the observation that "national stateways can indeed modify regional folkways"—may be more a product of inferential preference than of empirical proof.

Utilizing as foundation for his work all

the 80 governorships at issue between 1950 and 1973 in the eleven southern states, Professor Black probes the ways in which and degrees to which candidates for governor significantly altered traditional commitments to a racially segregated society. Voting data from all of the southern counties for Democratic first primaries, Democratic second primaries and closely contested final elections are compared so as to identify demographic and geographic factors affecting support for militant segregationists. Prototypes of his initiatives in data assembly and interpretation are Figures 24, 25, and 26 that plot indexes of changing racial stances of candidates and winners by state, region and subregion. Texas and Tennessee emerge as the only states in the post-*Brown* period in which nonsegregationists consistently exhibited greater strength than segregationists. Not surprisingly he finds racial change least evident in Deep South elections.

Professor Black is at his best when, having properly acknowledged his intellectual indebtedness to V.O. Key, he proceeds through data analysis to dispute Key's hypothesis about the relationship between Democratic factionalism and racial politics. Whereas Key indicated that insistence upon the racially segregated status quo would be more characteristic of multifactional than unifactional systems because "a cohesive faction has the power to discipline wild-eyed men," Black's data show no persistent relationships between factional structure and racial change. Once the threat to white supremacy materialized with the *Brown* decision, Black observes, some of the most centripetal state political organizations, such as Virginia's Byrd Organization, provided platforms for "wild-eyed men" of their own.

Professor Black's analyses will interest students of the current political scene as well as those seeking historical perspectives on change. After crediting Jimmy Carter with explicit repudiation of racial discrimination in Carter's gubernatorial inaugural, Black subsequently observes that Carter was "far from genuinely liberal on civil rights" and that "his subsequent performance ... failed to match the promise of his inaugural."

Whether or not author and reviewer have similar priorities, Professor Black has written a stimulating, innovative, and essentially optimistic volume that will be required reading for all who are concerned with the interactions of politics and human rights.

VICTOR G. ROSENBLUM
Northwestern University
Chicago
Illinois

MATTHEW A. CRENSON. *The Federal Machine: Beginnings of Bureaucracy in Jacksonian America.* Pp. xii, 186. Baltimore, Md.: The Johns Hopkins University Press, 1975. $10.00.

Americans have long disparaged bureaucracy and its "red tape." But no matter who is in power the day-to-day operations of the federal government remain constant in the attempt to move matters along. This book views the question of bureaucracy in the United States as it was handled during the Andrew Jackson presidency.

Crenson views the Jacksonian years as the true beginning of an entrenched political-minded bureaucracy. Certainly the Jacksonians were unlike any administrators in the federal government before 1829 although this book clearly shows many of the Jacksonians were wealthy and former Federalists. The old assumption of the spoils systems revolution is shown to be inaccurate by Crenson.

Before describing Jackson's administration the author devotes several chapters to a background analysis. Here he looks at the political beliefs and social institutions of the 1820s. There is an admirable section on what historians have said about "Jacksonian Democracy" which can be read by the novice or those needing an update on the issue.

The character of Jackson comes through as shrewd and subtle. Quite frequently he let others take the blame for his mistakes or do the dirty work. No one was more accomplished at this than Amos Kendall who occupies a good portion of the book.

In fact, Crenson narrows his study to the machinations of the Post Office Department and the General Land Office. The reader sees the corruption and difficulties facing the government when the nation was young, separated by time and space, and changing rapidly. Kendall's negotiations with railroads to carry the mails and the question of abolitionist literature in the mails is examined. Both instances afford a view of how matters were dealt with long ago.

This is not a lengthy book but the importance of it is twofold: first, the author tackles a largely previously neglected aspect of the Jackson Era and, secondly, he has something vital to say beyond the constant rehashing of the Jackson theme. For these reasons the book should be in research libraries and possessed by students of the American government.

LEWIS H. CROCE
Mankato State University
Minnesota

DAVID HOLBROOK CULBERT. *News for Everyman: Radio and Foreign Affairs in Thirties America*. Pp. xvi, 238. Westport, Conn.: Greenwood Press, 1976. $13.50.

One of the major preoccupations of the historiography of Franklin D. Roosevelt's foreign policies has been a debate on the degree to which they were or were not a reflection of public opinion. David Holbrook Culbert's *News for Everyman: Radio and Foreign Affairs in Thirties America* adds significantly to this literature by demonstrating that during the six years prior to Pearl Harbor, the broadcasts describing German aggression in Europe made "the news" an integral part of daily radio programming and "played a major role in creating a climate of opinion favorable to an interventionist foreign policy" (p. 5).

Culbert is concerned primarily with what six commentators—Boake Carter, H.V. Kaltenborn, Raymond Gram Swing, Elmer Davis, Fulton Lewis, Jr., and Edward R. Murrow—had to say about the ominous events in Europe. Far Eastern affairs, seldom mentioned by the six, receive only scant attention. Other newscasters are omitted because they either did not write their own copy, analyze the news, or include personal political comment. However selective in approach, the author does offer commanding assessments of these news analysts' style and impact.

Of the six, Culbert notes, only two—Carter and Lewis—were isolationists. Yet the others, all interventionists, exerted by far the greatest influence. In the process they sacrificed objectivity to the point of becoming tools of the administration. Each of the six was truly distinctive. Carter helped strengthen the pre-Munich isolationist mood in America and was forced off the air (in part, by administration pressure) for his trouble. Kaltenborn not only broadcast directly from a civil war battlefield in Spain but his eighteen-day commentary on the Munich Crisis established radio as the preeminent source news on foreign affairs. With a Wilsonian's determination to promote liberal ideas throughout the world, Swing became an unofficial spokesman of the Department of State. Davis demonstrated that a keen wit and impeccable credentials could overcome the worst speaking voice on the air. Addressing himself primarily to elites in order to advance his career, Lewis's main importance lay in the fact that he had so little influence on the average American. In his "This is London" broadcasts, carefully tailored to have the greatest aural appeal, Murrow made real such abstractions as patriotism and national honor.

Culbert is at his best in describing the quality and nuances of voices and images projected over the air. While he is convincing in demonstrating radio's impact on public opinion, his conclusions on its influence on foreign affairs are more tentative. His excellent bibliography should be consulted by all who study radio in the thirties. A product of prodigious research, *Radio for Everyman* is an important contribution to our understanding of the relationship between mass media and public opinion.

LARRY D. HILL
Texas A&M University
College Station

LOUIS FILLER. *Appointment At Armageddon: Muckraking and Progressivism in American Life*. Pp. xiii, 446. Westport, Conn.: Greenwood Press, 1976. $15.95.

Above all else this book is the author's attempt to place muckraking and progressivism in what he considers their proper context in American history. At one and the same time Filler sees progressivism and muckraking as dynamic forces in our history, for both good and bad, for idealism and, at the same time, for racism, warfare and other dark sides of our history. This reviewer wonders why not, for are not these two facets of our history themselves but microcosms of our totality? We are taught in undergraduate school that one of the cardinal sins in writing or thinking history is to forget to place events or themes in their historical context. What Filler is doing is just this—for examples, portraying Teddy Roosevelt, E.L. Godkin, Tom Watson and Henry Wallace in the light of their own particular times and needs.

What makes this book important is the way Filler "sees" the role of progressivism and muckraking in American history. Filler is an important historian, for he is the author of such major works as *The Crusade Against Slavery (1830–1860)*, in the Harper New American Nation series, and *Crusaders for American Liberalism*. What he thinks and writes of is important to historians as part of historiography and to those in the social sciences who are concerned with conceptualizations about American history.

The book is divided into three sections: "Past and Present," "Industry," and "Progressivism." In these sections, as well as in his introduction, Filler laments that "ours is not an era that has reason to anticipate progress" (p. xii). This is the essence, the theme of this book, that although progressivism is dead in our country and is criticized very harshly now, we still have much to learn from analyzing progressivism.

Filler downgrades some well-known progressives and resurrects others from the grave of obscurity. He attempts to place Theodore Roosevelt in historical perspective by reminding us not to judge T.R. on today's bases. He also reminds us that racism and progressivism were not one and the same in most instances, even in the case of Tom Watson of Georgia (p. 131).

Whether or not we accept many of Filler's statements and beliefs we can accept many of his assumptions. Progressivism could develop because of "meeting of minds and energies that reached from the bottom of the social order to the top" (p. 158). The "South was more than its demagogues" and "the South attained a more promising future for its blacks and whites" than what Watson represented (p. 138).

There are some minor flaws with the book, both as to interpretation and its production. Filler accepts that the "long count" in the Jack Dempsey-Gene Tunney fight was the result of mobster involvement with sports, enabling Tunney to keep the championship. I doubt if many historians subscribe to this position. There are several editing mistakes that should have been caught in galley proofs. For example, footnote three in the text is labeled number five (p. 14). But these really do not detract from the overall usefulness of the book. This work should be read in conjunction with Richard Hofstadter's *The Age of Reform: From Bryan to F.D.R.* (1955) which it contradicts, and somewhat supersedes.

HENRY MARKS

Huntsville
Alabama

TONY MARTIN. *Race First: The Ideological and Organizational Struggles of Marcus Garvey and the Universal Negro Improvement Association*. Pp. x, 421. Westport, Conn.: Greenwood Press, 1976. $17.50.

Dr. Tony Martin, born in Trinidad, educated at the University of Hull, England, Gray's Inn, London, and Michigan State University, is Associate Professor of History and Black Studies at Wellesley College. He asserted in his Preface (p. ix):

This book is based on the simple premise that no one could have organized and built up the largest black mass movement in Afro-American history, in the face of continuous onslaughts from communists on the left, black reactionaries on all sides, and the most powerful governments in the world, and yet be a buffoon or a clown, or even an overwhelming impractical visionary.

Equally debatable are his conclusions (p. x) that Garvey prevailed against his ideological opponents and that "it was only with his deportation from the United States that his organizational grip on the black masses in North America and, to varying degrees elsewhere, slowly began to loosen. Even then, his ideological legacy continued to be a major force in black communities." The author's conclusion about the feud between Garvey, on the one hand, W.E.B. DuBois, William Pickens, A. Philip Randolph, Chandler Owen and Robert Bagnall among others on the other hand, attributed "a major portion of the responsibility for Garvey's imprisonment and deportation . . . to the integrationist onslaught, especially as manifested in the campaigns of Du Bois and the NAACP, and the black Socialists Owen and Randolph" (p. 333). And in his observation that "there was no hint of racial arrogance" in the direct dealings of such advocates in the 1930s of white supremacy as Senator Theodore G. Bilbo of Mississippi and Ernest Sevier Cox of the White America Society with Garvey ignores the devastating effect of their support on large numbers of Americans. The author presents no proof that Garvey's ideological legacy of separatism and Back to Africa "continued to be a major force in black communities." The reviewer knows that the FBI has tried, unsuccessfully, to assess this influence.

If the author had not been imprisoned by his determination to prove that "Marcus Garvey has as good a claim as anyone to the distinction of being the greatest black figure of the twentieth century" (p. 359), his volume would have greater value. For instance, such scholars as Arthur A. Schomburg and Carter G. Woodson cooperated with Garvey in Promoting interest in "Black History."

The list of branches of the Universal Negro Improvement Association in the United States and abroad is valuable. The footnotes and the bibliography reveal comprehensive research.

RAYFORD W. LOGAN
Howard University
Washington, D.C.

PAUL DAVID NELSON. *General Horatio Gates: A Biography.* Pp. xiii, 319. Baton Rouge: Louisiana State University Press, 1976. $17.50.

After two centuries Horatio Gates remains one of the most controversial figures in our struggle for independence. Paul David Nelson has attempted an appraisal and a reevaluation of the military career of this paradoxical man. Born in England in 1728, Gates served with some distinction in the British army, seeing extensive service in America during the last of the wars with France. He moved to Virginia in 1772 and purchased a plantation there. On June 17, 1775, he was commissioned a Brigadier General and appointed adjutant-general of the newly formed Continental Army, and he reported to Washington at Cambridge on July 9th. Excelling in organization and administrative detail, Gates rendered valuable service to the Patriot army. In 1777 he won the spectacular and perhaps decisive victory at Saratoga. This, however, was followed by heated controversy with Washington. Service with the Board of War and in several minor capacities was followed by Congressional appointment to command the southern army following the American surrender at Charleston. Gates' disastrous defeat at Camden, probably the worst American debacle of the entire war, ruined his reputation and closed Gates' career as an independent commander. He served with Washington from 1782 to 1783. In Virginia and later in New York, Gates achieved some minor social and political success during the post-war years. He died in 1806.

Writing in 1931 Randolph G. Adams noted that the manuscript sources for a life of Gates were voluminous. This author has examined many of those sources and both his bibliography and footnotes vouch for their frequent use. A revision of a doctoral thesis, this book is perhaps mistitled. It is not a full-scale biography of Gates; rather it is a study of his military role during the Revolution. There is an almost total disregard of Gates' personal life. Ten percent deals with the life of Gates before his arrival in Virginia at the age of 44; fifteen pages are devoted to the last 23 years of his life.

As a study of Gates' military career, however, this book earns several kudos. The author examines, with care, his leadership at both Saratoga and Camden and the complex and troublesome story of his difficulties with Washington in 1777 and 1778, often referred to as the Conway Cabal. As such it deserves the attention of those studying the military history of our Revolution. The author is remarkably objective in his recognition of the mistakes and weaknesses of Gates. His appraisal of Schuyler, antagonist of Gates in 1776 and 1771, is forthright and balanced. Nelson justifies his assertion that Gates was "a modestly gifted military officer with both commendable and damaging traits of character" (p. xi).

The study is somewhat marred by occasional reliance on secondary sources and by an absence of documentation that would have been helpful (see p. 91). The accounts of Stanwix and Bennington, admittedly peripheral to a study of Gates' leadership, leave something to be desired. In general, however, the documentation is impressive and the analysis and evaluation are always interesting and often convincing.

RALPH ADAMS BROWN
State University of New York
Cortland

NORMAN H. NIE, SIDNEY VERBA and JOHN PETROCIK. *The Changing American Voter*. Pp. vii, 399. Cambridge, Mass.: Harvard University Press, 1976. $15.00.

*The Changing American Voter* is one of the really important books of recent years. Based on data collected from numerous national surveys conducted between 1939 and 1974, and including material from over 30,000 interviews, the authors have undertaken to update and bring into new perspective the findings of the 1960 classic *The American Voter*. That work was a pioneering effort in post-war political science and represented one of the first important adaptations of survey research techniques to voter behavior. Based on a University of Michigan/Survey Research Center study of the 1956 election, the researchers concluded that voters cast ballots based on personality and party affiliation rather than on issues.

The new study concludes that the American public is more issue-oriented than it has been in the past and that it is more detached from the political parties than at any time in the past four decades. The current study confirmed the earlier findings that party identification is a long-term commitment, established early in life and ordinarily maintained after that. The growth of the number of independents does not contradict that basic assumption although it does modify it. Partisan commitments, however, do interact with the issues of the day. The partisan attachments that arose out of the New Deal years remained dominant in the 1950s when the surveys upon which *The American Voter* was based were being conducted. Though the New Deal issues were not as salient as they had once been, they had not been replaced by new issues that were of deep concern to the electorate.

The 1960s and 70s however, brought to the fore a whole new range of intensive and emotional issues which upset the old system. The Vietnam War, the urban crisis, racial conflicts, Watergate and a major economic recession are all issues which cut across the old New Deal alliances and voting patterns. Part of the change in voter attitude is attributable to a change in the public belief systems. Candidates and parties have begun to be evaluated in terms of the issue positions which they represent to the voters. Furthermore, as the authors point out, the new issue-coherence and the increased level of concern over issues have been translated into a greater connection between issue positions and the vote.

Probably the second major finding in this study was the impressive decline in partisanship among the voters of America. The Independents now represent the largest group in society, slightly larger than the Democrats and twice as large as the Republicans. Even among those who claim a partisan identification, the allegiance is weak. Voters are more likely to desert their own party to vote for candidates of the other. Citizens are generally dissatisfied with the parties as they are presently constituted. And, at the same time, the voter has developed a more clearcut set of issue commitments and is using them as a voters' guide.

Most of those who are involved in teaching and research in American electoral politics will welcome this book. It is likely to take its place on that relatively short shelf composed of "important" books in political science.

ROBERT J. HUCKSHORN
Florida Atlantic University
Boca Raton

RICHARD L. RUBIN. *Party Dynamics: The Democratic Coalition and the Politics of Change*. Pp. 203. New York: Oxford University Press, 1976. $9.95. Paperbound, $3.95.

This is a book of two parts. The first part spends four chapters to make a point that could have been presented in one; but the second part is one of the most cogent analyses in print of the various conflicts that have been consuming the Democratic party for almost a decade. The features of the electorate that Richard Rubin turns to for an understanding of the recent history of the Democrats—suburbanization, the "Catholic factor," labor, southerners, blacks, the New Politics Democrats, and elite factionalism—are unquestionably the place to begin. The problem with the book is its strikingly uneven analysis of these elements.

The first chapter observes that the rise of the suburbs has not presaged a decline in the Democratic majority, because migration to the suburbs did not convert Democrats to Republicans. The major

finding in this chapter is the substantial difference between eastern and midwestern suburbs in the proportion of Republican supporters. He also shows that in the east the number of Republicans moving out of cities and into suburbs is proportionally greater than the number of Republicans moving into midwestern suburbs. As a result, the relatively greater Republican bias of eastern suburbs is maintained. The next two chapters repeat the finding that there are fewer and less loyal Democrats among Catholics and union members in the east compared to the midwest.

This eastern-midwestern difference is interesting and merits analysis. Unfortunately it is not analyzed; it is simply talked about, with the result that the chapters are overlong, repetitious, and boring. The basic finding is demonstrated too many times. The only attempted explanation of the regional variation is mounted in the chapter on "The Catholic Factor" when Rubin shows that regional differences in the social status of Catholics is not the explanation for the regional differences in partisanship. Redundant data and verbal overkill largely destroy the merit of this part of the book.

In Chapter four he finally offers an explanation of this regional difference that is both imaginative and theoretically intriguing. His basic thesis is that the Democratic party in the east has been less successful at holding the loyalities of some elements of the New Deal coalition because the eastern Republican party is substantially more liberal than its midwestern counterpart. In Rubin's view, smaller issue differences between eastern Democrats and Republicans have weakened the Democratic predisposition of some groups of voters. To test this explanation, Rubin compares eastern and midwestern Republican and Democratic Senators in terms of their welfare and racial liberalism. He finds that midwestern Republican Senators are substantially more conservative than their Democratic colleagues, while eastern Republicans are only mildly more conservative than eastern Democrats on welfare questions and a fraction more liberal than the Democrats on racial matters. Unfortunately, his use of these data is only illustrative, and his failure to analyze them systematically leaves his original insight untested. In short, the data that could redeem the first three chapters are not presented; and they are necessary since his explanation defies the convention that party identification is formed by references to national and not state politics (the south excepted, perhaps).

In the next two chapters the merit of the book is finally established. His analysis of the factionalism of Democratic elites and the changing Democratic electorate is excellent. The importance of the ideological orientation of the middle-class, New Politics Democrats to this factionalism is clearly drawn. The changing contribution of blacks, union members, Southerners, and city dwellers to the Democratic vote is woven into a persuasive explanation of the success of the "anti-regular" campaigns of McCarthy, Wallace, and McGovern. Overall, he offers a fine analysis of how changes in the Democratic electorate since the late Forties have fueled the turmoil of the party over recent elections. His discussion of the importance of racial questions for the South, for blacks, and the new middle-class Democrats is particularly good. The intra-party history which permitted the emergence of the race issue is also explained. Rubin's explanation of the concern with which blacks view Democratic factionalism is particularly interesting in light of black support for Jimmy Carter over several liberal Democrats in the 1976 primaries.

The impact of television and the expanding primary system on the Democratic party, and the greater permeability of its elite selection process is the focus of the last two chapters. These chapters provide an insightful discussion of the relationship between the selection of Democratic candidates and the character of intra-party conflict, especially with regard to the problem of meshing the preferences of Democratic activists with those of the general voting population.

If the data in the first half of this book had been as skillfully analyzed as the trends in the second half of the book are

insightfully interpreted, this would be a substantial contribution to the literature on party change. It is a tribute to the quality of the later chapters that it is worth buying the book just to read them.

JOHN PETROCIK
University of California
Los Angeles

WOODROW WILSON. *The Papers of Woodrow Wilson*, Vols. 20, 21: *1910*. Edited by Arthur S. Link et al. Pp. xxii, 604; xx, 644. Princeton, N.J.: Princeton University Press, 1975, 1976. $22.50, $25.00.

These are turning point volumes in the series as it depicts not only the full evolution of Wilson's life, but the conditions, personalities, and interests which gave him his major decade. Volume 20 begins and continues with a thick dossier of letters, minutes, charges and counter-charges about a matter which should have had minimum general interest: the location of a new graduate school at Princeton. It can be only because of Wilson's qualities that it stirred politicians and bystanders remote from Princeton and its projects.

What related the numerous participants in a movement which, by the end of Volume 21 elected Wilson governor of New Jersey? Clearly, it was their search for efficiency in government. They had experienced a decade of reform which had reached everywhere, forcing social decisions of every kind on almost everybody. That wave of reform was still activating talented people of every kind throughout New Jersey, and threatening its Republican and Democratic machines. The profoundly conservative George Harvey persuaded the Democratic boss, James Smith, Jr., that Wilson would be a brake on untidy reformers who, if they won power, would submerge parties in popular clamor. In effect, Wilson offered to be the people's representative within a political system too intricate for any individual to grasp. As one party worker put it: "I am like thousands of other Democrats . . . anxious to see the State in the hands of honest, unselfish and sane administrators. . . . The people are tired of demagogues, quacks and cure-alls" (XXI, 21, 86).

The critical fact was that Smith needed assurances that Wilson would not turn on those who made him governor. Wilson was glad to indicate that creating his own machine was "the last thing I should think of" (XX, 540). He set down other Delphic phrases which persuaded Smith and others that Wilson would meet other due political obligations. Smith did not take to heart Wilson's ". . . so long as I was left absolutely free . . . in the matter of measures and men."

Wilson's combination of strength and weakness displays him as wholly made by his times. He rouses hatred among Princeton elements who see his demand for a "democratic" graduate school harmful to their brand of elite interests. Had Wilson resigned under pressure, as he might have done, his saga would have ended there, with Wilson doubtless rounding out his career as a well-respected administrator elsewhere. His impassioned defense of policies before the Pittsburgh alumni, April 17, 1910, was received in silence. But it brought him national sympathy, even a vibrant letter which he did not answer from a "demagogue," David Graham Phillips, Princeton '87, who hoped "you will be able to make Princeton the university of the present and future, instead of a mockery of medievalism" (XX, 363ff., 372). Yet Wilson had retreated on the graduate school location and protested that it was his "ideals" which distinguished him from his opponent Dean Andrew F. West.

Wilson had a bad, querulous moment when it seemed there might be an open fight for the Democratic nomination, rather than, as he had insisted, having it handed to him by party bosses without qualifications, without struggle, without self-exposure of any kind. He rushed to his sponsor Harvey for reassurances. Yet he also consistently denied to reporters and inquirers that he sought the office of governor at all, and was ingenuous in voicing his surprise at being nominated. Wilson found phrases for everyone which did not outrage their party opponents whose suffrage he also needed.

Famous is the exchange between the reformer George L. Record and Wilson (XXI, 338 ff., 406 ff.) which won over Record without alarming Record's foe, Smith. Wilson also assuaged labor elements on one side, and corporations on the other. By the end of Volume 21, Wilson is receiving congratulations on victory from everybody, including Smith, and his campaign has been national news.

Wilson expresses his deep obligation to Harvey, and thanks Smith for his congratulations, though he had denounced the boss during the campaign. Later, Wilson will repudiate Smith and abandon Harvey, and be himself denounced as an ingrate. It is an open question, to be answered by scholars, how much difference Wilson's governorship, and the operations of his public service commissions, made, over what other Smith appointees might have done. Wilson was far from being the only sensitized instrument of change in New Jersey or elsewhere.

During his campaign, Wilson had argued that what the times needed was not new men but new programs, and indeed new programs—not necessarily identifiable with Wilson—would materialize in New Jersey, as elsewhere and in the Federal structure. The best of Wilson's eloquence is yet to come, and to be weighed for its pertinacity in his time and ours.

LOUIS FILLER

Antioch College
Yellow Springs
Ohio

ELMO R. ZUMWALT, JR. *On Watch: A Memoir*. Pp. vii, 568. New York: Quadrangle, 1976. $12.50.

During Admiral Zumwalt's four years "on watch" as Chief of Naval Operations, he struggled diligently to improve morale and efficiency in numerous ways. He earned a reputation as a thoughtful, farsighted, military administrator. His efforts to eliminate needlessly authoritarian practices ("Mickey Mouse") and pervasive racial discrimination in the Navy were hardly successful, but undeniably constructive. There has been a definite movement to implement equal career opportunities for women and blacks, particularly with increased respect for the rank and file of Navy personnel.

Zumwalt's memoirs include fascinating vignettes of a brief tour in China in 1945 where he first met his Russian-born wife, Mouza. There is, moreover, a thoughtful section about Naval vessels and weaponry. He discusses the politics of weapons procurement, the budgetary process, and bureaucratic politics from a military perspective. For foreign policy scholars deficient in any of these areas, there is a wealth of data to consider.

The author lays much of the blame for the failure of Naval shipbuilding programs in recent years on Hyman S. Rickover. Zumwalt concedes that the 76-year old Admiral with legendary influence in Congress rarely if ever pushes for ineffective weapons systems. As head of the relatively obscure Division of Nuclear Propulsion he is rarely the object of public attention. Nonetheless, Rickover's obsession with nuclear vessels and his powerful opposition to naval alternatives which might be considerably cheaper and relatively efficient, has resulted in much consternation in Washington. Rickover is not merely parochial, he is ruthless, according to Zumwalt. Thus, few oppose him openly. With allies throughout the Navy who have served under his tutelage and in the Joint Committee on Atomic Energy and the Armed Services Committees (in particular on the House Seapower Subcommittee), Rickover quietly promotes his favorite projects and personnel.

As yet another chronicle of internecine politics during the Nixon-Kissinger years it compares favorably to other accounts due to the author's detailed notes and keen memory of conversations between elites. Foreign policy scholars and students of civil military relations particularly will find these memoirs provocative and useful in the years ahead. Of interest may be Kissinger's alleged comments on Russia's ascendency *vis-à-vis* the U.S. (p. 319), Prince Bernard's "Catch-22"

rationale for a constant U.S. commitment in Western Europe (p. 358), and Soviet Ambassador Dobrynin's view of parity in strategic arms (p. 487).

On potentially critical foreign policy issues such as the endangered ecology of the seas, the question of a Palestinean State and projected conflict in Southern Africa, there is virtually no mention. Understandably, we have come to expect that military leaders (and Zumwalt clearly ranks among the most impressive in recent years) confine their thinking about America's future security to important power relationships.

Unfortunately, there is too much mental masturbation about the likely outcome of conventional naval war between the U.S. and the Soviet Union (Zumwalt believes that it is necessary to keep statistical odds on such hypothetical conflicts). Whereas, naval conflict between the superpowers is quite conceivable, the possibility that one side would accept defeat without utilizing all forces, including nuclear weapons, seems remote. One of the most important political developments which reduces the threat of an accidental war because overzealous commanders engage in macho confrontations ("playing chicken" on the seas) was an understanding concluded in 1972 (p. 391).

Zumwalt's concerns are similar to those of the Secretary of State whom he came to distrust so deeply. Thus, this book is primarily interesting because of Zumwalt's argument that "we should begin to gird ourselves for a harsher adversary relation with the Soviet Union." The focus on "the growing maritime power of the Soviets (was) the most immediate and formidable threat to the U.S. . . . ." is clear (p. 330). What some will consider his "worst-case analysis" of the military capabilities and political intentions of the U.S.S.R. others will consider an objective and thoughtful study. Readers should not neglect the search for alternatives to the policies that Zumwalt and Henry Kissinger represent in the text.

PAUL CONWAY
State University of New York
College at Oneonta

## SOCIOLOGY

ELIOT FREIDSON. *Doctoring Together: A Study of Professional Social Control*. Pp. xiii, 298. New York: Elsevier, 1976. $13.50.

Eliot Freidson has for some years been directing attention to the way in which medical care may be influenced by the settings in which it is offered. He has also raised questions about the effectiveness of professional social control in the medical field.

*Doctoring Together* reflects both these concerns. It is the first full-length account of an intensive study he conducted more than a decade ago in a large urban medical organization, summaries of which were published in article form in the '60s. Although somewhat belated, this new volume providing extended discussion of the findings, is a valuable addition to the literature. It includes for the first time a thorough description of the research methods employed in the study, gives verbatim excerpts from interviews with physicians, and presents its analysis within a systematic framework of concepts and theory. Much of this profits, no doubt, from Freidson's work on his recent Sorokin-Award winning volume, *Profession of Medicine* (1970).

The medical organization selected in the early '60s for study was a model of its type, incorporating features advocated by reformers. It operated under a prepaid-service-contract-plan in which some 45,000 persons were enrolled, and employed on a salary basis some 50 physicians. As a special protection, the insurance company which administered the organization made periodic checks on standards of medical care. Freidson's study tested the effectiveness of this emergent type of system.

Under the broad principle that "the way work is organized and controlled influences the nature of work itself," the study depended basically first, on an analysis of the organization, its rules and its structure, and secondly, on the opinions of the physicians about their work and that of their colleagues. The study aimed "not so much to measure results as

to understand how and why the organization operated as it did." Methods of research employed approximated the field-study type, including: observation ("just being there") attendance at staff meetings, review of medical and other records, and, most importantly, interviews. In order to obtain a more complete view, physicians were encouraged, at least initially, to talk at length about their problems as they saw them, rather than responding to fixed questions.

The analysis focusses primarily upon the processes of social control. Two models of social control are contrasted: the *bureaucratic model* associated with hierarchical organization and supervision, and the *professional model* in "a company of equals." Elements of both models were found in the medical organization. Complaints by physicians stemmed largely from bureaucratic restrictions enforcing required office hours, crowded schedules and a general "overload" which militated against optimal care. Problematic relations with patients resulted, moreover, from elimination of the fee barrier and from the fixed-panel system preventing choice of physicians.

Freidson takes a more serious view, however, of the failures of professional control to bar from practice those physicians known by their colleagues to be guilty of substandard practices. Occasional "talking-to" repeated offenders or boycotting them personally in referrals were the only measures taken.

The book is important in view of changes in medical care being considered by our country. It is stimulating reading and admirably well organized for teaching purposes.

CAROLYN ZELENY

Wilson College
Chambersburg
Pennsylvania

MURIEL GARDINER. *The Deadly Innocents: Portraits of Children Who Kill*. Pp. vii, 190. New York: Basic Books, 1976. $8.95.

In his preface Stephen Spender notes that the author is not so much concerned with explaining why young people commit homicides as describing the conditions in which some of them have done so. The tragic and deplorable backgrounds of these young offenders are almost beyond belief. Spender states that the author's purpose is to persuade readers to agitate for changes in the family, the schools, the law courts, and the rehabilitation centers. Her compassionate account will arouse her readers, although some may question her objectivity.

According to the dust jacket this book contains portraits of ten children, all under the age of eighteen, who have killed or attempted to kill. Yet two of the children are eighteen years of age and not all of them killed or attempted to kill. One committed armed robbery and kidnapping, but is brought within the fold by the assumption that he acted with the intent to kill himself. He wanted to threaten a police officer with his gun so that the officer would kill him. Another is described as a "bystander" at a murder.

The author, a psychoanalyst, read English literature at Oxford University, but her literary style may surprise her tutors. School grades drop catastrophically, delicious aromas come from the kitchen, tremendous sympathy springs up, and a heart pounds with joyful anticipation. Her psychoanalytic interpretations, fortunately few in number, may surprise her training psychoanalysts. A young sailor's intention to spend his last evening on leave with a girl friend may have meant choosing between heterosexuality and homosexuality. His mother by withholding money for this evening, may have become, at least symbolically, the instrument for depriving him of a normal heterosexual relationship, perhaps forcing him into homosexuality. The killing of his mother is described as having all the earmarks of a homosexual panic.

Long quotations of conversations, some of them extending back into early childhood, do not ring true. The "bystander" at the brutal beating of an elderly burglary victim, feeling letdown by the outcome, is reassured by one of his partners in crime: "Cheer up, old fellow. Here, have a beer. We can't make a big grab every time, you know. And that gold watch is a real beauty. Cuff links not bad either. We three are going to draw lots to see who gets what." After they learn that the victim has died they spend a jolly evening drinking, talking, and planning for the future.

JOHN M. MACDONALD
University of Colorado
School of Medicine
Denver

RICHARD KIECKHEFER. *European Witch Trials: Their Foundations in Popular and Learned Culture, 1300–1500.* Pp. x, 181. Berkeley: University of California Press, 1976. $13.50.

E. WILLIAM MONTER. *Witchcraft in France and Switzerland: The Borderlands During the Reformation.* Pp. 232. Ithaca, N.Y.: Cornell University Press, 1976. $15.00.

Some contemporary historians believe that testimonial accounts of devil-trafficking in fourteenth and fifteenth century Europe were in reality artifacts imposed by judges and Inquisitors upon the statements made by participants during the prosecution of alleged witches. *European Witch Trials* reports an empirical test of this thesis.

Professor Kieckhefer usefully distinguishes between *sorcery* (the magical use of conjurations and spells to achieve desired ends), *invocation* (calling up evil spirits to hear one's bidding), and *diabolism* (Satan-worship). He holds that the need among learned men, who in general dominated the agencies of justice, for an Aristotelian-rationalist explanation of how sorcery could cause hailstorms, crop-failures and other blights led them to reject the peasants' simple reasoning that "magic" did "magic" things. Instead, drawing upon matured Christian theory, the learned adopted the notion that the wondrous things done by sorcery resulted from willful dealings between the sorcerer and the underworld of incubi, succubi, demons and familiars, for help from such beings seemed a necessary causal link between